INNOVATIVE FINANCING
FOR DEVELOPMENT

INNOVATIVE FINANCING
FOR DEVELOPMENT

Edited by
Suhas Ketkar
Dilip Ratha

THE WORLD BANK
Washington, D.C.

This volume is a product of the staff of the International Bank for Reconstruction and Development / The World Bank. The findings, interpretations, and conclusions expressed in this volume do not necessarily reflect the views of the Executive Directors of The World Bank or the governments they represent.

The World Bank does not guarantee the accuracy of the data included in this work. The boundaries, colors, denominations, and other information shown on any map in this work do not imply any judgement on the part of The World Bank concerning the legal status of any territory or the endorsement or acceptance of such boundaries.

Rights and Permissions
The material in this publication is copyrighted. Copying and/or transmitting portions or all of this work without permission may be a violation of applicable law. The International Bank for Reconstruction and Development / The World Bank encourages dissemination of its work and will normally grant permission to reproduce portions of the work promptly.

For permission to photocopy or reprint any part of this work, please send a request with complete information to the Copyright Clearance Center Inc., 222 Rosewood Drive, Danvers, MA 01923, USA; telephone: 978-750-8400; fax: 978-750-4470; Internet: www.copyright.com.

All other queries on rights and licenses, including subsidiary rights, should be addressed to the Office of the Publisher, The World Bank, 1818 H Street NW, Washington, DC 20433, USA; fax: 202-522-2422; e-mail: pubrights@worldbank.org.

ISBN: 978-0-8213-7685-0
eISBN: 978-0-8213-7706-2
DOI: 10.1596/978-0-8213-7685-0

Library of Congress Cataloging-in-Publication Data

Innovative financing for development / Suhas Ketkar and Dilip Ratha (editors).
    p. cm.
  Includes bibliographical references and index.
  ISBN 978-0-8213-7685-0 — ISBN 978-0-8213-7706-2 (electronic)
  1. Developing countries—Finance. 2. Economic development—Developing countries—Finance. 3. Economic assistance—Developing countries. I. Ketkar, Suhas. II. Ratha, Dilip.
HG195.I555 2008
338.9009172'4—dc22

                                                                    2008029533

Cover design: Naylor Design

Contents

Boxes

Figures

Tables

Foreword

In the run-up to the "Follow-up International Conference on Financing for Development" to be held in Doha from November 28 to December 2, 2008, it seems particularly timely to collect in one book writings on the various market-based innovative methods of raising development finance. Although developing countries are well advised to use caution in incurring large foreign debt obligations, especially of short duration, there is little doubt that poor countries can benefit from cross-border capital whether channeled through the public or private sectors. For example, many countries need to rely on sizable foreign capital for infrastructure development. Achieving Millennium Development Goals by the 2015 deadline depends crucially on the availability of adequate financing. However, since official development assistance is expected to fall short of the requisite levels, market financing will be both necessary and appropriate.

The papers in this book focus on various recent innovations in international finance that allow developing countries to tap global capital markets in times of low risk appetite, thereby reducing their vulnerability to booms and busts in capital flows. Debt issues backed by future hard currency receivables and diaspora bonds fall into the category of mechanisms that are best described as foul-weather friends. By linking the rate on interest to a country's ability to pay, GDP-indexed bonds reduce the cyclical vulnerabilities of developing countries. Furthermore, these innovative mechanisms permit lower-cost and longer-term borrowings in international capital markets. Not only do the papers included in this book describe the innovative financing mechanisms; they also quantify the mechanisms' potential size and then identify the constraints on their use. Finally, the papers recommend concrete measures that the World Bank and other regional development banks can implement to alleviate these constraints.

Economists have analyzed the feasibility and potential of using various tax-based sources of development finance in the context of meeting the Millennium Development Goals. This has given rise to a new discipline of global public finance. This book complements those efforts by focusing on market-based mechanisms for raising development finance.

Uri Dadush
Director, Development Prospects Group
World Bank

Acknowledgments

This book grew out of the research initiated about 10 years back, in the aftermath of the Asian financial crisis, to explore market-based mechanisms that developing countries could use to raise financing in times of troubled global capital markets. We are grateful to Uri Dadush, director of the Development Prospects Group at the World Bank for his unconditional support of this research.

We would also like to thank the United Nations Department of Economic and Social Affairs as well as Stephany Griffith-Jones and Krishnan Sharma for permission to reprint their paper on GDP-indexed bonds in this book.

Zhimei Xu in the Development Prospects Group's Migration and Remittances Team worked tirelessly to meet the aggressive production schedule for the publication of this book. Stephen McGroarty, Aziz Gökdemir, and Andrés Meneses provided excellent editorial and production assistance. Kusum Ketkar and Sanket Mohapatra read early drafts of selected chapters and made useful comments. We owe all these individuals our profound thanks.

Finally, over the years we have presented many of the ideas described in this book at numerous international conferences and received many insightful comments. In particular, we benefited a great deal from extensive discussions with colleagues at the rating agencies Fitch, Moody's, and Standard & Poor's. Though too numerous to identify individually, we would be remiss if we failed to acknowledge all these contributions.

About the Editors

Suhas Ketkar is a recognized expert on the emerging markets of Asia, Europe, and Latin America. He is currently Professor of Economics and Director of the Graduate Program in Economic Development at Vanderbilt University. Previously he worked as a financial economist and strategist for 25 years with several Wall Street firms including RBS Greenwich Capital, Credit Suisse First Boston, Marine Midland Bank, and Fidelity Investments.

Dilip Ratha is a lead economist in the Development Prospects Group at the World Bank. His work reflects a deep interest in financing development in poor countries. He has been working on emerging markets for nearly two decades while at the World Bank and prior to that, at Credit Agricole Indosuez, Singapore; Indian Institute of Management, Ahmedabad; the Policy Group, New Delhi; and Indian Statistical Institute, New Delhi.

Abbreviations

Currency: All dollar figures are in U.S. dollars

Afreximbank	African Export-Import Bank
AMC	advance market commitment
ATI	African Trade Insurance Agency
BdB	Banco do Brasil
CDs	certificates of deposit
DCI	Development Corporation for Israel
DPRs	diversified payment rights
EBID	Economic Community of West African States Bank for Investment and Development
EMU	European Monetary Union
FCD	foreign currency deposit
FDI	foreign direct investment
GAVI	Global Alliance for Vaccines and Immunization
GDP	gross domestic product
Gemloc	Global Emerging Markets Local Currency Bond Fund
GNI	gross national income
HIPC	Heavily Indebted Poor Countries (Initiative)
IBRD	International Bank for Reconstruction and Development
ICRG	International Country Risk Guide
IDA	International Development Association

IDBs	India Development Bonds
IFIs	international financial institutions
IFFIm	International Finance Facility for Immunisation
IMDs	India Millennium Deposits
IMF	International Monetary Fund
IPO	initial public offering
LIBOR	London Interbank Offer Rate
MDGs	Millennium Development Goals
MDRI	Multilateral Debt Relief Initiative
ODA	official development assistance
OECD	Organisation for Economic Co-operation and Development
PPPs	public-private partnerships
RIBs	Resurgent India Bonds
SBI	State Bank of India
SEC	U.S. Securities and Exchange Commission
SPV	special purpose vehicle
S&P	Standard & Poor's
TIPS	Treasury Inflation-Protected Securities
UNDP	United Nations Development Programme

CHAPTER 1

Innovative Financing for Development: Overview

Suhas Ketkar and Dilip Ratha

A large funding gap looms on the horizon as the 2015 deadline for alleviating poverty and other internationally agreed-upon Millennium Development Goals (MDGs) draws closer. The United Nations' Monterrey Conference on Finance for Development in 2002 sought to increase official development assistance (ODA) from 0.23 percent of donors' gross national income (GNI) in 2002 to 0.7 percent of GNI. But ODA, excluding debt relief, was only 0.25 percent in 2007. Current commitments from donors imply that ODA will increase to only 0.35 percent of their GNI, half the target level, by 2010 (World Bank 2008). There is little doubt that developing countries need additional, cross-border capital channeled to the private sector. This is particularly true in the context of Sub-Saharan Africa.

Lacking credit history, and given the perception by investors that investments in these countries can be risky, developing countries need innovative financing mechanisms.[1] This book lends a helping hand to that purpose by bringing together papers on various innovative market-based methods of raising development finance.[2] Needless to say, developing countries must be prudent and cautious in resorting to market-based sources of finance. Such borrowings must be within the limits of each country's absorptive capacity. Otherwise they run the risk of accumulating excessive debt burden. Furthermore, developing countries should also avoid the temptation to incur large amounts of short-term debt, because such flows can be pro-cyclical, reversing quickly in times of difficulties, with potentially destabilizing effects on the financial markets (Dadush, Dasgupta, and Ratha 2000).

This chapter begins with a brief review of the early innovations—the advent of syndicated loans in the 1970s and the emergence of Brady bonds and other sovereign bonds in the late 1980s and 1990s. The intention is not to undertake a comprehensive analysis of the events that have changed the nature of capital flows to developing countries. Rather, it is to use the backdrop of these events to focus on the innovations that occurred in the provision of finance for development.

The chapter then presents a brief overview of the rest of the book. Chapters 2, 3, and 4 discuss the more recent innovations—securitization of future-flow receivables, diaspora bonds, and GDP-indexed bonds. Chapter 5 highlights the role of sovereign ratings in facilitating access to international capital markets, and uses econometric techniques to "predict" the sovereign credit ratings of a large number of unrated developing countries. The final chapter evaluates the significance of the various innovative financing mechanisms in mobilizing additional capital for development in Sub-Saharan Africa. After summarizing the chapters, the penultimate section of this overview chapter then discusses the role for public policy in promoting the various innovative financing options described in chapters 2 through 6. The final section of this chapter concludes with reflections on some additional innovations that are well established as well as those that are being developed and could help generate financing for developing countries.

Early Innovations

Developing countries have always looked for new and innovative ways of raising finance. For over 20 years following World War II, ODA was the principal source of foreign capital for developing countries. In 1970, for instance, it accounted for roughly 48 percent of total net capital flows, including grants, to all developing countries.[3] Bank loans were a distant second at 22 percent, while foreign direct investment (FDI) made up another 19 percent. Bond financing was nearly nonexistent. Although ODA grew strongly throughout the 1970s, with the World Bank leading the way under Robert S. McNamara's presidency, it was not adequate to meet the financing requirements of many oil-importing countries in Latin America and elsewhere that were adversely affected by the two oil price shocks. Large international banks stepped into the breach and recycled oil-exporters' petrodollar deposits. Believing that private financial markets would allocate resources efficiently, the United States and other creditor governments encouraged large international banks to recycle petrodollars aggressively.[4]

Large international banks used the syndicated loan market to provide massive amounts of credit to developing countries. A syndicated loan is a large loan in which a group of banks work together to provide funds to a single borrower. There is generally a lead bank that provides a share of the loan and syndicates the rest to other banks. Though syndicated loans emerged in the 1960s with the creation of the eurodollar market, its use in arranging loans to developing countries was the financial innovation of the decade (Ballantyne 1996). The typical loan consisted of a syndicated medium- to long-term credit priced with a floating-rate contract. The variable rate was tied to the London Interbank Offer Rate, which was repriced every six months. Thanks to the use of syndicated loans, bank lending to all developing countries expanded rapidly to $53.5 billion in 1980 from $5.5 billion in 1970. Bank lending to Latin America and the Caribbean rose from $4.0 billion in 1970 to $32.7 billion in 1980. The region's overall foreign debt stock shot up from $32.5 billion in 1970 to $242.8 billion in 1980 (World Bank 2008).

Because roughly two-thirds of this debt was on floating interest rates, the run-up in U.S. interest rates in the early 1980s led to a surge in the debt service burden and contributed to the emergence of Latin America's debt crisis. The crisis was eventually resolved, starting with the restructuring of Mexico's debt in 1989. The advent of innovative Brady bonds played a crucial role by converting the difficult-to-trade bank debt into tradable bonds. The Brady bonds were fashioned along JP Morgan's innovative "Aztec" bonds, which restructured $3.6 billion of Mexico's sovereign debt into $2.6 billion of 20-year principal-defeased bonds with a six-month coupon of LIBOR plus 1.625 percent (Ketkar and Natella 1993).

The Brady Plan was first articulated by U.S. Treasury Secretary Nicholas F. Brady in March 1989. It created two principal types of bonds to give banks a choice between debt forgiveness over time or up front. The par bond option converted one dollar of debt into one dollar in bonds, which carried below-market interest rates over the security's 30-year life. The debt relief came in the form of the below-market coupon on par bonds. In contrast, discount bonds, which carried market-related interest rates, converted one dollar of debt into less than one dollar of bonds, thereby providing up-front debt relief. Both par and discount bonds were collateralized by zero-coupon 30-year U.S. Treasury bonds. Countries restructuring their debts under the Brady Plan purchased the U.S. zero-coupon Treasuries either with their own resources or with funds borrowed from multilateral creditors. In addition to this principal securitization, both types of bonds provided rolling interest guarantees for 12 to 18 months. Thus, both par and discount bonds mitigated the risks of default on the restructured principal as well as on two or three coupon payments. The 12 to 18 months of time bought with rolling interest guarantees was thought to be adequate to renegotiate the restructuring deal in case a country could not abide by the terms and conditions of its Brady Plan.

As part of the Brady Plan, debtor nations also implemented debt-equity swaps, debt buybacks, exit bonds, and other solutions.[5] The International Monetary Fund (IMF) and the World Bank provided substantial funds to facilitate these debt reduction activities. To qualify for borrowing privileges, debtor countries had to agree to introduce economic reforms within their domestic economies in order to promote growth and enhance debt-servicing capacity.

The innovative Brady Plan proved quite successful in providing sizable permanent debt relief and in finally resolving the Latin American debt crisis. It is estimated that under the Brady Plan agreements, between 1989 and 1994 the forgiveness of existing debts by private lenders amounted to approximately 32 percent of the $191 billion in outstanding loans, or approximately $61 billion for the 18 nations that negotiated Brady Plan reductions (Cline 1995, 234–35). This debt reduction returned Latin America's debt to sustainable levels.

The success of the Brady Plan went beyond the resolution of the debt crisis. First and foremost, the conversion of hard-to-trade bank debt into tradable bonds made the developing countries' debts available to many institutional investors, such as insurance companies, hedge funds, mutual funds, and pension funds. This expanded the investor base interested in the formerly debt-ridden countries and ameliorated their almost exclusive dependence on bank credits. Second, the implementation of the Brady Plan paved the way for the issuance of global and euro bonds by developing countries. Over time, more and more developing countries received sovereign credit ratings from agencies such as Fitch, Moody's, and Standard & Poor's, which accelerated sovereign debt issuance. Finally, the benchmark established by the issuance of sovereign bonds subsequently permitted many developing-country corporations to tap international debt capital markets.[6]

The benefits of the Brady Plan are evident in the rapid rise in the developing countries' stock of outstanding guaranteed and nonguaranteed bonds since 1990. As depicted in figure 1.1, outstanding bonds surged from a modest $12.8 billion in 1980 to $104.6 billion in 1990 and to a massive $705.4 billion by 2007 (World Bank 2008). Similarly, trading in developing-country debt jumped from its negligible level in 1985 to $6.0 trillion in 1997 (figure 1.2); and following a decline during the Asian currency crisis and the Argentine debt crisis, trading volumes returned to these levels in 2007 (EMTA 2007).

The switch from bank loans to bonds increased the availability of capital; in all likelihood it also increased the volatility of financial flows to developing countries. Banks were much more captive providers of funds to developing countries than were bond investors. Banks valued relationships in total rather than returns on specific activities. Furthermore, they were not required to mark their assets to market on a daily basis. As a result, banks often remained engaged in a country even when it was expe-

FIGURE 1.1
Value of Bonded Debt in All Developing Countries, 1970–2005

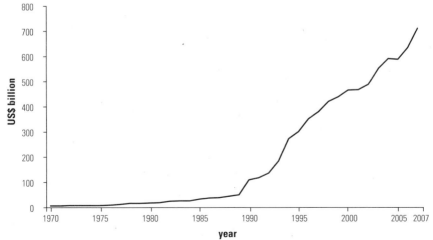

Source: World Bank 2008.

FIGURE 1.2

Debt-Trading Volume of Developing Countries, 1985–2007

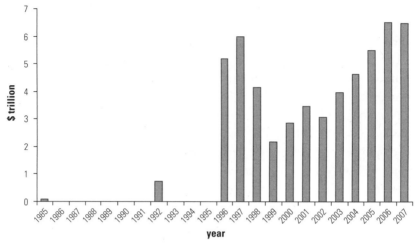

Source: EMTA.

riencing debt-servicing difficulties. Bond investors, in contrast, are likely to move out of a country at the first sign of trouble because they are required to mark their assets to market on a daily basis. Having taken a hit by sell-ing the bonds that are falling in price, however, bond investors can be expected to lick their wounds and repurchase sovereign bonds that have suffered a sharp enough decline in price. All in all, the switch from bank loans to bonds may have made capital flows to developing countries much more volatile than before. Certainly, debt crises since 1990 have been fre-quent and sharp, but also short-lived as opposed to the 1980s crisis that dragged on for nearly a decade. Little wonder that developing countries and financial markets have attempted to come up with innovations that provide access to funding during times of financial stress.[7]

Recent Innovations

The next three chapters in this book explore the recent innovations aimed at stabilizing financial flows to developing countries—the asset-backed securitization of future-flow receivables, diaspora bonds like those issued by the Development Corporation for Israel (DCI) and the State Bank of India (SBI), and GDP-indexed bonds. Securitization of future-flow receivables is a method of tapping international capital markets in times of deteriorating risk perception and low risk appetite among investors. The securitization structure allows sovereign, subsovereign, and private sector entities in developing countries to pierce the sovereign credit ceiling and obtain financing at significantly lower interest costs and for longer duration. Diaspora bonds constitute yet another source of finance in difficult times. These bonds appeal to the diasporas' patriotism to make the sale. In addition, diaspora investors are expected to show a greater degree of forbearance than dollar-based investors if the issuer were to encounter financial difficulties. As a result, it is possible to sell diaspora bonds at a significant price premium (yield discount). Finally, the GDP-indexed bonds link the coupon to the economy's performance, that is, its ability to pay. This feature of GDP-indexed bonds allows the issuing countries to follow countercyclical economic policies, thereby reducing the risk of default. The reduced risk of default is one major reason why issuers can be expected to pay a yield premium on these bonds. For the same reason, creditors may be willing to accept a yield discount.

Future-Flow Securitization

The first future-flow securitized transaction was undertaken by Mexico's Telmex in 1987.[8] Since then, the principal credit rating agencies have rated over 400 transactions, with the aggregate principal amount totaling $80 billion. A wide variety of future receivables have been securitized (table 1.1).[9] While heavy crude oil exports are the best receivables to securitize, diversified payment rights (DPRs) are not far behind. Securitization of DPRs, which include all hard currency receivables that come through the Society for Worldwide Interbank Financial Telecommunication system, is a more recent innovation. DPRs are deemed attractive collateral because the diversification of their source of origin makes such flows stable. For example, during 2002–04, when the fear of the Luis Inacio (Lula) da Silva presidency all but dried up Brazil's access to international capital markets, many Brazilian banks securitized future hard currency DPRs to raise $5.1 billion.

In chapter 2, Suhas Ketkar and Dilip Ratha describe how future-flow-backed transactions are structured to mitigate the sovereign risk of exposure to a developing-country borrower; that is, its government will take steps to disrupt timely debt servicing. This disruption is accomplished by

TABLE 1.1
Hierarchy in Future-Flow-Backed Transactions

1. Heavy crude oil receivables
2. Diversified payment rights, airline ticket receivables, telephone receivables, credit card receivables, and electronic remittances
3. Oil and gas royalties and export receivables
4. Paper remittances
5. Tax revenue receivables

Source: Fitch Ratings and Standard & Poor's.

ensuring that the payments on the receivables do not enter the issuer's home country before obligations to bond investors are met. Thus, the special purpose vehicle that issues the debt and through which the receivable is sold is set up offshore. Furthermore, designated international customers are directed to make payments into an offshore trust whose first obligation is to pay the bondholders and send only the excess collection to the issuer. Although this structure mitigates the sovereign transfer and convertibility risks, several other risks remain. These include (1) performance risk related to the issuer's ability to generate the receivable, (2) product risk associated with the stability of receivable flows due to price and volume fluctuations, and (3) diversion risk of the issuer's government compelling sales to nondesignated customers. Ketkar and Ratha point out how some of these risks can be mitigated through choice of the future-flow receivables and excess coverage.

After reviewing the evolution of this financing vehicle over the past 20 years, Ketkar and Ratha examine the rationale for future-flow securitization. They conclude that the issuing entities find such transactions appealing because they reduce the cost of raising finance, particularly in times of distress in global capital markets. Investors find future-flow-backed securities attractive because of their impeccable performance; there have been few defaults on securitized bonds. Notwithstanding these advantages, the actual issuance of securitized bonds is far below the potential for this asset class. In the final section of their paper, Ketkar and Ratha identify several constraints that have held back the issuance of future-flow-backed transactions. These include paucity of good receivables as well as strong (that is, investment grade) local entities, and absence of clear laws, particularly bankruptcy laws. Some of the constraints—such as high legal and other fixed costs and long lead times—that were binding in the 1990s have now become much less restrictive as investment banks have built up skills, template structures have developed, and issuers have learned to use master trust arrangements and to pool receivables.

Also in the final section of chapter 2, Ketkar and Ratha explore the scope for public policy to lift some of the constraints on the issuance of future-flow-backed securities from developing countries. Clearly, multilateral institutions like the World Bank and the International Finance Corporation can educate government officials and private sector managers in developing countries on the role that this asset class can play in times of crisis and how best to identify and structure future-flow-backed transactions. Those institutions can also provide assistance and advice to countries on developing appropriate legal infrastructure. Finally, they can defray some of the high costs associated with doing these transactions for the first time.

Diaspora Bonds

In chapter 3, Ketkar and Ratha discuss the track record of the Development Corporation for Israel and the State Bank of India in raising foreign capital by tapping the wealth of the Jewish and Indian diasporas, respectively. The DCI's diaspora bond issuance has been a recurrent feature of Israel's annual foreign funding program, raising well over $25 billion since 1951. The SBI has been much more opportunistic. It has issued diaspora bonds on only three occasions—following the balance-of-payments crisis in 1991, subsequent to the nuclear tests in 1998, and in 2000—raising a total of $11.3 billion. The Jewish diaspora paid a steep price premium (or offered a large patriotic yield discount) in buying DCI bonds. Although the Indian diaspora provided little in the way of patriotic discounts, they purchased SBI bonds when ordinary sources of funding had all but vanished. Yet another major difference between the Israeli and Indian experience has to do with U.S. Securities and Exchange Commission (SEC) registration. Whereas the DCI bonds were registered at the SEC, the SBI quite deliberately decided to eschew SEC registration due to the perception that the U.S. courts and laws are exceptionally plaintiff friendly. The SBI sold its bonds to retail U.S. investors in 1998. When the SEC insisted on registration in 2000, the SBI refrained from selling the bonds in the United States.

In the fourth section of chapter 3, Ketkar and Ratha provide the rationale for diaspora bonds. For countries, diaspora bonds represent a stable and cheap source of external finance, especially in times of financial stress.

Diaspora bonds offer investors the opportunity to display patriotism by doing good in the country of their origin. Beyond patriotism, however, diaspora bonds allow for better risk management. Typically, the worst-case scenario involving diaspora bonds is that the issuer makes debt service payments in local currency rather than in hard currency terms. But since diaspora investors are likely to have actual or contingent liabilities in their country of origin, they are likely to view the risk of receiving payments in local currency with much less trepidation.

On the basis of the large diaspora communities in the United States and a set of minimum preconditions for success in selling diaspora bonds, Ketkar and Ratha identify potential issuers of diaspora bonds: the Philippines, India, China, Vietnam, and the Republic of Korea, from Asia; El Salvador, the Dominican Republic, Jamaica, Colombia, Guatemala, and Haiti, from Latin America and the Caribbean; and Poland, from Eastern Europe. Diaspora presence is also significant in other parts of the world, for example, Korean and Chinese diasporas in Japan; Indian and Pakistani diasporas in the United Kingdom; Turkish, Croatian, and Serbian diasporas in Germany; Algerian and Moroccan diasporas in France; and large pools of migrants from India, Pakistan, the Philippines, Bangladesh, Indonesia, and Africa in the oil-rich Gulf countries.

All of the above countries, therefore, are potential issuers of diaspora bonds. However, Israeli and Indian experience shows that countries will have to register their diaspora bonds with the SEC if they want to tap the retail U.S. market. The customary disclosure requirements of SEC registration may prove daunting for some countries, although some of the African and East European countries and Turkey—with their significant diaspora presence in Europe—will be able to raise funds on the continent where the regulatory requirements are relatively less stringent than in the United States. Arguably, diaspora bonds could also be issued in the major destination countries in the Gulf region and in Hong Kong, China; Malaysia; the Russian Federation; Singapore; and South Africa.

GDP-Indexed Bonds

Stephany Griffith-Jones and Krishnan Sharma make the case for GDP-indexed bonds in chapter 4. The debt service payments on fixed-coupon bonds are potentially negatively correlated with a country's ability to pay. When an internal or external shock cuts growth, revenues fall and social safety net expenditures rise. The resulting rise in fiscal pressure forces a country to either adopt pro-cyclical fiscal policies or default on foreign debt. Both options can be quite traumatic for a developing country. GDP-indexed bonds are designed to avert this trauma. Coupons on such bonds are set to vary according to the economy's growth performance, that is, its ability to pay. This feature of GDP-indexed bonds limits the cyclical vulnerabilities of developing countries. The resultant reduction in the likelihood of defaults and debt crises is beneficial for investors as well. Furthermore, GDP-indexed bonds allow investors in low-growth (developed) countries to take a stake in higher-growth (developing) countries. In addition, investments in GDP-indexed bonds of many developing countries provide diversification benefits to investors because growth rates across developing countries tend to be generally uncorrelated. Finally, GDP-indexed bonds also benefit the global economy and the international financial system at large by reducing the incidence of disruptions arising from formal defaults and debt crises. This "public good" characteristic of GDP-indexed bonds implies that all of the benefits of the bonds are not captured by issuers and investors. As a result, markets alone may not have adequate incentive to issue GDP-indexed bonds, and public policy intervention may be required and justified.

Despite their apparent attractiveness, GDP-indexed bonds have not caught on. Only a few developing countries—Bosnia and Herzegovina, Bulgaria, and Costa Rica—have incorporated clauses or warrants in their Brady Plans that increase the payoff to bondholders if GDP growth exceeds a threshold. The more recent Argentine debt restructuring following the collapse of convertibility in 2001 also included warrants indexed to growth. Still, widespread use of GDP-indexed bonds has been held back because of several concerns, including accuracy of GDP data, the potential for deliberate underreporting and possibly even underproduction of growth, and the excessive complexity of the bonds. Griffith-Jones and Sharma go on to discuss these concerns and find them to be far from compelling obstacles. But they concede that low liquidity for GDP-indexed bonds due to their newness and complexity could be a valid constraint. They see a role for public policy in not only improving the accuracy and transparency of GDP data, but more crucially in creating a critical mass for the new instrument. The latter would require a coordinated effort by international organizations to persuade several governments (preferably both developed and developing) to start issuing GDP-indexed bonds more or less simultaneously.

Griffith-Jones and Sharma offer additional suggestions to jump-start the issuance of GDP-indexed bonds. First, multilateral institutions could develop a portfolio of loans whose repayment is indexed to growth rates in the debtor countries and then securitize these loans for placement in international capital markets. Second, issuers could offer GDP-indexed bonds with a "sweetener"; that is, a bond that pays a higher return when GDP growth exceeds its trend level. Finally, multilateral institutions could provide partial guarantees on a case-by-case basis to first issuers of GDP-indexed bonds to jump-start the program.

A persuasive argument can be made that developing countries would be willing to pay a yield premium on indexed bonds in relation to fixed-coupon bonds as insurance for avoiding the trauma resulting from pro-cyclical fiscal policies and a potential debt default. Borensztein and Mauro (2002) have used the capital asset pricing model to calculate this insurance premium at a relatively low rate of about 1 percentage point per year. But there is a risk of a large disparity between the premiums that issuers are willing to pay and what investors are willing to accept. The disparity could be large for highly volatile and indebted countries, which are likely to find GDP-indexed bonds particularly attractive. The problem could be even more serious if such countries are the first issuers from whom investors are likely to demand additional novelty premiums. Keeping all this in mind, Griffith-Jones and Sharma believe that the first issuers should be stable countries such as Chile and Mexico or possibly even developed European Monetary Union countries.

Returning to Argentina's GDP-indexed warrants, Griffith-Jones and Sharma note that this was the first large-scale issuance of a GDP-linked security. Following the debt moratorium at the end of 2001 and the collapse of currency convertibility in early 2002, Argentina began a long drawn-out process of debt renegotiations. The issuance was finally concluded in June 2005 when the participating creditors swapped $62 billion in face value of their claims for a new set of bonds with a face value of $35.3 billion. A GDP-linked warrant was attached to each one of these new bonds. The warrants represented an obligation by the Argentine government to pay 5 percent of the excess annual GDP in any year in which the GDP growth rate rises above the trend. The warrants became detachable in November 2005.

Written in 2006 by Griffith-Jones and Sharma, chapter 4 of this book contains only preliminary analysis of Argentina's GDP-indexed warrants.

But there exists by now more definitive evidence on the valuation of these warrants, which initially elicited a rather tepid response from the market. Most investment banks placed a value of about $2 per $100 of notional value (*Euromoney* 2006). The initial low valuation perhaps reflected low growth expectations as well as the high novelty premium. However, the valuation subsequently improved a great deal as Argentina posted strong growth rates of 9.2 percent in 2005, 8.5 percent in 2006, and an estimated 8.7 percent in 2007 (Brown 2008). The peak valuation of $15.82 was reached in early June 2007. The valuation has declined since then as higher oil prices have dampened growth projections and the Argentine risk spread has increased. Still, the warrants were trading at about $12.50 in early January 2008 (Costa, Chamon, and Ricci 2008). This good performance of Argentine warrants should improve the market reception to GDP-indexed bonds and act as a catalyst for additional issuance.

Shadow Ratings and Market Access

In chapter 5, Dilip Ratha, Prabal De, and Sanket Mohapatra begin by highlighting the importance of sovereign credit ratings for accessing international capital markets. In general, sovereign debt spreads are found to fall as sovereign credit ratings improve. But the transition to investment grade brings large discrete contractions in spread, from 191 basis points in 2003 to 67 basis points in 2007, for an average of 107 basis points during the period depicted in figure 1.3. Ratha, De, and Mohapatra also argue that not having a sovereign rating may be worse than having a low rating. In 2005, foreign direct investment accounted for 85 percent of private capital flows to unrated countries, with bank loans making up most of the rest. In comparison, capital flows were much more diversified even in B-rated countries—roughly 55 percent from FDI, 15 percent from bank loans, as much as 25 percent from bonds, and nearly 5 percent from equity flows.

Notwithstanding the benefits that sovereign ratings bring, some 70 developing countries—mostly poor—remain unrated at present. Ratha et al. set out to remedy this situation by estimating shadow sovereign ratings for unrated developing countries. Before embarking on this task, they highlight some stylized facts related to sovereign ratings. Two salient facts stand out. First, the principal rating agencies—Standard & Poor's, Moody's, and Fitch Ratings—began to rate developing countries in the late 1980s, following the debt crisis in Latin America. Second, sovereign ratings issued

FIGURE 1.3
Launch Spreads Decline with an Increase in Sovereign Rating

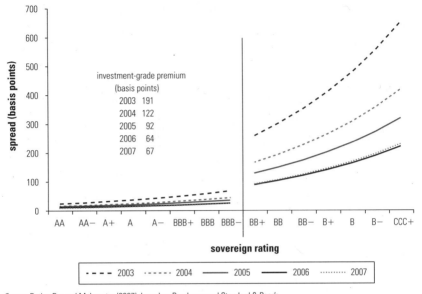

Source: Ratha, De, and Mohapatra (2007), based on Bondware and Standard & Poor's.

Note: Assuming a $100 million sovereign bond issue with a seven-year tenor. Borrowing costs have fallen steadily since 2003 with a slight reversal more recently, reflecting changes in the global liquidity situation. The investment-grade premium indicates the rise in spreads when the rating falls below BBB–. The relationship between sovereign ratings and spreads is based on the following regression:

log(launch spread) = 2.58 − 1.2 investment grade dummy + 0.15 sovereign rating + 0.23 log(issue size) + 0.03 maturity − 0.44 year 2004 dummy − 0.73 year 2005 dummy − 1.10 year 2006 dummy − 1.05 year 2007 dummy

N = 200; Adjusted R^2 = 0.70

All the coefficients were significant at 5 percent. A lower numeric value of the sovereign rating indicates a better rating.

by the three rating agencies tend to be highly correlated, with the bivariate correlation coefficients as high as 0.97 to 0.99 at year-end 2006.

Turning to the shadow ratings exercise, Ratha et al. recognize that a lot of care, rigor, and judgment go into determining sovereign ratings. Any econometric model-based determination of ratings, therefore, must be viewed as a second-best approach. Its use can be justified only in the context of the considerable time and resources that rating agencies would require to assign ratings to the 70 currently unrated developing countries.

The model specifications used by Ratha et al. draw on eight previous studies. Sovereign ratings are first converted into numerical scores with a score of 1 for all AAA-rated countries and 21 for C-rated countries. These rating scores are then regressed on seven independent country characteristics—per capita gross national income (−), GDP growth rate

$(-)$, debt-to-exports $(+)$, reserves in relation to imports plus short-term debt $(-)$, growth volatility $(+)$, inflation $(+)$, and the rule-of-law variable $(-)$. The expected influence of the independent variables on sovereign ratings is shown in parentheses.

Ratha et al. estimate four specifications of the model for each agency's sovereign ratings. In a departure from some of the earlier studies, only developing-country ratings are included in the estimations. In the benchmark specification 1, ratings at the end of 2006 are regressed on the values of the independent variables lagged one year. Just over 80 percent of the variation in ratings is explained by the independent variables. All of them have the expected signs, and except inflation, all are statistically significant at 1 percent. Other estimated specifications confirm the relationships revealed in specification 1.

Using the benchmark regression results, the authors then predict sovereign ratings on 55 unrated developing countries. These predicted ratings indicate that not all the unrated countries are hopeless; many appear to be more creditworthy than previously believed. For example, eight of the 55 countries are likely to be above investment grade, while another 18 are likely to be in the B to BB category. This suggests that there is hope for some of the unrated developing countries to obtain financing in global capital markets.[10]

Financing for Development in Sub-Saharan Africa

In chapter 6, Dilip Ratha, Sanket Mohapatra, and Sonia Plaza first examine the nature of capital flows to Sub-Saharan Africa and then explore the scope for innovation in raising additional cross-border financing for the region. In addition to securitization of future-flow receivables and diaspora bonds, the authors also explore the role that partial risk guarantees, International Finance Facility for Immunisation (IFFIm), and advance market commitment (AMC) structures can play in front-loading financing.

In the second section of chapter 6, Ratha, Mohapatra, and Plaza analyze the sources of capital for Sub-Saharan Africa, excluding South Africa, to conclude that the region's external finances are much less diversified than in other developing regions. In stark contrast to other regions of the developing world, Sub-Saharan Africa remains heavily dependent on official development assistance and foreign direct investment. ODA to Sub-Saharan Africa excluding South Africa amounted to $37.5 billion in 2006, some 8 percent of the region's GDP. But multilateral and bilateral debt relief accounted for a large share of the reported ODA. In fact, net official debt flows to the region have declined in recent years, from 1.5 percent of GDP in the early 1980s to 0.3 percent of GDP during 2000–05. New donors such as China and India could fill some of the funding gap, but their delinking of aid from political and economic reforms may dilute the effectiveness of ODA.

As for FDI, its 2.4 percent share in the region's GDP is about the same as in other developing regions, but that masks the fact that the FDI in Sub-Saharan Africa is concentrated in enclave sectors such as oil and natural resources and hence less supportive of broad-based growth. Other medium- and long-term private debt and equity flows to the region (excluding South Africa) are minuscule, and short-term debt flows have been very volatile. Personal and institutional remittances are rising. Recorded personal remittances rose from $3.2 billion in 1995 to $10.3 billion in 2006. But these flows made up roughly 2.1 percent of the region's GDP, significantly below the 3.5 percent of GDP in other developing countries. Institutional remittances from foundations, however, are becoming increasingly important.

On the basis of the pool of African migrants in Organisation for Economic Co-operation and Development countries and of reasonable assumptions about their incomes (average income in the host country) and saving rates (20 percent of income), the potential diaspora savings are estimated at $28.5 billion. Diaspora bonds could tap into these savings. Such bonds would also offer the region's flight capital—an estimated $8.1 billion annually from 1990 to 2005—a vehicle to return home. Thus, the region could raise $5 to $10 billion through diaspora bonds. Future-flow securitization is even larger. Using the methodology developed by Ketkar and Ratha in chapter 2, Ratha et al. estimate Sub-Saharan Africa's potential securitization at about $17 billion. Ketkar and Ratha put the most likely securitization volume at about $14 billion, with remittances accounting for its largest share.

Turning to other innovative mechanisms, Ratha et al. argue that there is potential for extending the scope of guarantees beyond large infrastructure projects and beyond sovereign borrowers. Making guarantees available to private sector ventures could bring in large amounts of private financing to Sub-Saharan Africa. IFFIm, essentially a financial structure for securitizing future aid commitments, could also yield significant funding up front. Since the aid commitments are from rich countries, IFFIm received high investment-grade credit ratings, well above the ratings of countries borrowing the funds. Using future aid commitments (from France, Italy, Norway, South Africa, Spain, Sweden, and the United Kingdom), IFFIm raised $1 billion in 2006, and plans are in place to raise an additional $4 billion. The AMC structure for vaccines launched last year is unlikely to increase aid flows to poor countries, but it could bring together private and public donors in an innovative way to help raise resources for development.

Innovations Classified by Intermediation Functions

Table 1.2 classifies both the early and recent innovations on the basis of the intermediation functions they facilitated. Thus, the switch from fixed- to floating-rate debt transferred the price risk from creditors to debtors. The advent of syndicated loans enhanced liquidity for developing countries. Debt-equity swaps pioneered by Chile gave creditors equity stakes in companies. The principal and rolling interest guarantees of the Brady bonds partially transferred credit risk from developing countries to the U.S. Treasury. The conversion of bank loans into bonds enhanced liquidity for developing countries, allowing those countries to subsequently issue global bonds. Future-flow securitizations are designed to transfer credit risk from borrowers, thereby enhancing credit ratings and expanding liquidity. Diaspora bonds are meant to enhance liquidity by appealing to their patriotism and by giving them a better risk-management tool. Finally, GDP-indexed bonds are also expected to enhance liquidity by giving creditors an option on the growth performance of developing countries.

A Role for Public Policy

International financial institutions (IFIs) like the World Bank Group and the regional development banks can play an important role in promoting the use of innovative financing mechanisms by developing countries. First and foremost, IFIs can educate public sector bureaucrats and private sector managers in the intricacies of and the potential for the new market-based techniques of raising development finance. Second, they can offer assistance in producing reliable and timely data needed to do innovative financing deals. This would include help to banks in tracking inflows of

TABLE 1.2

Innovations Classified by Financial Intermediation Function

Innovation	Price-risk transference	Credit-risk transference	Liquidity enhancement	Credit enhancement	Equity generation
	Function				
Floating-rate debt contracts	X				
Syndicated loans			X		
Debt-equity swaps					X
Brady bonds					
Par		X		X	
Discount	X	X		X	
Global bonds			X		
Future-flow securitization		X	X		
Monoliner guarantees				X	
Diaspora bonds			X		
GDP-indexed bonds			X		X

Source: Authors, following Levich 1988.

diversified payment rights (DPRs) including workers' remittances, and help to other companies in tracking export receivables. Securitization of future-flow receivables cannot be achieved without an adequate history of the relevant flows. Also, countries are likely to find it difficult to issue GDP-indexed bonds in the absence of reliable and timely GDP statistics. Again, IFIs can provide a great deal of assistance to developing countries in collecting GDP data and certifying the data's accuracy, if necessary. Third, IFIs, especially the International Monetary Fund, should issue clear guidelines as to whether future-flow-backed debt, often legally interpreted as "true-sale," should be excluded from debt limits set under IMF programs. IFIs can also assist developing countries in building appropriate legal and institutional structure, including bankruptcy laws. Fourth, IFIs can provide seed money to create legal templates to facilitate debt issuance using various innovative financing techniques. Fifth, IFIs could go a step further and underwrite the likely high costs to be incurred by the first issuers of future-flow-backed debt and GDP-indexed bonds. Sixth, IFIs could undertake coordinated issuance of GDP-indexed bonds by a number of countries to overcome the problems of critical mass and liquidity. Finally, IFIs can help countries obtain sovereign ratings from the major rating agencies. Even when the sovereign is not interested in borrowing, having a sovereign rating will serve as a benchmark for subsovereign borrowers and help them access international capital markets.

The Future of Innovative Financing

The preceding overview of recent market-based innovations in raising development finance offers a variety of approaches that sovereign, sub-sovereign, and private sector entities in middle- as well as low-income developing countries can use to obtain additional funding. Countries that are rated up to five notches below investment grade and have sizable desirable receivables such as oil exports or DPRs, including workers' remittances, are the ideal candidates to benefit from securitization. A securitized transaction from such a country can receive investment-grade rating because its structure mitigates the usual convertibility and transfer risks. In addition, oil companies are generally considered good credit risks, and banks that generate large amounts of DPRs are in a special position insofar as they are unlikely to be allowed to fail lest there be systemwide negative implications.

The potential offered by diaspora bonds is also considerable for many developing countries. Those with a significant diaspora in the United States will have to meet the requirements of U.S. SEC registration, which may impose serious burdens of time and resources on smaller countries. Some of the North African and East European countries and Turkey, with their large diaspora presence in Europe, however, will be able to raise funds more easily on the continent, where the regulatory requirements are less stringent than in the United States.

The prospect of shadow ratings opening up access to international capital markets is particularly relevant for poor countries in Africa, many of which remain unrated. Innovations such as IFFIm and AMC are also more relevant for Africa. Although the expansion of partial official guarantees can galvanize private capital flows to all developing countries, Sub-Saharan Africa is once again likely to be the biggest beneficiary.

In addition to the above innovative financing mechanisms, several developed and developing countries have long used public-private partnerships (PPPs) to supplement limited official budgets and other resources to accelerate infrastructure development. Public-private partnerships typically refer to contractual agreements formed between a public sector entity and a private sector entity to generate private sector participation in infrastructure development projects. PPPs are designed to enable public sector entities to tap private sector capital, technology, and management expertise, as well as other resources. Their ultimate aim is to enhance infrastructure development in a more timely fashion than is possible with only public sector resources. Although PPP structures originated to speed up the construction of highways in developed countries, they are now increasingly used by developing countries in several sectors, including water and wastewater, education, health care, building construction, power, parks and recreation, technology, and many others. Many developing countries have used PPP structures in recent years—Brazil, China, Croatia, the Arab Republic of Egypt, Lebanon, Malaysia, Poland, Romania, and South Africa, to name a few.

Public-private partnerships, which are promoted by the World Bank, should continue to play an increasingly important role in generating funds for infrastructure projects in the developing world. The reasons PPP schemes are underutilized in many developing countries, but particularly in Sub-Saharan Africa, include lack of a relevant legal framework (an appropriate concession law, for instance) and economic and political stability. The World Bank can certainly provide the necessary support in drafting the appropriate laws. Furthermore, the World Bank can also use its guarantee instruments to cover the government performance risks that the market is unable to absorb or mitigate, thereby mobilizing private sector financing for infrastructure development projects in developing countries (Queiroz 2005).

In conclusion, it is worth reiterating that financing MDGs would require increasing the investment rate above the domestic saving rate, and the financing gap has to be bridged with additional financing from abroad. Official aid alone will not be sufficient for this purpose. The private sector has to become the engine of growth and employment generation in poor countries, and official aid efforts must catalyze innovative financing solutions for the private sector.

Notes

1. Innovative financing involves risk mitigation and credit enhancement through the provision of collateral (either existing or future assets), spreading risk among many investors, and guarantees by higher-rated third parties. Innovative financing is not limited to financial engineering. Tufano (2003) defined it as "the act of creating and then popularizing new financial instruments as well as new financial technologies, institutions and markets" (310). Innovations often take place when lenders and borrowers seek to improve price-risk trans-

ference, credit-risk transference, liquidity enhancement, credit enhancement, and equity generation (Levich 1988).

2. This book can be viewed as a companion to the book edited by Anthony B. Atkinson, New Sources of Development Finance (2004), which explores the potential for a tax on short-term capital and currency flows (Tobin tax), global environmental taxes, a global lottery, creation of new special drawing rights, increased private donations for development, increased remittances from emigrants, and the International Finance Facility recently proposed by the U.K. government. But none of these represents a market-based approach, which is the principal focus of the current book.

3. Data are from Global Development Finance and its predecessor, World Debt Tables, as cited in Williamson 2005, 40.

4. L. William Seidman, former chairman of the Federal Deposit Insurance Corporation, has admitted telling large banks that "the process of recycling petrodollars to the less developed countries was beneficial, and perhaps a patriotic duty" (Seidman 1993, 38).

5. Chile started the debt-equity swap program in 1985, allowing foreign and Chilean investors to buy Chile's foreign debt at the discounted price at which it traded in the secondary market, and then to negotiate prepayment in pesos at a rate somewhere between its nominal and market values. Foreigners were required to use the pesos in investments approved by the central bank.

6. The earlier advent of junk bonds also helped pave the way for the issuance of Brady and global bonds by the typically below-investment-grade developing countries. Prior to 1977, the junk bond market consisted of "fallen angels," or bonds whose initial investment-grade ratings were subsequently lowered. But the market began to change in 1977, when bonds that were rated below investment grade from the start were issued in large quantities.

7. The switch from bank lending to bonds has also made debt restructuring much more difficult than ever before, leading Eichengreen and Portes (1995) to recommend the inclusion of collective action clauses in bond contracts and the IMF to champion the sovereign debt restructuring mechanism (Krueger 2002).

8. Future-flow securitization deals have held up very well during the recent mortgage debt difficulties. Future-flow securitization transactions are very different from mortgage loan securitization. The latter are based on existing loans, typically denominated in local currency terms. The former refer to future flows, and typically raise cross-border foreign currency financing.

9. A salient characteristic of this asset class is that a variety of existing or future assets can be securitized. In the Unites States, for example, assets that have been securitized (or used as collateral) include revenues from existing or future films of a studio; music royalty rights, often including a catalog of revenues from a single artist or a group; franchise loans and leases; insurance premiums to be earned from customers; life settlements (the issuer is usually a life settlement company that monetizes a pool consisting of life insurance policies—gen-

erally from individuals over the age of 65 and with various ailments—that may otherwise be permitted to lapse); patent rights (intellectual property); small business loans; stranded cost (financing used by a utility to recover certain contractual costs that would otherwise not be recovered from rate payers due to deregulation of the electric power industry); structured settlements (bonds are secured by rights to payments due to a claimant under a settlement agreement); and tobacco settlements and legal fees (bonds are secured by tobacco settlement revenues—over $200 billion over the first 25 years—payable to states under the Master Settlement Agreement; also legal fees awarded to attorneys who represented the states are being securitized). In 2007, Deutsche Bank, with the support of KfW, securitized microfinance loans to raise 60 million euros from private investors to support 21 microfinance institutions in 15 countries. Securitizing future aid commitments and charitable contributions is yet another innovation currently being developed.

10. This rating model successfully predicted the rating upgrades of Brazil, Colombia, and Peru, and first-time ratings of Ghana, Kenya, and Uganda in 2007 and 2008 (see annex table 5A.1 on p. 129). Since then, Albania, Belarus, Cambodia, Gabon, and St. Vincent and the Grenadines have also been rated—exactly or closely aligned with the predictions in table 5.7 on p. 124.

References

Atkinson, Anthony B., ed. 2004. *New Sources of Development Finance*. Oxford: Oxford University Press.

Ballantyne, William. 1996. "Syndicated Loans." *Arab Law Review* 11 (4): 372–82.

Borensztein, Eduardo, and Paolo Mauro. 2002. "Reviving the Case for GDP-Indexed Bonds." IMF Policy Discussion Paper No. 02/10, International Monetary Fund, Washington, DC.

Brown, Ernest W., ed. 2008. "Strictly Macro," June 18. Latin American Economics Research, Santander, New York.

Cline, William R. 1995. *International Debt Reexamined*. Washington, DC: Institute for International Economics.

Costa, Alejo, Marcos Chamon, and Luca Antonio Ricci. 2008. "Is There a Novelty Premium on New Financial Instruments? The Argentine Experience with GDP-Indexed Warrants." IMF Working Paper WP/08/109, International Monetary Fund, Washington, DC.

Dadush, Uri, Dipak Dasgupta, and Dilip Ratha, 2000. "The Role of Short-Term Debt in Recent Crises." *Finance and Development*, December.

Eichengreen, Barry, and Richard Portes. 1995. "Crisis? What Crisis? Orderly Workouts for Sovereign Debtors." Center for Economic Policy Research, London, i-xviii.

EMTA (Trade Association for Emerging Markets), http://www.emta.org, New York. Various EMTA press releases.

Euromoney. 2006. "Argentine GDP Warrants," January 25.

Griffith-Jones, Stephany, and Krishnan Sharma. 2006. "GDP-Indexed Bonds: Making It Happen." Working Paper No. 21, Department of Economic and Social Affairs. United Nations, New York.

Ketkar, Suhas, and Stefano Natella. 1993. *An Introduction to Emerging Countries Fixed Income Instruments*. New York: Credit Suisse First Boston.

Krueger, Anne. 2002. *A New Approach to Sovereign Debt Restructuring*. Washington, DC: International Monetary Fund.

Levich, Richard M. 1988. "Financial Innovations in International Financial Markets." In *The United States in the World Economy*, ed. Martin Feldstein, 215–77. Cambridge, MA: National Bureau of Economic Research.

Queiroz, Cesar. 2005. "Launching Public Private Partnerships for Highways in Transition Economies." TP-9, September, Transport Sector Board, World Bank, Washington, DC.

Ratha, Dilip, Prabal De, and Sanket Mohapatra. 2007. "Shadow Sovereign Ratings for Unrated Developing Countries." Policy Research Working Paper 4269, World Bank, Washington, DC.

Ratha, Dilip, Sanket Mohapatra, and Sonia Plaza. 2005. "Beyond Aid: New Sources and Innovative Mechanisms for Financing Development in Sub-Saharan Africa." WPS4609, Development Prospects Group, World Bank, Washington, DC.

Seidman, L. William. 1993. *Full Faith and Credit: The Great S & L Debacle and Other Washington Sagas*. New York: Crown.

Tufano, Peter. 2003. "Financial Innovation." In *Handbook of Economics and Finance*, ed. George M. Constantinides, Milton Harris, and Rene M. Stulz, 307–35. Amsterdam, The Netherlands: Elsevier.

Williamson, John. 2005. *Curbing the Boom-Bust Cycle: Stabilizing Capital Flows to Emerging Markets*. Washington, DC: Peterson Institute for International Economics.

World Bank. 2007. *Global Monitoring Report 2007: Confronting the Challenges of Gender Equality and Fragile States*. Washington, DC: World Bank.

———. 2008. *Global Development Finance 2008*. Washington, DC: World Bank.

CHAPTER 2

Future-Flow Securitization for Development Finance

Suhas Ketkar and Dilip Ratha

Securitization is a fairly recent financial innovation. The first securitized transactions in the United States occurred in the 1970s and involved the pooling and repackaging of home mortgages for resale as tradable securities by lenders. Since then, securitized markets have grown in sophistica-

The research reported in this chapter was undertaken over the past 10 years and resulted in four publications (Ketkar and Ratha 2001a, 2001b, 2004–2005; Ratha 2006). We would like to thank Uri Dadush and Ashoka Mody of the Economic Prospects and Policy Group for extensive discussions and Arun Sharma and Hans Paris of IFC for providing important insights. Anthony Bottrill, Sara Calvo, and Alejandro Izquierdo also made useful comments. This research relies extensively on interviews with professionals from rating agencies, investment banks, legal firms, and insurance companies active in the market for future-flow securitization. In particular, we would like to thank the following organizations and individuals for sharing their knowledge, information, and views: Ambac (Daniel Bond, Michael Morcom); Asset Guaranty Insurance Company (David Bigelow, Eric R. Van Heyst); Banco Santander (Shailesh S. Deshpande); Chase Securities Inc. (Mark A. Tuttle); Citibank (Radford C. West); Cleary, Gottlieb, Steen and Hamilton (Andres de la Cruz); Credit Suisse First Boston (David Anderson); Davis Polk & Wardwell (E. Waide Warner Jr., Sartaj Gill); Fitch IBCA, Duff and Phelps (Jill Zelter, Patrick Kearns, Suzanne Albers, Christopher Donnelly); JP Morgan (Hillary Ward); Moody's (Maria Muller, Susan Knapp); Morgan Stanley Dean Witter (Sadek M. Wahba); Standard & Poor's (Laura Feinland Katz, Gary Kochubka, Rosario Buendia, Kevin M. Kime, Eric Gretch); and TIAA CREF (Sanjeev Handa).

tion to cover a wide range of assets. In developing countries, the focus has been on securitizing a wide spectrum of future-flow receivables, including exports of oil and gas, minerals and metals, and agricultural raw materials as well as electronic and paper remittances, credit card vouchers, airline tickets, net international telephone charges, and even tax revenues. More recently, banks have started securitizing diversified payment rights (DPRs), that is, all payments that flow through the SWIFT system.[1] Several sovereign, subsovereign, and private sector borrowers have used future-flow securitization to raise some $80 billion since the first securitization of net international telephone receivables by Mexico's Telmex in 1987. Developing-country issuers have found market placements backed by hard currency receivables particularly useful in times of financial stress because their structure allows issuers to escape the sovereign credit ceiling.

This chapter describes the typical structure of a future-flow-backed securitization in the following section and discusses how this structure and the choice of the receivable can mitigate many of the risks involved in taking on exposure to issuers from developing countries. The third section elaborates the rationale for securitization, followed by the history of future-flow securitizations from developing countries and an evaluation of the potential for this asset class. Given the sharp rise in workers' remittances to developing countries in recent years and concerns that such flows may not really be good for the recipient countries, the chapter then examines the role that securitization can play in magnifying the development impact of remittances. The chapter concludes by describing the constraints that inhibit the issuance of debt backed by future-flow receivables and by exploring the remedial role for public policy.

Risk Mitigation in Future-Flow Securitization

A typical future-flow structure involves the borrowing entity (or originator) selling its future product (receivable) directly or indirectly to an offshore special purpose vehicle (SPV; see figure 2.1). The SPV issues the debt instrument. Designated international customers (or obligors) are directed to pay for exports from the originating entity directly to an offshore collection account managed by a trustee. The collection agent allocates these receivables to the SPV, which in turn makes principal and interest payments to the investors. Excess collections are then directed to the originator.

FIGURE 2.1

Stylized Structure of a Typical Future-Flow Securitization

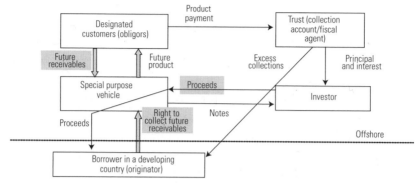

Source: Authors.

In short, this structure ensures that the hard currency receivable does not enter the country until the bondholders have been paid. As a result, the government of the borrower cannot impede timely servicing of securitized bonds. Thus, the structure mitigates the usual transfer and convertibility risks, allowing borrowers in developing countries to pierce the sovereign credit ceiling and obtain financing at lower interest costs and for longer duration. Additional examples of future-flow securitization structures are provided in the annex.

Risk mitigation in securitized transactions occurs through the structure of the transaction as well as the choice of the future-flow receivable (S&P 2004c). By obtaining a legally binding consent from designated customers that they would make payments to the offshore trust, the structure mitigates sovereign transfer and convertibility risks. The structure also mitigates the bankruptcy risk because the SPV typically has no other creditors and hence cannot go bankrupt. Of course, the risk of the originator going bankrupt exists. Such risk is mitigated in part when originators have high local-currency credit ratings and low performance risk, which captures the ability and willingness of the originator to produce and deliver the product that generates the receivables. Rating agencies have also come to accept the argument that an entity may continue to generate receivables even when it is in financial default. This "true sale" principle has now become an expected feature in future-flow securitized transactions. Furthermore, Fitch Ratings uses the "going concern" and Standard & Poor's (S&P) uses "survival" assessments in awarding asset-backed transactions of certain entities, such as banks, higher credit ratings than the issuers' local currency ratings. Both the going concern and survival assessments reflect the belief that, in many countries, entities like banks are not liquidated even when they experience financial default.

Though a securitized transaction can be structured so as to minimize the transfer and convertibility risks, some other elements of sovereign risk cannot be totally eliminated. For instance, the sovereign can insist on the originator selling the product in the domestic market rather than in the export market or selling the product to customers other than those who sign the consent agreement. This product-diversion risk is generally greater for commodities such as agricultural staples. It is relatively low for crude oil (such as Mayan crude oil from Mexico), which is sold to a limited number of buyers who have the requisite refining capacity. It is also low for credit card receivables, since there are only a handful of credit card companies (such as Visa, MasterCard, and American Express).

The product risk arising from price and volume volatility, and hence fluctuations in cash flow, cannot be totally eliminated, but it can be mitigated by using excess coverage or overcollateralization. Typically, it is easier to control product risk for commodities like oil, gas, metals, and minerals, for which there is demand from many diverse sources. In contrast, custom-made products are likely to have high product risk unless the parties have adequately enforceable long-term sales contracts.

Keeping in mind the performance, diversion, and product risks, the rating agencies have arrived at the hierarchy of future-flow receivable transactions detailed in table 2.1. Securitization of heavy crude oil receivables is deemed to be the most secure. DPR flows that come through the SWIFT system represent a new collateral that has been securitized since 2000. Such SWIFT flows include qualified export earnings, foreign direct investment inflows, and workers' remittances. This diversification in the source of origin makes DPRs the second-best collateral. In contrast, securitization of future tax receipts is thought to be the least secure.

It is possible to securitize future-flow receivables even at the lowest end of the hierarchy shown in table 2.1. An example of this is the securitization of co-participation tax revenues (through federal revenue sharing) by several Argentine provinces (S&P 1999). But given the problems experienced by such tax-backed transactions since Argentina's currency collapse and sovereign default in 2001, securitization of future local-currency tax receivables to raise foreign capital is unlikely unless many more safeguards can be put in place.

TABLE 2.1
Hierarchy in Future-Flow-Backed Transactions

1. Heavy crude oil receivables
2. Diversified payment rights, airline ticket receivables, telephone receivables, credit card receivables, and electronic remittances
3. Oil and gas royalties and export receivables
4. Paper remittances
5. Tax revenue receivables

Sources: Fitch Ratings and Standard & Poor's.

Insurance companies played a rising role in the 1990s in structured finance transactions by providing complete financial guarantees. For example, Ambac Assurance Corp. provided guarantees in a 2002 credit card merchant voucher securitization in Central America, which involved five countries: Costa Rica, El Salvador, Guatemala, Honduras, and Nicaragua. While Standard & Poor's assigned this multiple-jurisdiction Credomatic transaction a stand-alone investment-grade credit rating of BBB−, the Ambac guarantees of timely payment of interest and principal raised the transaction rating to AAA.[2] The Multilateral Investment Guarantee Agency has also provided insurance against political risks in several future-flow deals.

Rationale for Securitization

From the investors' point of view, the attractiveness of future-flow securities lies in their good credit rating and their stellar performance in good as well as bad times. Because much of secured debt paper is traded infrequently, there is a lack of adequate information on secondary market price and spread on securitized debt. Nevertheless, the available information (as well as the perceptions of market players) suggests that future-flow securities tend to have smaller average spreads as well as lower volatility in price and spread than unsecured debt of developing countries (Ketkar and Ratha 2001a, 17–18). Defaults on rated future-flow asset-backed securities issued by developing countries have also been very infrequent. In general, the asset class has performed well despite the Mexican peso crisis in 1994–95, the Asian liquidity crisis in 1997–98, and the Russian and Ecuadoran debt defaults in 1998 and 1999. An interesting example is the

Pakistan telephone receivable deal that continued to perform even in the face of selective default on sovereign debt (see box 2.1).

Indeed, the asset class was default free until Argentina's sovereign debt default at the end of 2001 (Fitch Ratings 1999c). Subsequently, Argentina devalued the currency, imposed restrictions on hard currency transfers, and pesified most contracts (that is, it compulsorily converted certain dollar obligations into pesos at a one-to-one exchange rate). Pesification in Argentina in January 2002 adversely affected mortgage-backed securities as well as companies that were local currency generators, such as utilities. Their structured dollar-denominated debt obligations ran into difficulties. Utilities, for instance, were unable to raise tariffs adequately to cover the bloated local currency costs of servicing dollar-denominated debt. The dollar-denominated debt of Argentine provinces that was backed by peso-denominated revenue-sharing arrangements also ran into trouble. But securities backed by future hard-currency receivables continued to perform on schedule, proving their resiliency against transferability and convertibility controls (S&P 2003). Both the oil export–backed debt of Argentina's oil company YPF and the oil royalty–backed bonds issued by the province of Salta continued to perform. The full repayment of the Aluar Aluminio Argentino S.A.I.C. transaction in mid-2004 confirmed once again that hard currency future-flow-backed securitizations remain a strong and reliable financing alternative for developing countries (S&P 2004a).

BOX 2.1

Pakistan Telecommunications Company Limited (PTCL)—No Default on Asset-Backed Papers Even in the Face of Selective Default on Sovereign Debt

In 1997, the PTCL issued $250 million in bonds backed by future telephone settlement receivables from AT&T, MCI, Sprint, British Telecom, Mercury Telecommunications, and Deutsche Telekom. Even though PTCL is 88 percent owned by the government of Pakistan, this issue was rated BBB− by Standard & Poor's, four notches higher than the B+ sovereign rating.

Following the detonation of nuclear devices in May 1998, Pakistan's economy and creditworthiness deteriorated rapidly. Investors became con-

BOX 2.1 (continued)

cerned that faced with increasing official demands for equal burden sharing, the government might place the future-flow receivable-backed securities in a single basket with all other sovereign debt and interfere with PTCL's debt servicing. The government of Pakistan rescheduled its Paris Club debt obligations on January 30, 1999, and signed a preliminary London Club agreement on July 6, 1999, to reschedule $877 million of sovereign commercial loan arrears. But PTCL's future-flow net receivable–backed bonds were not subjected to any rescheduling or restructuring, although their rating was downgraded several times during 1997–98 (see table below). Partly this was because the amount required to service these obligations made up only 30 percent of the total net telephone receivables of the company. But the main reason PTCL's bonds were not rescheduled or restructured was that there was a strong incentive on the sovereign's part to keep servicing the bonds and not jeopardize the operation of the local telephone network, and even more important, to not risk severing Pakistan's telecommunication link to the rest of the world.

History of PTCL Credit Rating

Date	Pakistan sovereign rating	PTCL rating	Comment
Aug. 1997	B+	BBB−	At issuance due to its structure
June 1998	B−	BB+/− outlook	Following the detonation of a nuclear device, which led to the imposition of trade sanctions and the freezing of $13 billion in foreign-currency bank deposits
July 1998	CCC	B−	Following a downgrade of Pakistan's rating from B− to CCC
Dec. 1998	CC	CCC+	Following a tentative agreement with the International Monetary Fund, which opened the way for debt restructuring while it left uncertain the precise fate of PTCL debt
Jan. 1999	SD	CCC+	Following the rescheduling of $969 million of commercial loans in default since July 1998
Dec. 1999	B−	CCC+	Expected to be upgraded to BB

Source: Standard & Poor's 1999b.

While this near-perfect track record (of no default) is encouraging for this asset class, the test has not been stringent until now because future-flow asset-backed debt still represents a very small percentage of total debt. One of the few cases of investor dispute involving an airline receivable securitization deal by Colombia's Avianca was settled out of court, without default on the underlying securities.[3]

Future-flow securitization transactions are appealing to issuers because their above-sovereign-credit rating reduces the cost of raising financing, particularly in times of distress in global capital markets. The cost saving is the largest when securitization results in an investment-grade rating for a transaction from a speculative sovereign. Since investment-grade debt can be purchased by many more classes of institutional investors, the transition to investment grade brings in a sizable reduction in spread. The extent of cost saving also depends on conditions in the international capital markets and the reception to the plain vanilla sovereign bonds from the country. This is best illustrated with a few examples.

First, when the fear of the Workers' Party candidate, Luis Inacio Lula da Silva, being elected Brazil's president sent spreads on Brazilian debt soaring and all but cut off access to international finance for Brazilian public and private sector entities, Brazilian banks began to securitize DPR flows. The state-owned Banco do Brasil got the ball rolling in early 2002 by doing the first securitization of DPRs to raise $450 million. Moody's and Standard & Poor's rated this transaction investment grade at Baa1 and BBB+, respectively. Brazil's sovereign ratings at that time were B1 by Moody's and BB− by Standard & Poor's. Other major Brazilian banks—Banespa, Bradesco, Itau, and Unibanco—followed suit and together did 24 DPR-backed transactions to raise a total of $5.1 billion ($2.1 billion in 2002, $1.8 billion in 2003, and $1.2 billion in 2004). Of these 24 transactions, 10 were rated AAA thanks to insurance coverage by Ambac and others. Of the remaining 14, eight were rated BBB, two were BBB−, and four were BBB+. For eight transactions on which data are available, the spread at issuance averaged 334 basis points over U.S. Treasury bonds. The spread on the Brazil component of the JP Morgan–tracked Emerging Markets Bond Index (EMBI+) during those years averaged 1,116 basis points over Treasuries. Thus, the DPR securitization resulted in savings of over 700 basis points.

Another example illustrates how cost savings to issuers depend on conditions in the global financial markets. In late 1998, when financing to developing countries dried up as a result of the crises in Asia and the Russian Federation, Pemex Finance Ltd., a special-purpose vehicle established to finance capital expenditures of Mexico's state-owned oil and gas company (Pemex), issued a series of oil-export-backed securities that were rated BBB by Standard & Poor's, three notches above the Mexican sovereign and Pemex unsecured debt. Through securitization Pemex saved over 100 basis points from what it would have had to pay on senior Pemex debt. By 2000, global risk appetite for developing-country debt had improved, and the spread on the unsecured Pemex senior debt had declined to 325 basis points from 462.5 basis points in 1998 in the aftermath of the East Asian currency crisis. The interest cost saving to Pemex on a similar transaction was 50 basis points in 2000. This shows that future-flow-backed transactions offer greater spread advantage in bad rather than good times in the international capital markets.[4]

In addition to providing lower-cost funding, securitization also allows issuers to extend maturity of their debt and improve risk management as well as balance-sheet performance (e.g., return on equity). Securitization also permits issuers from developing countries to tap a wider class of investors. For example, this asset class is attractive to insurance companies that are required to buy only investment-grade assets. These investors also tend to buy and hold an asset until maturity. Moreover, by establishing a credit history for the borrower, these deals enhance the borrower's ability to access the market in the future and reduce the costs of that access.

Governments may find this asset class attractive because it can provide a way of accessing markets during times of liquidity crisis. Because of their investment-grade rating, future-flow deals attract a much wider class of investors than unsecured deals. Thus, future-flow deals can improve market liquidity and reduce market volatility. That can generate added interest on the part of international investors in other asset classes or on the part of other borrowers. For many developing countries, future-flow receivable-backed securitization may be the only way to begin accessing international capital markets.[5]

Perhaps the most important incentive for governments to promote this asset class lies in the externalities associated with future-flow deals. Future-flow deals involve a much closer scrutiny of the legal and institutional environment—the existence as well as the implementation of laws relating to property rights and bankruptcy procedures—than do unsecured transactions. In trying to structure away various elements of sovereign risk, highly trained professionals from investment banks, legal firms, and international rating agencies spend enormous amounts of time and energy examining the investment climate in a country, paying special attention to ways in which the sovereign can affect the performance of private or public sector issuers. They also closely study the risks facing the sovereign itself. Thus, these deals can produce enormous informational externalities by clarifying the legal and institutional environment and the investment climate in a developing country. Besides, the preparation of a future-flow transaction, if backed by the government, may involve structural reforms of the legal and institutional environment. These reforms would facilitate domestic capital market development and encourage international placements, as in the aftermath of the Brady deals in the early 1990s. Such results are evident from Mexico's experience (S&P 2004b).

Securitization Track Record

Developing countries have been securitizing future-flow receivables for about 20 years. The three rating agencies—Fitch Ratings, Moody's, and Standard & Poor's—have by now rated more than 400 transactions. Data compiled from the three agencies show that over $80 billion has been raised using future-flow securitization.[6] As figure 2.2 shows, the issuance of future-flow receivable-backed securities increased especially after the Mexican crisis in 1994–95. It peaked at just about $12 billion in 1996, thanks to Pemex's $6 billion oil export receivable transaction.[7] While down from that high level, securitized issuance has stayed robust, since then averaging $6.1 billion per year.

FIGURE 2.2
Asset-Backed Securitization Issuance, 1992–2006

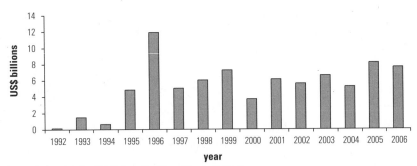

Sources: Authors; based on Fitch Ratings, Moody's, and Standard & Poor's.

Latin American issuers dominate the market for future-flow securitization (figure 2.3). Mexico alone accounts for roughly 30 percent of asset-backed transactions in nominal dollar terms. Thanks to robust activity of Brazilian banks in securitizing DPRs in the early years of this decade, Brazil has now moved into second place with 19.3 percent market share. Turkish banks have also tapped international capital markets by aggressive DPR securitization in recent years, increasing the country's market share to 16.9 percent at present, from 3.5 percent in the 1990s. Securitization is not limited to large countries. A number of small countries, such as El Salvador, Jamaica, Panama, and Peru, have also been active in securitizing remittances and credit card vouchers. In addition to Turkey, the Arab Republic of Egypt, Kazakhstan, Russia, and South Africa represent the non–Latin American presence in this market.

Although some 32 percent of future-flow transactions in dollar terms are backed by oil and gas export receivables, the asset class has demonstrated an enormous scope for creativity. Since 2002, DPRs have increased in importance and now account for 28 percent market share by amount raised. The role of credit card vouchers in providing securitized finance has declined somewhat, to 16 percent. Mineral and metal export receivables, agricultural raw materials exports, airline ticket receivables, and telecommunications receivables also remain important sources of collateral. The

FIGURE 2.3
Major Issuers, 1992–2006

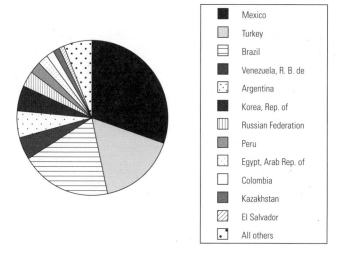

Source: Authors; based on Fitch Ratings, Moody's, and Standard & Poor's.

share of non-oil deals is much larger in terms of number of transactions, given the large difference in the size of oil and gas versus non-oil-backed transactions. The average size of oil-and–gas-based transactions has been as large as $417 million. The average size of transactions securitized by DPRs and other receivables has been much smaller (see table 2.2).

Potential for Future-Flow Securitization

The future-flow-secured transactions allow issuers to pledge receivables over a number of years and hence open up the possibility of raising funds in capital markets that are a multiple of a given year's receivables. As discussed earlier, exports of oil and gas, minerals and metals, and agricultural raw materials, plus receivables from credit card vouchers, workers' remittances, and net international telephone charges, are suitable for future-flow securitization. In deriving the potential, the objective is not to forecast, but to obtain a benchmark against which the severity of constraints on such issuance could be gauged.[8]

Developing countries exported $490.9 billion worth of oil and gas and $129.9 billion worth of minerals and metals on average between 2003 and 2006. In addition, they received about $179.6 billion in travel receipts from nonresidents. These three items plus agricultural raw materials (about $51 billion) provided on average over $850 billion worth of foreign

TABLE 2.2
Future-Flow Securitization Worldwide, by Asset, 1992–2006

Sources of collateral	Volume (US$ millions)	Share (%)	No. of transactions	Average size (US$ millions)
Oil and gas	26,250	31.3	63	417
DPRs	23,084	27.5	122	189
Remittances	1,782	2.1	16	111
Credit card vouchers	13,044	15.6	63	207
Minerals and metals	9,164	10.9	55	167
Agriculture	2,705	3.2	22	123
Ticket receivables	1,486	1.8	8	187
Telecoms	1,310	1.6	15	87
Others	4,978	5.9	23	216
Total	83,803	100.0	387	212

Sources: Authors; based on Fitch Ratings, Moody's, and Standard & Poor's.

exchange to developing countries in 2003–06. Applying an overcollateralization ratio of 5:1—that is, assuming only $1 of debt is backed by $5 of future export revenue—the potential size of future-flow-backed securitization could exceed $150 billion per year (table 2.3). This calculation assumes that only half of the future flows of foreign visitors' expenditures are paid in credit cards.[9] Oil and gas exports from Saudi Arabia are excluded from these calculations, reflecting its role as a net exporter of capital. Also many countries that did not report balance-of-payments data to the International Monetary Fund (IMF) are excluded.

A more realistic assessment of securitization potential is provided in table 2.4. It is built on the previously stated premise that the biggest benefit from securitization occurs when a transaction from a speculative-grade country receives an investment-grade rating. Consequently, the prime candidates for securitization are countries that are rated B or better, because pledging of a future receivable allows the transaction to be rated up to five notches above the sovereign credit ceiling. Limiting securitization to countries rated B or better but below investment grade still implies a total potential issuance of $57 billion per year.

Tables 2.3 and 2.4 confirm that oil and gas exports are the dominant source for potential securitization across all regions and income classes. These account for just over 60 percent of total potential issuance from all

TABLE 2.3

Securitization Potential of Regions and Sectors, 2003–06 (average)
(US$ billions)

Country/region	Oil and gas exports	Agricultural exports	Minerals and metals exports	Credit card vouchers	Total
All developing countries	98.2	10.2	26.0	18.0	152.3
Low-income countries	12.7	1.3	2.4	1.3	17.7
Lower-middle-income countries	31.7	3.8	7.6	7.7	50.8
Upper-middle-income countries	53.8	5.1	16.0	9.0	83.9
East Asia and the Pacific	12.8	3.6	5.1	5.4	26.9
Europe and Central Asia	32.1	2.5	6.5	5.0	46.0
Latin America and the Caribbean	19.5	2.3	9.3	3.3	34.3
Middle East and North Africa	22.0	0.2	0.7	2.2	25.1
South Asia	1.6	0.3	1.1	0.9	3.9
Sub-Saharan Africa	10.3	1.3	3.3	1.3	16.1

Source: Authors' calculations. Data on exports are from the World Bank's *World Development Indicators,* various years.

TABLE 2.4

Most Likely Issuers' Securitization Potential, 2003–06 (average)

(US$ billions)

Country/region	Oil and gas exports	Agricultural exports	Minerals and metals exports	Credit card vouchers	Total
All developing countries	35.1	4.2	9.2	8.5	57.0
Low-income countries	4.4	1.0	1.9	1.2	8.5
Lower-middle-income countries	19.0	1.9	0.9	3.5	25.3
Upper-middle-income countries	11.7	1.3	4.3	3.8	21.1
East Asia and the Pacific	5.7	1.1	1.1	5.4	13.3
Europe and Central Asia	2.8	0.4	0.5	5.0	8.5
Latin America and the Caribbean	13.7	1.5	4.3	3.3	22.7
Middle East and North Africa	10.3	0.2	0.5	2.2	13.2
South Asia	1.6	0.3	1.1	0.9	3.9
Sub-Saharan Africa	1.0	0.8	0.5	1.3	2.2

Source: Authors' calculations. Data on exports are from the World Bank's *World Development Indicators,* various years.

developing countries. The potential for securitizing minerals and metals exports is relatively large in upper-middle-income countries and in Latin America and the Caribbean as well as South Asia. The potential for securitizing credit card vouchers, in contrast, appears to be relatively high in lower-middle-income countries and for countries in South Asia.

In summary, the size of future-flow receivables of developing countries from exports of oil and gas, minerals and metals, and agricultural raw materials and from credit card vouchers could be as large as $150 billion, but more likely about $57 billion per annum. Interestingly, Latin America accounts for a quarter to one-half of this potential size, which is in sharp contrast to its absolute dominance at present (figure 2.3). This is not to imply that the potential for securitization is exhausted in Latin America. But this exercise indicates a sizable potential for growth of this asset class in other regions. In particular, the greatest potential seems to be in the East Asia and Pacific and the Middle East and North Africa regions. Many countries in these regions are also middle-income countries that need external financing. Several countries in the Middle East have large amounts of oil collateral that could potentially be securitized if these countries needed external capital. Countries in East Asia and the Pacific (particularly Indonesia, Malaysia, and the Philippines) also have large amounts of receivables that could potentially be securitized. In South Asia, the potential for this asset class lies in minerals and metals exports and credit card vouchers from tourism.

Magnifying the Development Impact of Remittances

Workers' remittances to developing countries have increased enormously in recent years, to an estimated $239.7 billion in 2007, up from $84.5 billion in 2000 (World Bank, *Global Development Finance* 2008). Despite their positive role in reducing poverty and supporting investment in human capital, the evidence of their development impact is mixed (Chami, Fullenkamp, and Jahjah 2003). While the thesis that remittances retard growth suffers from many theoretical and empirical problems, there is little doubt that developing countries could do more to leverage remittances. Banks can raise funds by securitizing remittance receivables and then use the proceeds to increase lending.

Remittance securitization typically involves a bank (see box 2.2 for an example involving Banco do Brasil) pledging its future remittance receivables to an offshore special purpose vehicle. The SPV issues the debt. Designated correspondent banks are directed to channel remittance flows of the borrowing bank through an offshore collection account managed by a trustee. The collection agent makes principal and interest payments to the investors and sends excess collections to the borrowing bank. Since remittances do not enter the issuer's home country, the rating agencies believe that the structure mitigates the usual sovereign transfer and convertibility risks. Such transactions also often resort to excess coverage to mitigate the risk of volatility and seasonality in remittances.

By mitigating currency convertibility risk, a key component of sovereign risk, the future-flow securitization structure allows securities to be rated better than the sovereign credit rating. As discussed before, the ratings on these transactions are still capped by the issuer's local currency credit rating. This is where banks have an advantage. Large local banks with significant market shares, in particular, are likely to be rated investment grade in local currency terms. Governments can hardly allow them to fail, fearing widespread systemic ripple effects. As long as large banks are favored to remain in business as going concerns, they are likely to continue to receive workers' remittances and hence retain the ability to service their securitized debt. Large banks, therefore, can use securitized

BOX 2.2

Banco do Brasil's (BdB) Nikkei RemittanceTrust Securitization

Amount: US$250 million. Collateral: U.S. dollar– or Japanese yen–denominated worker remittances. Transaction rating BBB+ versus BdB's and Brazil's local currency rating of BB+/Stable and foreign currency rating of BB–/Stable.

This deal involved Banco do Brasil selling its future remittance receivables from Brazilian workers in Japan directly or indirectly to a Cayman Is- land–based offshore SPV named Nikkei Remittance Rights Finance Compa- ny. A New York City–based SPV issued and sold the debt instrument to in- vestors, receiving US$250 million. BdB Japan was directed to transfer remittances directly to the collection account managed by the New York–based trust. The collection agent was to make principal and interest payments to the investors. Excess collections were to be directed to the originator BdB via the SPV.

Since remittances did not enter Brazil, the rating agencies believed that the structure mitigated the usual sovereign transfer and convertibility risks. The structure also mitigated the bankruptcy risk because the SPV had no other creditors and hence could not go bankrupt. Of course, the risk of BdB go- ing bankrupt existed, but such risk was minimal given the government- owned BdB's dominant position in Brazil. Furthermore, legal opinion held that creditors would continue to have access to the pledged security (that is, remittances) even if BdB were to file a bankruptcy petition.

However, a number of residual risks remained, and they were difficult to structure away. These included the performance risk—the ability and will- ingness of BdB to garner remittances and deliver them to the collection ac- count managed by the New York–based trustee; the product risk—the abil- ity and willingness of Japan to generate remittances; and the diversion risk—the possibility of BdB selling the remittance rights to another party. The performance risk is generally captured in the issuer's local currency rat- ing. For entities such as banks, Fitch Ratings uses the going concern and Standard & Poor's uses the survival assessment of the originating entity in rating an asset-backed transaction higher than the issuer's local currency rating. This was the case for the BdB's Nikkei Remittance Trust transaction, which was rated BBB+ by Standard & Poor's, whereas BdB had a BB+ local rating. In reaching this decision, Standard & Poor's took into account (1) BdB's position as the largest financial institution in Brazil (with a 2,900-strong branch network), which makes it the most natural conduit for funds transfers, (2) the long-established presence of BdB in Japan since 1972, and (3) the importance of worker remittances in generating foreign exchange for the Brazilian government.

Structure of BdB Remittance Securitization

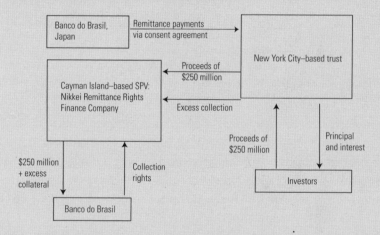

Source: Standard & Poor's 2002.

The product risk from volatility and seasonal fluctuations in remittances was mitigated via overcollateralization or excess coverage, with a debt service coverage ratio of 7.64x. Another element of the product risk was partially mitigated by recognizing Japan's need for workers to supplement the native workforce, and the availability of Brazilians of Japanese descent to fill this demand. Standard & Poor's, however, recognized as constraints on the rating the possibilities of Japan obtaining workers from countries other than Brazil, and of BdB selling remittance rights to another party. It expressly identified the latter as an event of default, triggering early amortization.

(Box continues on the following page.)

BOX 2.2 (continued)

Some elements of the sovereign risk also cannot be totally eliminated. For example, Banco Central do Brasil can compel BdB to pay remittances directly to the central bank instead of the trust. A degree of protection against this risk is provided by the fact that BdB is majority owned by the government of Brazil. In other instances, remittance securitized transactions have made designated correspondent banks sign a Notice and Acknowledgement, binding under U.S. law (or the law of a highly rated country), that they will make payments to the offshore trust. That would make the sovereign reluctant to take the drastic step of requiring payments into the central bank. Currency devaluation is yet another element of sovereign risk that cannot be totally eliminated, even in structured transactions. For instance, currency devaluation may affect the size and timing of remittances, particularly through formal channels.

Source: Standard & Poor's 2002.

---

structures to achieve investment-grade ratings on their remittance-backed foreign currency debt. In the case of El Salvador, for example, the remittance-backed securities were rated investment grade, four notches above the sub-investment-grade sovereign rating of BB. As table 2.5 shows, the various remittance- or DPR-backed transactions were rated two to five notches above the sovereign ratings.

Skeptics have raised a number of concerns about the stability of remittances, the incentives the governments may have to divert remittance flows from banks involved in securitization, and the ability of banks to securitize remittances that don't belong to them. These concerns are addressed in the next three sections.

Will remittances stay up in a crisis?

Whether remittances will hold up in a crisis appears to depend on the type of crisis. Crises caused by natural disasters often bring about a rise in remittances. Thus, countries in Asia that were hit by the tsunami in December 2004 collectively experienced a 33 percent surge in remittances in 2005 to $21 billion. Similarly, the massive earthquakes in Turkey in August 1999 and Gujarat, India, in January 2001 raised rather than reduced remit-

TABLE 2.5
Remittance- and DPR-Backed Transaction Ratings

Year	Issuer	Amount (US$ millions)	Transaction rating	Sovereign rating	Rating gain (no. of notches)
2007	Banco Bradesco, Brazil	400	A−	BB	5
2005	Banco de Credito del Peru	50	BBB	BB+	2
2004	Banco Salvadoreno	25	BBB	BB+	2
2002	Banco do Brasil	250	BBB+	BB−	5
1998	Banco Cuscatlan, El Salvador	50	BBB	BB	3

Source: Standard & Poor's.

tances to Turkey and India, though by not as much as the rise in remittances to the tsunami-affected countries in the Far East. The destructive earthquake in Mexico City in 1985 also caused remittances to rise (figures 2.4 and 2.5).

Crises caused by economic mismanagement, in contrast, seem to yield mixed results. Mexico's currency crisis at the end of 1994 did not lead to a decline in remittances. In fact, remittances rose from $3.98 billion in 1994 to $4.12 billion in 1995. But the currency crisis in the Far East in 1997–98 did result in a modest decline in remittances. The combined remittances in Indonesia, the Republic of Korea, the Philippines, and Thailand fell to $8.5

FIGURE 2.4
Rises in Remittances Following National Disasters

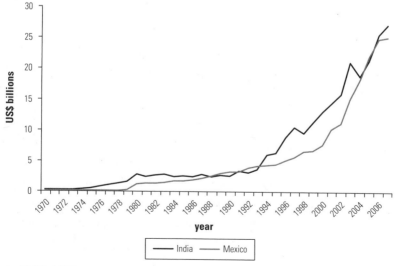

Source: World Bank 2007.

FIGURE 2.5

Recovery of Remittances after Tsunamis

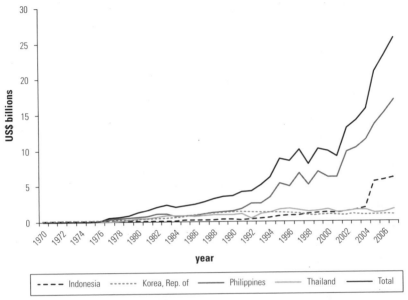

Source: World Bank 2007.

billion in 1998 from $10 billion in 1997; however, remittances recovered quickly and returned to their precrisis level in 1999. In contrast, Russia's debt default in 1998 caused a sizable 33 percent reduction in remittances, to $1.3 billion in 1999, and the flows did not overtake their precrisis level until 2004.

On the whole, the altruistic nature of remittances increases the prospects of their resistance to cyclicality. The evidence on the determinants of remittances to India shows that such flows are determined by the number of migrants and their total earnings. India-specific factors such as political uncertainty, interest rates, or exchange rate depreciation have little impact on these flows (Gupta 2005).

In any case, the risk of fluctuations in remittance flows can be easily mitigated via overcollateralization in securitized transactions. The Banco do Brasil Nikkei Remittance Trust securitization highlighted earlier provided for an excess debt service coverage ratio of 7.64x. Of course, a wildly overvalued domestic currency that creates a massive parallel market premium can dry up remittance flows through official bank channels. This is one risk that cannot be mitigated.

Will the state take steps to divert remittances from private to state-owned banks?

The risk of the state taking steps to divert remittances away from private banks exists. There is good reason to believe, however, that such risk is relatively low. The state, after all, has no interest in inducing a default on the remittance-securitized debt of a private bank because of its wider implications for the stability of the financial system. The larger the private bank is, the greater are such systemwide implications. Hence, it is to be expected that only large banks in developing countries would be able to convincingly mitigate the risk of adverse state action.

Will the central bank of the recipient country permit the payment of remittances into an offshore escrow account?

This is a crucial question. Quite clearly, such a transaction can only be undertaken with the blessing of the central bank. The belief is that the central bank will recognize the value of a domestic bank accessing international capital markets via securitization at a lower spread and longer maturity, and hence will not insist that all remittance dollars be sold to the central bank. Central banks in Brazil, Mexico, Turkey, and elsewhere have shown such willingness despite the prevalence of significant capital controls.

How can a recipient bank show remittances as deposits for the benefit of local residents if they are paid into an offshore escrow account?

It is true that the remittances of, for example, Bangladeshis in the United States to their relatives in Dhaka belong to either the senders or receivers. The bank through which such remittances are channeled acts as an intermediary in converting the dollars remitted into taka payments to recipients in Dhaka. Hence, a question is often raised as to how the intermediating bank in Bangladesh can use the dollar remittances that it does not own to securitize its dollar-denominated bond issuance? This question has been raised now in two alternative ways—one, how can a bank securitize flows that it does not own? Or two, how can a bank create deposit liabilities in favor of recipients if the remittance dollars are paid into an offshore escrow account?

The answer to both these questions comes from the intermediation function of the bank in a securitized transaction. What the securitization structure allows the bank in Bangladesh to do is to purchase dollars from the originators of remittances by promising to pay the recipients of remittances the requisite amount of takas. The latter is done by creating deposit liabilities in favor of remittance recipients. It makes little difference that the dollars are paid into an offshore escrow account, because the bank in Bangladesh has voluntarily surrendered the first claim on those dollars in favor of the bondholders. The securitized bonds are the bank's dollar-denominated liabilities that are funded with future (purchased) flows of dollar remittances. The taka liabilities of the bank in regard to the recipients of remittances can be funded with cash reserves and other assets.

If the potential issuance is linked to the aggregate amount of workers' remittances to developing countries, it could be as high as $24 billion per year on the basis of the estimated 2007 remittances to all developing countries of $239.7 billion.[10] But it seems appropriate to limit the scope of remittance securitization to obtain a more realistic estimate of the potential. First, only banks from speculative-grade countries rated at least B would be able to achieve investment-grade ratings to their securitized transactions by structuring away the sovereign risk. Second, only the top two or three banks from countries with a minimum of $500 million in remittances are likely to be big enough generators of remittances to make securitization cost-effective. Limiting remittance securitization in this fashion to 25 countries sharply reduces the potential issuance to about $12 billion per year. In deriving this potential, it is further assumed that only one-half of the reported remittances are generated by the top two or three banks in each qualifying country. Finally, once again the 5:1 overcollateralization ratio is used to estimate the potential amounts reported in table 2.6.

All the major countries in South Asia are recipients of large amounts of remittances. Of these, India is rated BB+, and both Pakistan and Sri Lanka are rated B+ by Standard & Poor's as regards their foreign currency long-term creditworthiness. While Bangladesh is not rated at present, its rating is estimated to be in the B− to B range on the basis of the shadow ratings methodology developed by Ratha, De, and Mohapatra (2007). Given that this is an estimate with up to one notch error on either side, Bangladesh is also included among the potential issuers of bonds securitized by future remittances. The total potential from South Asia is estimated at $4.2 billion per year. Countries in East Asia and the Pacific, led by the Philippines,

TABLE 2.6
Potential for Remittance-Backed Securitization
(US$ billions)

Country	S&P Rating	Remittances 2007	Potential
East Asia and the Pacific			
Indonesia	BB−	6.0	0.6
Philippines	BB−	17.0	1.7
Vietnam	BB−	5.0	0.5
		28.0	2.8
Europe and Central Asia			
Albania	BB	1.5	0.1
Georgia	B+	0.5	0.1
Serbia and Montenegro	BB−	4.9	0.5
Tajikistan	B+	1.3	0.1
Turkey	BB−	1.2	0.1
Ukraine	BB−	0.9	0.1
		10.3	1.0
Latin America and the Caribbean			
Brazil	BB	4.5	0.5
Colombia	BB	4.6	0.5
Costa Rica	BB	0.6	0.1
El Salvador	BB+	3.6	0.4
Guatemala	BB	4.1	0.4
Peru	BB	2.0	0.2
		19.4	1.9
Middle East and North Africa			
Egypt, Arab Rep. of	BB+	5.9	0.6
Jordan	BB	2.9	0.3
Morocco	BB+	5.7	0.6
Yemen, Rep. of	BB	1.3	0.1
		15.8	1.6
South Asia			
Bangladesh	B	6.4	0.6
India	BB+	27.0	2.7
Pakistan	B+	6.1	0.6
Sri Lanka	B+	2.7	0.3
		42.2	4.2
Sub-Saharan Africa			
Nigeria	BB−	3.3	0.3
Senegal	B+	0.9	0.1
		4.2	0.4
All developing countries		119.9	12.0

Source: Authors' calculations based on World Bank 2007 and Standard & Poor's.

have the second largest potential of $2.8 billion in remittance-backed securitizations. The other regions of the world that are likely candidates for the issuance of remittance-backed debt include, in declining order of importance, Latin America and the Caribbean ($1.9 billion), the Middle East and North Africa ($1.6 billion), Europe and Central Asia ($1.0 billion), and Sub-Saharan Africa ($0.4 billion). The potential of Latin America and the Caribbean is dampened somewhat because Mexico, the biggest recipient of remittances in the region, has graduated to investment-grade rating. Ecuador, another recipient of remittances estimated at $3.2 billion in 2007, is rated CCC+, and hence is unlikely to receive investment-grade rating via securitization.

Constraints on Securitization and the Role for Public Policy

The estimated potential for asset-backed securitization reveals that there is ample scope for developing countries to raise significant amounts of capital by securitizing future-flow receivables. Yet the actual size of such debt issuance has been relatively small. This section explores the principal reasons for this state of affairs. It then focuses on the role public policy can play in alleviating some the constraints inhibiting issuance of debt backed by future hard currency receivables.

Given that the transaction rating is capped by the issuer's local currency credit rating, the best candidates for future-flow-backed transactions are typically investment-grade issuers (in local currency terms) from below-investment-grade sovereigns. However, a paucity of investment-grade companies in below-investment-grade sovereigns inhibits developing countries' ability to issue securitized debt.[11] This is where banks have an advantage. Most governments are unlikely to allow banks to fail lest a systemwide problem would emerge. Such inclination on the part of authorities should keep banks going concerns, which would permit banks to keep on generating workers' remittances.

Though investment-grade issuers in below-investment-grade countries are the best candidates for future-flow asset-backed deals, it is essential that the issuer countries provide certain institutional and legal protections if such deals are to occur. In general, it is difficult to structure securitized transactions in countries that have few laws on their books. Typically, less law implies greater doubt and uncertainty, which makes it more difficult to structure a deal. Bankruptcy law, in particular, is crucial for securitized trans-actions. Ideally, the bankruptcy law should permit "true sale" of a future-flow asset. However, it is possible to structure a securitized transaction by examining the country's history of adherence to existing laws or by deter-mining if the law is ambiguous enough to permit a "true sale" opinion.[12]

Another significant constraint on the issuance of all future-flow receiv-able-backed securities used to come from long lead times and the very spe-cialized skills involved in putting together structures that mitigate various elements of risk and allow rating agencies to rate these bonds above the sovereign ceiling. The long lead times—often anywhere from six months to over one year—deterred investment banks from pursuing such deals aggressively. Also, the specialized skills necessary to structure asset-backed transactions, together with the long lead times, implied that promoting this business would be an expensive proposition for investment banks and issuers who would eventually bear these costs. Legal costs involved in structuring these transactions were reported to be particularly steep, at $2 million to $3 million per transaction. Furthermore, these high costs were fixed. Thus, future-flow-backed issuance became affordable only when large amounts of financing were raised. Consequently, only large issuers who could justify raising large amounts of financing in the international capital markets were expected to be viable candidates for this asset class. A paucity of such entities among developing countries was therefore yet another constraint on the growth of this asset class.

The above constraints have become much less relevant in recent years thanks to the experience gained by issuers and investment banks alike. Now international investment banks have the ability to structure future-flow-backed deals in very short periods of time. Highly skilled and special-ized professionals are no longer required as the asset class has become amenable to the proverbial cookie-cutter approach. This is reflected in the fact that all international investment banks, large and small, are now pro-moting this product, often in teams of one or two professionals. The com-petition among banks is so keen that structuring fees have reportedly fallen sharply, to as little as 40 basis points. Rating agencies now charge about $200,000 to rate such transactions. While 144A registration costs for issuance have declined to between $250,000 and $300,000, Reg. S regis-tration is even less expensive. Legal fees have also come down, especially for repeat transactions, because lawyers can use the same documentation developed earlier.[13]

Absence of an appropriate legal infrastructure is yet another constraint on the issuance of future-flow-backed securities. In addition to the absence of appropriate legal structures, there is also a lack of consensus in developing countries and multinational institutions on the accounting treatment of such transactions. For instance, should securitized debt be included in determining debt limits under IMF programs? Since such debt is asset backed, there is room to believe that it does not constitute net debt. But the IMF often has been unwilling to exhibit any flexibility. Some countries—Colombia and República Bolivariana de Venezuela, for instance—are known to lack the necessary legal framework to undertake DPR securitization. Clearly, there is scope for public policy in this area to establish appropriate legal frameworks as well as flexible accounting rules. Instead of attempting a grand overhaul of the legal system, countries should be encouraged to have a focused approach. The most crucial law is one governing bankruptcy. It is even more vital that the bankruptcy law allows the pledged assets to remain pledged in the event of default, which is the true sales principle. Beyond the bankruptcy code, developing countries should be encouraged to follow the general rule that more is better, since less law means more doubt and greater cost in structuring securitized transactions.

International financial institutions (IFIs) can also play a role in promoting this asset class. The World Bank or the International Finance Corporation, for example, could provide credit enhancement (Corbi 2008). This could come in the form of a "credit wrap" of the type that monoline insurance companies make available to commercially driven transactions. In a wrapped transaction, lower-rated tranches are elevated to a higher rating by virtue of the guarantee from the credit enhancer. Because transactions can be structured in different tranches, the World Bank could participate in the senior or mezzanine or junior tranches, depending on the risk volatility and its own objectives. Obviously, the ultimate objectives are (1) to facilitate access to funding for unrated or low-rated institutions, and (2) to reduce the international capital market asymmetries and constraints for new issuers from developing countries.

Alternatively, IFIs could boost the growth of future-flow remittance securitization by providing direct or indirect guarantees. A direct guarantee to the structured transaction may include a risk-sharing agreement between the intermediary and the World Bank that limits the maximum exposure to say 50 percent of a tranche. The risk-sharing agreement may also include pari-passu provisions that limit the risks in the case of insolvency of the originator by limiting the maximum exposure upon default, thereby improving the recovery rates for the World Bank. An indirect guarantee results in the World Bank providing a counter-guarantee to other intermediaries that issue guarantees for the benefit of the transaction's bondholders. Finally, the World Bank can also get involved by providing a credit default swap or other equivalent instrument to enhance the rating of the transaction. Any World Bank participation brings at least two immediate benefits to the investor. First, it provides a triple-A rating to the affected tranches. Second, it reduces regulatory capital requirement for any bank investors. Capital adequacy requirements are zero percent under Basel II versus 100 percent otherwise.

Finally, and at the very least, IFIs like the World Bank can play a useful function of educating public sector bureaucrats and private sector managers in developing countries on the role that this asset class can play in times of crisis and how best to identify and structure future-flow-backed transactions.

Annex: Additional Examples of Securitization

Example 1: Banco de Credito del Peru's Securitization of Credit Card Receivables

Amount: $100 million. Issue date: 11/12/1998. Maturity: 11/14/2005. Future U.S. dollar receivables owed to Banco de Credito del Peru by Visa International. Credit Rating AAA from Standard & Poor's.

Credit card holders traveling to Peru buy goods and services and obtain an advance in local currency from an ATM. The merchants sell the resulting vouchers to a local voucher-acquiring bank, which pays them cash. The voucher-acquiring bank then obtains dollars from Visa.

In a structured transaction, the voucher-acquiring bank (Banco de Credito del Peru, in this instance) issues irrevocable instructions to the credit card company (Visa, in this instance) to transfer all future payments on credit card vouchers to an offshore account under the control of a trustee. The trustee uses the monies paid into this account to make payments to the bondholders. This structured transaction is not subject to the same sovereign risks as unstructured transactions.

As figure 2A.2 shows, the Banco de Credito Overseas Ltd. (BCOL) Master Trust, which receives payments from Visa, is outside the Peruvian jurisdiction. The first claim on BCOL is from the bondholders. The Peruvian Central Bank is not involved in the process. After paying principal and interest to the bondholders, the BCOL Master Trust pays excess Visa payments on vouchers to Banco de Credito Overseas Ltd. in the Bahamas, which in turn pays the excess to Banco de Credito del Peru in Peru. The proceeds from the issuance of the structured bonds flow to Banco de Credito del Peru via BCOL Master Trust and Banco de Credito Overseas Ltd. in the Bahamas.

While this structure mitigates the usual convertibility and transfer risks, two risks still remain. First, there is the risk of fluctuations in the volume of vouchers due to (1) variation in tourism, (2) relations with vendors, and (3) devaluation of Peru's currency, nuevo sol. Second, there is the risk of Banco de Credito del Peru becoming insolvent.

These risks can be reduced (not eliminated) through excess collateral. The rating agencies examine data on tourist arrivals and expenditures and subject the data to stress tests. The results of these tests are used to determine the necessary excess coverage. In the case of Banco de Credito del Peru (see figure 2A.1), the amount of future-flow receivables transferred

to the BCOL Master Trust were set at 2.5 times the debt service requirements. The structure described above plus the excess collateralization
resulted in the transaction receiving a AAA credit rating from Standard &
Poor's as opposed to the BB sovereign credit rating of Peru in 1998.

Example 2: Pemex Finance Limited Securitization of Crude Oil Receivables

Amount: Nine issuances during 1998 and 1999, each up to $500 million.
Future U.S. dollar receivables owed to Pemex Finance Ltd. by designated
customers who will receive Mayan crude oil from Pemex Exploración y
Producción (PEP), via Petroleos Mexicos Internacional (PMI). Rating BBB.

PMI arranges to sell Mayan crude oil, or some other crude oil type if
Mayan becomes unavailable, to designated customers who agree to deposit
their payments into an offshore collection account. PMI, a subsidiary of
Pemex, is the distributor for Mayan crude oil, which is produced by PEP.
Pemex Finance Ltd. is the offshore issuer of notes. It purchases the receiv-
ables from PMI via the offshore Pemex subsidiary, PMI Services.

Figure 2A.2 shows that sales of the crude oil to designated customers
and of receivables to PMI Services are out of the jurisdiction of the Mexi-

FIGURE 2A.1
Credit Card Receivables Structure

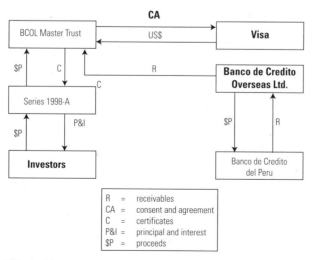

R	=	receivables
CA	=	consent and agreement
C	=	certificates
P&I	=	principal and interest
$P	=	proceeds

Source: Standard & Poor's 1999a, 80.

FIGURE 2A.2
Crude Oil Receivables Structure

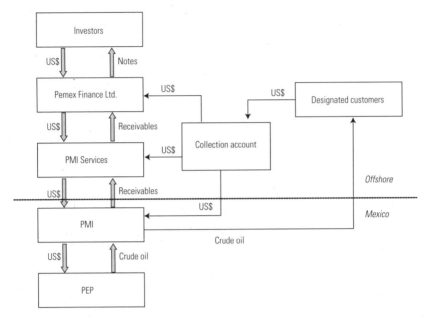

Source: Standard & Poor's 1999a, 114.

can government. The first claim on the receivables is from the note holders, and the Mexican central bank is not involved in the process. Chase Manhattan Bank has agreed to administer the issuance of all debt and the payment of interest and principal on such debt in accordance with Pemex's agreements. After paying note holders principal and interest, excess payments, based on fluctuation in crude oil prices, are paid to PMI Services and PMI, via the offshore collection account.

While this structure mitigates the usual convertibility and transfer risks, other risks still remain. Primarily, there is a risk that a fluctuation in crude oil prices will result in revenues insufficient to cover the interest and principal due to note holders. The overcollateralization of the notes minimizes this risk—PMI will provide a minimum coverage ratio of three times the amount needed for payment of interest and principal. Designated customers have also signed agreements acknowledging their commitment to purchase crude oil and to make any future payments into the offshore collection account. Further enhancing the strength of such issuance is Pemex's track record of timely servicing of debt in the past. As a result of these enhancements, Standard & Poor's rated the credit of 1998 and 1999 tranches A-2 and A-4 and 1999 tranche A-5 as BBB. Rated as AAA are 1998 and 1999 tranches A-1 and A-3, as they are insured by MBIA and AMBAC. These ratings are clearly favorable relative to the BB foreign currency rating of the United Mexican States.

Notes

1. SWIFT, the Society for Worldwide Interbank Financial Telecommunication, is the global provider of secure financial messaging services.
2. Monoline insurance companies that provide guarantees to issuers may not be able to play a big role in providing wraparound insurance to issuers from developing countries in the near future, given their current credit problems.
3. This out-of-court settlement also prevented a test of the "true sales" principle supported by widespread legal opinion from developing countries.
4. Note that even a 50 basis points saving on spread can be significant due to the compounding effect. For example, a 100 basis points spread saving translates into roughly $5 million interest saving after four years on a $100 million loan.
5. International capital flows are a way of smoothing adjustments to shocks. In a developing country, the link with international capital markets tends to be weak, and also the domestic capital market tends to be underdeveloped. Both these weaknesses limit the role of international capital in smoothing adjustment to shocks (Caballero 2000).
6. But this understates the true size of the asset class, because little information is available about unrated transactions. Data were compiled from the International Structured Finance Special Reports for various years from Fitch Ratings, Structured Finance Special Reports from Moody's, and Structured Finance Emerging Markets Ratings List from Standard & Poor's.
7. The Pemex oil exports deal was part of the conditions in the U.S. Treasury's rescue package for Mexico, following the 2004 Tequila crisis, which ended the Mexican peso's parity against the U.S. dollar (see Rubin and Weisberg 2004. The deal was funded using the U.S. Exchange Stabilization Fund.
8. Given the recent rapid rise in workers' remittances to developing countries, the potential for remittance-backed securitization is discussed in detail in the following section.
9. The above calculation does not include many sources of foreign exchange earnings for developing countries. One omission, for example, is telephone receivables, although with falling costs of international phone calls, the potential is decreasing in this sector.
10. Although excess coverage helps mitigate elements of product risk, it also reduces the total amount of funds that can be raised with future-flow receivables.
11. This calculation is based on data from the World Bank's Remittance Data from November 29, 2007 (World Bank 2007). It also assumes that only one-half of

the estimated remittances are channeled through banks. Finally, it assumes that the overcollateralization ratio is 5:1.

12. For instance, S&P had local currency ratings on 95 nonfinancial-sector companies in speculative-grade Latin American and Caribbean countries in mid-2007. Of these, only 15 were rated investment grade.

13. If a developing country were to adopt the U.S. bankruptcy code, which does not give creditors access to future-flow assets once a bankruptcy petition is filed, the potential for future-flow securitizations from that country is likely to be greatly reduced.

14. Based on the author's discussions at Deutsche Bank, Moody's Investor Services, and Standard & Poor's.

References

Caballero, Ricardo. 2000. "Aggregate Volatility in Modern Latin America: Causes and Cures." Paper prepared for the World Bank report *Dealing with Economic Insecurity in Latin America.* World Bank, Washington, DC.

Chami, Ralph, Connel Fullenkamp, and Samir Jahjah. 2003. "Are Immigrant Remittance Flows a Source of Capital for Development?" IMF Working Paper No. 03/189, International Monetary Fund, Washington, DC.

Corbi, Antonio, 2008. "Securitization of Future Flow Assets: Diversified Payments and Workers' Remittances." Working Paper, Economic Policy and Prospects Group, World Bank, Washington, DC.

Fitch Ratings. 2006. "Future Flow Securitization Rating Methodology." International Criteria Report, February 15. http://www.fitchratings.com.

———. Structured Finance. Various years. International Special Reports on Latin American Structured Finance. http://www.fitchratings.com.

Gupta, Poonam. 2005. "Macroeconomic Determinants of Remittances—Evidence from India." IMF Working Paper No. 05/224, International Monetary Fund, Washington, DC.

IMF (International Monetary Fund). Various years. *Balance of Payments Statistics.* http://www.imfstatistics.org/bop/.

Ketkar, Suhas, and Dilip Ratha. 2001a. "Development Financing during a Crisis: Securitization of Future Receivables." Policy Research Working Paper 2582, World Bank, Washington, DC.

———. 2001b. "Securitization of Future Flow Receivables: A Useful Tool for Developing Countries." *Finance & Development* (March), International Monetary Fund, Washington, DC.

———. 2004–2005. "Recent Advances in Future-Flow Securitization." *The Financier* 11/12: 1–14.

Moody's, Structured Finance. Various years. Special Reports on Latin American ABS/MBS. http://www.moodys.com.

Ratha, Dilip. 2006. "Leveraging Remittances for International Capital Market Access." Mimeo. Development Prospects Group, World Bank, Washington, DC.

Ratha, Dilip, Prabal De, and Sanket Mohapatra. 2007. "Shadow Sovereign Ratings for Unrated Developing Countries." Mimeo, April 20. Development Prospects Group, World Bank, Washington, DC.

S&P (Standard & Poor's). 1999a. "Securitization in Latin America 1999." http://www2.standardandpoors.com/spf/pdf/fixedincome/latin99_102004.pdf ?vregion=us&vlang=en.

———. 1999b. "Lessons from the Past Apply to Future Securitizations in Emerging Markets." July. http://www.standardandpoors.com/ratingsdirect.

———. 2000. "New Bank Survivability Criteria Should Aid Emerging Market Financial Future Flow Issuers." *Standard & Poor's Credit Week,* September 27. http://www2.standardandpoors.com/portal/site/sp/en/us/page.article/2,1,1,0, 1204836566348.html?vregion=us&vlang=en.

———. 2002. "Rating Assigned to 1st Future Flow Transaction in Brazil and Japan." August 10. http://www.standardandpoors.com/ratingsdirect.

———. 2003. "Economic Hurdles Continue to Plague Argentine Structured Market." May 15. http://www.standardandpoors.com/ratingsdirect.

———. 2004a. "Export Future Flows Thrive After Repayment of Argentine Aluar." June 16. http://www.standardandpoors.com/ratingsdirect.

———. 2004b. "Mexico's Subnational Securitization Market Entering Second Stage of Development." November 3. http://www.standardandpoors.com/ ratingsdirect.

———. 2004c. "The Three Building Blocks of an Emerging Markets Future Flow Transaction Rating," November 16. http://www.standardandpoors.com/ ratingsdirect.

———. 2007. "Structured Finance: Emerging Markets Ratings List," June 27. http://www.standardandpoors.com/ratingsdirect.

World Bank. 2007. "Remittances Data," November 29. http://go.world bank.org/QOWEWD6TA0.

———. Various years. *Global Development Finance.* Washington, DC: World Bank.

———. Various years. *World Development Indicators.* Washington, DC: World Bank.

CHAPTER 3

Development Finance via Diaspora Bonds

Suhas Ketkar and Dilip Ratha

Diasporas and their economic status in their adopted countries are fast becoming a source of pride as well as financial resources for developing countries. If seeking remittances is a way of tapping into diaspora income flows on a regular basis,[1] issuance of hard currency–denominated bonds to the diaspora is a way of tapping into the latter's wealth accumulated abroad. This chapter examines Israel's and India's track records to draw generalized conclusions about the viability of diaspora bonds as a development financing instrument.

Diaspora bonds are not yet widely used as a development financing instrument. Israel since 1951 and India since 1991 have been on the forefront in raising hard currency financing from their respective diasporas. Bonds issued by the Development Corporation for Israel, established in 1951 to raise foreign exchange resources from the Jewish diaspora, have totaled well over $25 billion. Diaspora bonds issued by the government-owned State Bank of India have raised over $11 billion to date. The gov-

We gratefully acknowledge discussions with David Beers of Standard & Poor's, Pratima Das of the State Bank of India, V. Gopinathan of SBICAP Securities, Deepak Mohanty of the International Monetary Fund, Jonathan Schiffer of Moody's, Asher Weingarten of the Bank of Israel, Shirley Strifler of Israel's Ministry of Finance and Tamar Roth-Drach from its Economic Mission to the United Nations, and Sanket Mohapatra of the World Bank.

ernment of Sri Lanka has also sold Sri Lanka Development Bonds since
2001 to several investor categories, including nonresident Sri Lankans,
raising a total of $580 million to date.[2] South Africa is reported to have
launched a project to issue Reconciliation and Development bonds to both
expatriate and domestic investors (Bradlow 2006). Although the Lebanese
government has had no systematic program to tap its diaspora, anecdotal
evidence indicates that the Lebanese diaspora has also contributed capital
to the Lebanese government.[3]

Diaspora bonds are different from foreign currency deposits (FCDs) that
are used by many developing countries to attract foreign currency
inflows.[4] Diaspora bonds are typically long-dated securities to be redeemed
only upon maturity. FCDs, in contrast, can be withdrawn at any time. This
is certainly true of demand and saving deposits. But even time deposits can
be withdrawn at any time by forgoing a portion of accrued interest. Therefore, FCDs are likely to be much more volatile, requiring banks to hold
much larger reserves against their FCD liabilities, thereby reducing their
ability to fund investments. Diaspora bonds, in contrast, are a source of
foreign financing that is long term. Hence, the proceeds from such bonds
can be used to finance investment.

Diaspora bonds may appear somewhat similar to the Islamic bonds. But
unlike diaspora bonds, Islamic bonds are governed by Islamic laws (*sharia*)
that forbid paying or receiving interest. The Islamic bonds are structured as
asset-backed securities of medium-term maturity that give investors a share
of the profit associated with proceeds from such issuance. The international
Islamic bond market is divided into sovereign (and quasi-sovereign) and
corporate sukuk markets. In 2001, the Bahrain Monetary Agency was the
first central bank to issue Islamic bonds with three- and five-year maturities. The German state of Saxony-Anhalt was the first non-Muslim issuer of
sukuk bonds when it tapped the global Islamic debt market in 2004 for 100
million euros. The largest issue of Islamic bonds to date, with a seven-year
maturity, was the sale of Qatar global sukuk for $700 million. Two factors
have contributed to the recent rapid rise in Islamic bond issuance: growing
demand for sharia-compliant financial instruments from Muslim immigrant and non-immigrant populations around the world, and the growing
oil wealth in the Gulf region (El Qorchi 2005).

The diaspora purchases of bonds issued by their country of origin are
likely to be driven by a sense of patriotism and the desire to contribute to
the development of the home country. Thus, there is often an element of

charity in these investments. The placement of bonds at a premium allows the issuing country to leverage the charity element into a substantially larger flow of capital. To the investors, diaspora bonds provide an opportunity to diversify asset composition and improve risk management.

The rest of the chapter is organized as follows. The next two sections examine the experiences of diaspora bond issuance by Israel and India. Then the chapter elaborates why issuers as well as investors find diaspora bonds attractive. Minimum conditions for the issuance of diaspora bonds are discussed next, with the objective of identifying several potential issuers. The final section provides a summary of findings and discussion of future research.

Israeli Experience

The Jewish diaspora in the United States (and to a lesser extent Canada) has supported development of Israel by buying bonds issued by the Development Corporation for Israel (DCI). The DCI was established in 1951 with the express objective of raising foreign exchange for the state of Israel from Jewish diaspora abroad (as individuals and communities) through issuance of nonnegotiable bonds. Israel views this financial vehicle as a stable source of overseas borrowing as well as an important mechanism for maintaining ties with diaspora Jewry. Nurturing of such ties is considered crucial, as reflected in the fact that the DCI offerings of diaspora bonds are quite extensive, with multiple maturities and minimum subscription amounts that range from a low of $100 to a high of $100,000. The diaspora is also valued as a diversified borrowing source, especially during periods when the government has difficulty borrowing from other external sources. Opportunity for redemption of these bonds has been limited, and history shows that nearly all DCI bonds are redeemed only at maturity. Furthermore, some $200 million in maturing bonds were never claimed (Chander 2005).

The Israeli Knesset passed a law in February 1951 authorizing the flotation of the country's first diaspora bond issue, known as the Israel Independence Issue, thereby marking the beginning of a program that has raised over $25 billion since inception (figure 3.1). In May 1951, David Ben-Gurion, Israel's first prime minister, officially kicked off the Israeli diaspora bond sales drive in the United States with a rally in New York and then undertook a coast-to-coast tour to build support for it. This first road show was highly successful and raised $52.6 million in bond sales. The DCI bonds make up roughly 32 percent of the government's outstanding external debt of $31.4 billion as of end-December 2005.

The history of DCI bond issuance reveals that the characteristics of such bond offerings have changed with time. Until the early 1970s, all DCI issues were fixed-rate bonds with maturities of 10 to 15 years (table 3.1). In the mid-1970s, DCI decided to target small banks and financial companies in the United States by issuing 10-, 7- and 5-year notes in denominations of $150,000, $250,000, and $1,000,000 at prime-based rates. Subsequently, the DCI changed its policy and began to retarget Jewish communities rather than banks and financial companies. The DCI also sold floating-rate bonds from 1980 to 1999. The minimum amount on floating-rate bonds was set at $25,000 in 1980 and reduced to $5,000 in December 1986. The maturity terms on these bonds were set at 10 to 12 years, and interest rates were calculated on the basis of the prime rate. Of the total DCI bond sales of $1.6 billion in 2003, fixed-rate bonds made up 89.5 percent, floating-rate bonds totaled 2.9 percent, and notes were 7.6 percent (figure 3.2).

FIGURE 3.1
Total Bond Sales by Israel, 1996–2007

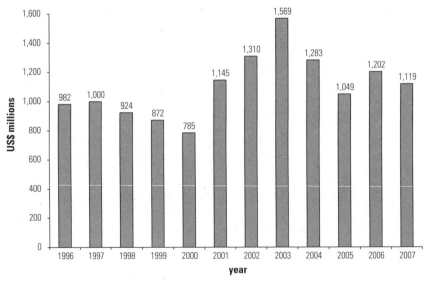

Source: Bank of Israel.

TABLE 3.1
Bond Offerings by Israel

Bond type	Dates	Maturity	Minimum (US$)	Rate basis
Fixed rate	1951–80	10–15 yrs	N/A	4.0
Fixed rate	1990 on	10 yrs	N/A	Market based
Fixed rate—EDI	1993	10 yrs	25,000	Market based, 6-month
Fixed rate—Zero Coupon	1993	10yrs	6,000	Market based, at redemption
Fixed rate—Jubilee	1998	5–10 yrs	25,000	Market based, 6-month
Notes	Mid-1970s	10 yrs	150,000	Prime based
		7 yrs	250,000	
		5 yrs	1,000,000	
Floating rate	1980–92	10-12 yrs	25,0000, 5,000	Prime based
Floating rate	1993–99	10 yrs	5,000	Prime based
Floating rate	Since end-1999	10 yrs	N/A	Libor based

Source: Bank of Israel.

Currently, Israel uses proceeds from bond sales to diaspora Jewry to finance major public sector projects such as desalination, construction of housing, and communication infrastructure. The Ministry of Finance defines DCI's annual borrowing policy in accordance with the govern-

FIGURE 3.2
Israeli Bond Sales by Type, 1951–2007

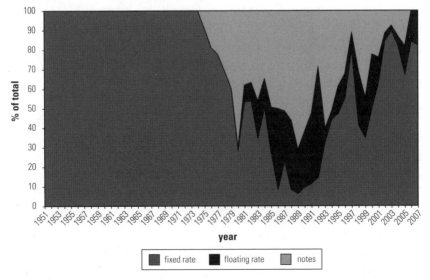

Source: Bank of Israel.

ment's foreign exchange requirements. The Finance Ministry periodically sets interest rates and more recently other parameters on different types of DCI bonds to meet the annual borrowing target. Still, the Israeli government does not consider borrowings from diaspora Jewry as a market-based source of finance. Accordingly, it does not seek credit ratings on these bonds from rating agencies such as Standard & Poor's and Moody's.

Comparison of interest rates on fixed-rate DCI bonds versus those on 10-year U.S. Treasury notes shows the large extent of discount offered by the Jewish diaspora in purchasing these bonds. Interest rates on DCI fixed-rate bonds averaged about 4 percent from 1951 to 1989. Although the 10-year U.S. Treasury rates were lower than 4 percent only from 1951 to 1958, they have been higher than 4 percent since. Of course, as the U.S. Treasury rates kept on rising rapidly in the 1980s, and buying DCI bonds at 4 percent implied steep discounts, demand for the fixed-rate issues waned in favor of floating-rate debt (figures 3.2 and 3.3). The sharp decline in U.S. rates since 2002 has rekindled investor interest in fixed-rate DCI bonds, however. The degree of patriotic discount has dwindled in recent years, and rates on fixed-rate DCI bonds have exceeded 10-year U.S. Treasury yields. This is perhaps owing to the fact that younger Jewish investors are seeking market-based returns. Perhaps more important, the decline in patriotic discount is also due to the Ministry of Finance developing alternative sources of external financing such as negotiable bonds guaranteed by the U.S. government, nonguaranteed negotiable bonds, and loans from banks. These instruments, which trade in the secondary market, provide alternative avenues for acquiring exposure to Israel. Consequently, interest rates on DCI bonds have to be competitive—in fact a tad higher than those on the above alternative instruments, given that DCI bonds are nonnegotiable (Rehavi and Weingarten 2004).

The over-50-year history of DCI bond issuance reveals that the Israeli government has nurtured this stable source of external finance that has often provided it foreign exchange resources at a discount to the market price. Over the years, the government has expanded the range of instruments available to Jewish diaspora investors. The pricing of these bonds has also recognized the changing nature of the target investor population. In the early years, the DCI sold bonds to diaspora Jewry (principally in the United States) who had a direct or indirect connection with the Holocaust and hence were willing to buy Israeli bonds at deep discount to market. But the old generation is being replaced by a new one, whose focus is

FIGURE 3.3
Discount on Israeli DCI Bonds Compared with U.S. Treasuries, 1953–2007

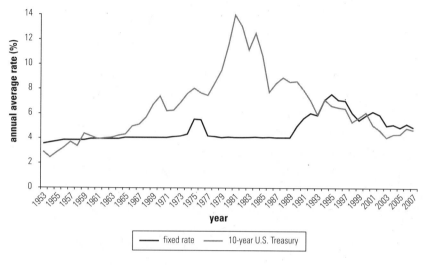

Sources: Bank of Israel and U.S. Federal Reserve.

increasingly on financial returns. Accordingly, the DCI bond offerings have had to move in recent years toward market pricing.

No commercial or investment banks or brokers have been involved in the marketing of Israeli diaspora bonds. Instead, these bonds are sold directly by DCI, with the Bank of New York acting as the fiscal agent. Currently, about 200 DCI employees in the United States maintain close contacts with Jewish communities in the various regions of the United States so as to understand investor profiles and preferences. They host investor events in Jewish communities with the express purpose of maintaining ties and selling bonds.

Indian Experience

On three separate occasions the Indian government has tapped its diaspora base of nonresident Indians for funding: India Development Bonds (IDBs) following the balance-of-payments crisis in 1991 ($1.6 billion), Resurgent India Bonds (RIBs) following the imposition of sanctions in the wake of nuclear testing in 1998 ($4.2 billion), and India Millennium Deposits (IMDs) in 2000 ($5.5 billion). The conduit for these transactions was the government-owned State Bank of India (SBI). The India Development Bonds provided a vehicle to nonresident Indians to bring back funds that they had withdrawn earlier that year as the country experienced a balance-of-payments crisis. The IDBs, and subsequently the Resurgent India Bonds and India Millennium Deposits, paid retail investors a higher return than they would have received from similar financial instruments in their country of residence. India also benefited because the diaspora investors did not seek as high a country risk premium as markets would have demanded. While this may have reflected different assessments of default probabilities, a more plausible explanation resides in investors of Indian origin viewing the risk of default with much less trepidation.[5]

The IDBs, RIBs, and IMDs all had five-year bullet maturity. The issues were done in multiple currencies—U.S. dollar, British pound, Deutsche mark/euro. Other relevant characteristics of the offerings are set out in table 3.2.

Unlike the Jewish diaspora, the Indian diaspora provided no patriotic discount on RIBs and only small ones on IMDs. When RIBs were sold in August 1998 to yield 7.75 percent on U.S. dollar–denominated bonds, the yield on BB-rated U.S. corporate bonds was 7.2 percent. Thus, there was

TABLE 3.2
Diaspora Bonds Issued by India

Bond type	Amount (US$ billions)	Year	Maturity	Minimum	Coupon (%)
India Development Bonds (IDBs)	1.6	1991	5 yrs		
U.S. dollar				—	9.50
British pound				—	13.25
Resurgent India Bonds (RIBs)	4.2	1998	5 yrs		
U.S. dollar				2,000*	7.75
British pound				1,000**	8.00
Deutsche mark				3,000*	8.25
India Millennium Deposits (IMDs)	5.5	2000	5 yrs		
U.S. dollar				2,000*	8.50
British pound				2,000**	7.85
Euro				2,000*	6.85

Source: State Bank of India.

Note: — not available.

* plus multiples of 1,000 in U.S. dollars and euros; ** plus multiples of 500 in British pound sterling.

no discount on the RIBs. As for the IMDs, the coupon was 8.5 percent, while the yield on the comparably rated U.S. corporate bonds was 8.9 percent for a 40-basis-points discount. In any case, Indian diaspora bonds provided much smaller discounts in comparison to Israel's DCI bonds.

From a purely economic perspective, the SBI's decision to restrict access to RIBs and IMDs to investors of Indian origin appears a bit odd. Why limit the potential size of the market? First, restricting the RIB and IMD sales to the Indian diaspora may have been a marketing strategy introduced in the belief that Indian investors would be more eager to invest in instruments that are available exclusively to them. Second, the SBI perhaps believed that the Indian diaspora investors would show more understanding and forbearance than other investors if India encountered a financial crisis. Having local currency–denominated current and/or contingent liabilities, the Indian diaspora investors might be content to receive debt service in rupees. In addition to the above reasons, however, the KYC (know your customer) reasoning offered by SBI officials to restrict market access to the Indian diaspora appears quite convincing. The SBI concluded that it knew its Indian diaspora investor base well enough to feel comfortable that the invested funds did not involve drug money.

India's diaspora bonds differ from Israel's in several ways (table 3.3). First, Israel views diaspora Jewry as a permanent fountain of external capital, which the DCI has kept engaged by offering a variety of investment vehicles on terms that the market demanded over the years. India, however, has used the diaspora funding only opportunistically.

TABLE 3.3
Comparison of Diaspora Bonds Issued by Israel and India

Israel	India
Annual issuance since 1951	Opportunistic issuance in 1991, 1998, and 2000
Development-oriented borrowings	Balance-of-payments support
Large though declining patriotic discount	Small patriotic discount, if any
Fixed, floating-rate bonds and notes	Fixed-rate bonds
Maturities from 1 to 20 years with bullet repayment	Five year with bullet maturity
Direct distribution by DCI	SBI distribution in conjunction with international banks
Targeted toward but not limited to diaspora	Limited to diaspora
SEC registered	No SEC registration
Nonnegotiable	Nonnegotiable

Source: Authors.

Second, the SBI has restricted the sales of its diaspora bonds only to investors of Indian origin. Israel, in contrast, has not limited the access to only the diaspora Jewry. Finally, while the DCI has registered its offerings with the U.S. Securities and Exchange Commission (SEC), the SBI has opted out of SEC registration.

As Chander (2001) points out, the SBI decision to forgo SEC registration of RIBs and IMDs raises several interesting issues. As for the RIBs, India managed to sell them to Indian diaspora retail investors in the United States without registering the instrument with the SEC. India made the argument that RIBs were bank certificates of deposits (CDs) and hence came under the purview of U.S. banking rather than U.S. securities laws. Indeed, the offer document described the RIBs as "bank instruments representing foreign currency denominated deposits in India." Like time CDs, the RIBs were to pay the original deposit plus interest at maturity. RIBs were also distributed through commercial banks; there were no underwriters. Though the SEC did not quite subscribe to the Indian position, the SBI still sold RIBs to U.S.-based retail investors of Indian origin. However, the bank was unable to use the same approach when it came to the IMDs, which were explicitly called deposits. Still, the SBI chose to forgo U.S. SEC registration. Instead of taking on the SEC, the SBI placed IMDs with Indian diaspora in Europe, the Gulf States, and the Far East.

Generally, high costs, stringent disclosure requirements, and lengthy lead times are cited as the principal deterrents to SEC registration; but these were probably not insurmountable obstacles. Costs of registration could not have exceeded $500,000, an insignificant amount compared with the large size of the issue and the massive size of the U.S. investor base of Indian origin to which the registration would provide unfettered access. The disclosure requirements also would not likely have been a major constraint for an institution like the SBI, which was already operating in a stringent regulatory Indian banking environment. The relatively long lead time of up to three months was an issue and weighed on the minds of SBI officials, especially when RIBs were issued in the wake of the nuclear tests and resulting sanctions. However, SBI officials instead pointed to the plaintiff-friendly U.S. court system in relation to other jurisdictions as the principal reason for eschewing SEC registration. As Roberta Romano explained: "In addition to class action mechanisms to aggregate individual claims not prevalent in other countries, U.S. procedure—including rules of discovery, pleading requirements, contingent fees, and the absence of a 'loser pays' cost rule—are far more favorable to plaintiffs than those of foreign courts" (Romano 1998, 2424). Finally, high-priced lawyers also make litigation in the United States quite expensive. A combination of these attributes poses a formidable risk to issuers bringing offerings to the U.S. market (Chander 2001).

India's decision to forgo SEC registration implied the avoidance of both U.S. laws and U.S. court procedures. Chander (2001) presented four reasons why an issuer involved in a global offering might seek to avoid multiple jurisdictions. First, compliance with the requirements of multiple jurisdictions is likely to escalate costs quite sharply. Second, the substantive features of the law may be unfavorable or especially demanding for particular types of issuers or issues. For example, countries have differing definitions of what constitute securities. Third, compliance with the requirements of multiple jurisdictions can delay offerings because of the time involved in making regulatory filings and obtaining regulatory approvals. While the prefiling disclosure requirements under Schedule B of the Securities Act in the United States are very limited, a market practice has developed to provide a lot of detailed economic and statistical information about the country, possibly to avoid material omissions. Putting together such information for the first time can prove daunting. Finally, the application of multiple regulatory systems to a global offering can potentially subject the issuer to lawsuits in multiple jurisdictions.

Perhaps an argument can be made, as in Chander (2001), that investors should be allowed to divest themselves from U.S. securities law in their international investments if they so choose. This approach could be generalized by giving investors the choice of law and forum, which is a principle recognized by U.S. courts for international transactions. The law and forum would then become another attribute of the security, which would influence its market price. Giving investors the choice of law and forum can be supported on efficiency grounds, provided that rational and well-informed investors populate the market. Proposals giving such a choice to investors were floated toward the end of the 1990s (Choi and Guzman 1998; Romano 1998). But markets were roiled since then by the collapse of Enron and MCI, signaling that markets were not always working in the best interest of investors. In view of this, it is highly unlikely that the SEC or the U.S. Congress would in the near future relax regulations and permit international investors to opt out of U.S. laws and courts (Chander 2005).

Nonetheless, an eventual shift toward a more permissive environment may occur as more and more investors vote with their feet and adopt laws and courts of a country other than the United States. This is already happening. Of the 25 largest stock offerings (initial public offerings, or IPOs) in 2005, only one was made in the United States (Zakaria 2006). Furthermore, nine of 10 IPOs in 2006 were also done in overseas markets. Indeed, a new effort has been launched in New York to recommend changes to the 2002 Sarbanes-Oxley Act and other laws and regulations that are believed to hinder the competitiveness of U.S. capital markets.[6] Chinese companies often cite the latter as the principal concern that leads them to issue stocks outside the United States (Murray 2006). In the short term, however, countries wishing to raise capital from diaspora investors will have to register their offerings with the U.S. SEC if they wish to have access to the retail U.S. diaspora investor base. If they opt to eschew SEC registration, they will then lose their ability to sell in the retail U.S. market.

Rationale for Diaspora Bonds

Diaspora bonds are as attractive to issuers as they are to investors. From the issuer's point of view, they are a reliable source of financing during times of difficulty. From the investor's perspective, they offer an attractive alternative for diversifying risk.

Rationale for the Issuer

Countries are expected to find diaspora bonds an attractive vehicle for securing a stable and cheap source of external finance. Since patriotism is the principal motivation for purchasing diaspora bonds, diaspora bonds are likely to be in demand in fair as well as foul weather.[7] Also, the diaspora is expected to provide a "patriotic" discount in pricing these bonds. The Israeli and to a lesser extent the Indian experience is clearly in keeping with this hypothesis.

The patriotic discount, which is tantamount to charity, raises an interesting question as to why a country should not seek just charitable contributions from their diaspora instead of taking on debt associated with the diaspora bonds. Seeking handouts may be considered politically degrading in some countries. More important, diaspora bonds allow a country to leverage a small amount of charity into a large amount of resources for development.

Yet another factor that might play into the calculus of the diaspora bond–issuing nation is the favorable impact it would have on the country's sovereign credit rating. Nurturing a reliable source of funding in good as well as bad times improves a country's sovereign credit rating. Rating agencies believe that Israel's ability to access the worldwide Jewry for funding has undoubtedly supported its sovereign credit rating. But Standard & Poor's does not view this source of funding as decisive in determining Israel's credit rating. In reaching this conclusion, Standard & Poor's cites Israel's inability to escape a painful adjustment program in the 1980s. In other words, the availability of financing from the Jewish diaspora did not allow Israel to avoid a crisis rooted in domestic mismanagement. Although the Jewish diaspora investors have stood by Israel whenever the country has come under attack from outside, they have not been as supportive when the problems were caused by economic mismanagement at home.

While concurring with the above assessment, Moody's analysts also point out that the mid-1980s' economic adjustment, which brought down inflationary expectations, and the 2002–03 structural reforms have improved Israel's economic fundamentals such that the country has sharply reduced its dependence on foreign financing. Furthermore, diaspora bonds and the U.S. government–guaranteed debt make up the bulk of Israel's total external indebtedness; market-based debt is only about 13 percent of total public sector foreign debt at end-December 2005. As a result, Israel's ability to issue diaspora bonds is now much more important in underpinning Israel's sovereign credit rating than it was in the 1980s when the country had much larger financing requirements.

India's access to funding from its diaspora did not prevent the rating agencies from downgrading the country's sovereign credit rating in 1998 following the imposition of international sanctions in the wake of nuclear testing. Moody's downgraded India from Baa3 to Ba2 in June 1998, and Standard & Poor's cut the rating to BB from BB+ in October 1998. But the excellent reception that RIBs and IMDs received in difficult circumstances has raised the relevance of diaspora funding to India's creditworthiness. Unlike Israel, however, India has not made diaspora bonds a regular feature of its foreign financing forays. Instead, diaspora bonds are used as a source of emergency finance. Without explicitly acknowledging as much, India has tapped this funding source whenever the balance of payments has threatened to run into deficit. The country's ability to do so is now perceived as a plus.

Rationale for the Investors

Why would investors find diaspora bonds attractive? Patriotism, in large part, explains why investors purchase diaspora bonds. The discount from market price at which Israel, India, and Lebanon have managed to sell such bonds to their respective diaspora is a reflection of the charity implicit in these transactions. Up to the end of the 1980s, Israel's DCI sold bonds with 10- to 15-year maturities to Jewish diaspora in the United States (and Canada to a lesser extent) at a fixed rate of roughly 4 percent without any reference to changes in U.S. interest rates. U.S. 10-year yields over the same time period averaged 6.8 percent, implying a significant discount to market rates. It was only in the 1990s that interest rates paid by the DCI started to rise in the direction of market interest rates.

Beyond patriotism, however, several other factors may also help explain diaspora interest in bonds issued by their country of origin. Principal among these is the opportunity such bonds provide for risk management. The worst-case default risk associated with diaspora bonds is that the issuing country would be unable to make debt service payments in hard currency. But the issuing country's ability to pay interest and principal in local currency terms is perceived to be much stronger, and therein lies the attractiveness of such bonds to diaspora investors. Typically, diaspora investors have current or contingent liabilities in their home country and hence may not be averse to accumulating assets in local currency. Consequently, they view the risk of receiving debt service in local currency terms with much less trepidation than purely dollar-based investors. Similarly, they are also likely to be much less concerned about the risk of currency devaluation. SBI officials have been quite explicit in stating that the Indian diaspora knew SBI to be rupee rich and hence never questioned its ability to meet all debt service obligations in rupees.[8]

Still other factors supporting purchases of diaspora bonds include the satisfaction that investors reap from contributing to economic growth in their home country. Diaspora bonds offer investors a vehicle to express their desire to do good in their country of origin through investment. Furthermore, diaspora bonds give investors the opportunity to diversify their assets away from their adopted country. Finally and somewhat speculatively, diaspora investors may also believe that they have some influence on policies at home, especially on bond repayments.

Conditions and Candidates for Successful Diaspora Bond Issuance

The sizable Jewish and Indian diasporas in the United States, Europe, and elsewhere have contributed to the success of Israel and India in raising funds from their respective diaspora. Many members of these diaspora communities have moved beyond the initial struggles of immigrants to become quite affluent. In the United States, for example, Jewish and Indian communities have among the highest levels of per capita income. In 2000, the median income of Indian-American and Jewish households in the United States was $60,093 and $54,000, respectively, versus $38,885 for all U.S. households.[9] Like all immigrants, they are also known to have savings higher than the average U.S. savings rate. As a result, they have a sizable amount of assets invested in stocks, bonds, real estate, and bank deposits.

Many other nations have large diaspora communities in the high-income Organisation for International Co-operation and Development (OECD) countries (table 3.4).[10] The presence of tens of millions of Mexican nationals in the United States is quite well known. Three regions—Asia, Latin America and the Caribbean, and Eastern Europe—have significant diaspora presence in the United States. The principal countries from each region in declining order of numerical strength include the Philippines, India, China, Vietnam, and Korea, from Asia; El Salvador, the Dominican Republic, Jamaica, Colombia, Guatemala, and Haiti, from Latin America and the Caribbean; and Poland, from Eastern Europe. Diaspora presence is also significant in other parts of the world, for example, Korean and Chinese diasporas in Japan; Indian and Pakistani diasporas in the United Kingdom; Turkish, Croatian, and Serbian diasporas in Germany; Algerians and Moroccans in France; and large pools of migrants from India, Pakistan, the Philippines, Bangladesh, Indonesia, and Africa in the oil-rich Gulf.

For diaspora investors to purchase hard currency bonds issued by their countries of origin, it would seem that there has to be a minimum level of governability. Absence of governability, as reflected in civil strife, is clearly a detriment to selling diaspora bonds. Though this requirement would not disqualify most countries in the Far East and many in Eastern Europe, countries such as Cuba, Haiti, and Nigeria (and several others in Africa),

TABLE 3.4

Countries with Large Diasporas in the High-Income OECD Countries

| Country | Emigrant stock | | Rule-of-law indicator |
	Population (thousands)	% of population	
Mexico	10,476	10.16	−0.51
Turkey	3,725	5.17	0.08
China	2,705	0.21	−0.42
Philippines	2,475	2.93	−0.44
India	2,380	0.22	0.13
Morocco	2,228	7.39	−0.08
Vietnam	1,839	2.21	−0.41
Serbia and Montenegro	1,815	22.56	−0.86
Poland	1,702	4.46	0.33
Colombia	1,082	2.41	−0.72
El Salvador	979	14.68	−0.44
Romania	938	4.33	−0.23
Jamaica	929	34.98	−0.60
Dominican Republic	922	9.74	−0.67
Russian Federation	916	0.64	−0.88
Pakistan	915	0.59	−0.87
Brazil	852	0.46	−0.45
Iran, Islamic Rep. of	780	1.13	−0.76
Ukraine	753	1.60	−0.57
Peru	609	2.23	−0.78
Lebanon	446	11.13	−0.33
South Africa	444	0.95	0.18
Egypt, Arab Rep. of	402	0.55	0.03
Trinidad and Tobago	323	24.38	−0.11
Cuba	1,135	10.08	−1.13
Haiti	558	6.00	−1.70
Nigeria	377	0.27	−1.41

Sources: Rule of law data from Kaufman, Kraay, and Mastruzzi (2006); emigrant stock data from Ratha and Shaw (2007).

which have large diasporas abroad but have low levels of governability, may be found wanting. Israeli and Indian experience also shows that countries will have to register their diaspora bonds with the U.S. SEC if they want to tap the retail U.S. market. The customary disclosure requirements of SEC registration may prove daunting for some countries. Some of the African and East European countries and Turkey, with significant diaspora presence in Europe, however, will be able to raise funds on the continent, where the regulatory requirements are relatively less stringent than in the United States. Arguably, diaspora bonds could also be issued in the major destination countries in the Gulf region and in Hong Kong, China; Malaysia; the Russian Federation; Singapore; and South Africa.

The Israeli track record reveals how the patriotic discount is the greatest from first-generation diasporas than from subsequent generations. Thus, the DCI secured large elements of charity in bonds issued in the immediate wake of the birth of the nation. As the Jewish diaspora with intimate connection to the Holocaust dwindled over time, the DCI pricing of diaspora bonds moved closer to the market. This is likely to be even more important where the diaspora ties are based on country of origin rather than religion. The second- and subsequent generation country diaspora can be expected to have much weaker ties to their ancestral countries. This suggests that, more than the aggregate size of the diaspora, the strength of the first-generation immigrants with close ties to the home country would be a better yardstick of the scope for diaspora bonds. Also, skilled migrants are more likely to invest in diaspora bonds than unskilled migrants.

While not a prerequisite, the sale of diaspora bonds would be greatly facilitated if the issuing country's institutions, such as the DCI from Israel, or its banks had a significant presence to service their diaspora in the developed countries of Europe and North America. Such institutions and bank networks would be much better positioned to market diaspora bonds to specific diaspora individuals and communities. Clearly, the presence of Indian banks in the United States helped with the marketing of RIBs. Where the Indian diaspora was known to favor specific foreign banks, such as Citibank and HSBC in the Gulf region, the SBI outsourced to them the marketing of RIBs and IMDs.

Conclusion

This chapter discusses the rationale, methodology, and potential for issuing diaspora bonds as instruments for raising external development finance, mostly drawing on the experiences of Israel and India. The government of Israel has nurtured this asset class by offering a flexible menu of investment options to keep the Jewish diaspora engaged since 1951. The Indian authorities, in contrast, have used this instrument opportunistically to raise financing during times when they had difficulty in accessing international capital markets (for example, in the aftermath of their nuclear testing in 1998). While thus far only state-owned entities have issued diaspora bonds, there is no reason why private sector companies cannot tap this source of funding. In terms of process, the issuers of diaspora bonds were able to bypass U.S. SEC registration in the past; however, that may not happen in the near future, as U.S. investors are unlikely to be allowed to choose the law and the forum governing bond contracts. Finally, factors that facilitate—or constrain—the issuance of diaspora bonds include having a sizable and wealthy diaspora abroad, and a strong and transparent legal system for contract enforcement at home. Absence of civil strife is a plus. While not a prerequisite, presence of national banks and other institutions in destination countries facilitates the marketing of bonds to the diaspora.

It has been difficult to gather facts and data on diaspora bonds, although anecdotally a number of countries are believed to have issued such bonds in the past (for example, Greece after World War II). One difficulty that confounds data gathering is the confusion between diaspora bonds and foreign currency deposits, and sometimes between diaspora bonds and local currency deposits. Exhorting the diaspora members to deposit money in domestic banks is different from asking them to purchase foreign currency–denominated bonds in international capital markets. Indeed, as pointed out in this chapter, diaspora bonds are also different from Islamic bonds, even though both are targeted to investors belonging to a specific group rather than to all investors. There is a need for better data gathering, including on pricing of these bonds, and on the cyclical characteristics of the flows associated with these bonds.

There is also a need for clarity on regulations in the host countries that allow diaspora members to invest in these bonds or constrain their investing. A pertinent question in this respect is, should these bonds be nonnegotiable, or should countries make an effort to develop a secondary market for these bonds? An argument can be made for the latter on the grounds that tradability in the secondary market would improve liquidity and pricing of these bonds.

Notes

1. Remittance flows to developing countries have increased steadily and sharply in recent years to reach over $200 billion in 2006 (Ratha 2007). The World Bank believes that unrecorded remittance flows to developing countries are one-half as large (World Bank 2005).

2. According to the Central Bank of Sri Lanka press release of September 13, 2006, the last issue of Sri Lanka Development Bonds for $105 million was sold through competitive bidding on September 12, 2006, at an average yield of the London interbank offered rate plus 148.5 basis points.

3. Indirect evidence may be that the Lebanese government bonds are priced higher than the level consistent with the country's sovereign credit rating.

4. A Bloomberg search of FCD schemes identifies well over 30 developing countries. Moody's and Standard and Poor's have foreign currency short-term debt ratings for 60 and 68 developing countries, respectively.

5. This point is taken up again in explaining SBI's decision to restrict the access to Resurgent India Bonds and India Millennium Deposits to investors of Indian origin.

6. The Committee on Capital Markets Regulation is an independent and bipartisan group consisting of 23 leaders from the investor community, business, finance, law, accounting, and academia. On November 30, 2006, the committee issued its interim report, highlighting areas of concern about the competitiveness of U.S. capital markets and outlining 32 recommendations in four key areas to enhance that competitiveness. For more information on this high-powered committee see http://www.capmktsreg.org.

7. Indeed, the purchases of bonds issued by Israel's DCI rose during the six-day war. Similarly, India was able to raise funds from its diaspora in the wake of the foreign exchange crisis in 1991 and again following the nuclear testing in 1998, when the country faced debilitating sanctions from the international community.

8. V. Gopinathan of SBICAP Securities made this point strongly in an interview in New York in December 2006.

9. National Jewish Population Survey (NJPS) of 2000/01 and the U.S. Census Bureau.

10. Data on migration stocks tend to be incomplete and outdated. Recent efforts to collect bilateral migration data in major migration corridors are summarized in Ratha and Shaw (2007).

References

Bradlow, Daniel D. 2006. "An Experiment in Creative Financing to Promote South African Reconciliation and Development," American University Washington College of Law.

Chander, Anupam. 2001. "Diaspora Bonds." *New York University Law Review,* 76 (October).

———. 2005. "Diaspora Bonds and U.S. Securities Regulation: An Interview." *University of California at Davis Business Law Review,* Interview, May 1.

Choi, Stephen J., and Andrew T. Guzman. 1998. "Portable Reciprocity: Rethinking the International Reach of Securities Regulation." *Southern California Law Review* 71 (July): 903, 922.

El Qorchi, Mohammed. 2005. "Islamic Finance Gears Up." *Finance & Development* 42 (4).

Kaufmann, Daniel, Aart Kraay, and Massimo Mastruzzi. 2006. "Governance Matters V: Aggregate and Individual Governance Indicators for 1996–2005." Policy Research Working Paper 4012, World Bank, Washington, DC.

Murray, Alan. 2006. "Panel's Mission: Easing Capital Market Rules." *Wall Street Journal,* September 12.

Ratha, Dilip. 2007. "Leveraging Remittances for Development." Mimeo. Development Prospects Group, World Bank, Washington, DC.

Ratha, Dilip, and William Shaw. 2007. "South-South Migration and Remittances." Working Paper 102, World Bank, Washington, DC.

Rehavi, Yehiel, and Asher Weingarten. 2004. "Fifty Years of External Finance via State of Israel Non-negotiable Bonds." Foreign Exchange Activity Department, Assets and Liabilities Unit, Bank of Israel, Tel Aviv, September 6.

Romano, Roberta. 1998. "Empowering Investors: A Market Approach to Securities Regulation." *Yale Law Journal* 107: 2359, 2424.

World Bank. 2005. *Global Economic Prospects 2006: Economic Implications of Remittances and Migration.* Washington, DC: World Bank.

Zakaria, Fareed. 2006. "How Long Will America Lead the World?" *Newsweek,* June 12.

CHAPTER 4

GDP-Indexed Bonds:
Making It Happen

Stephany Griffith-Jones and Krishnan Sharma

The introduction of GDP-indexed bonds could have a number of positive effects for developing countries, for investors, and for the international financial system. The proposal for such an instrument is not new, and a first wave of interest in indexing debt to GDP emerged in the 1980s, propounded by economists such as John Williamson (2005). In later years, this practice has been encouraged by the work of economists such as Shiller (1993, 2005a),[1] Borenzstein and Mauro (2004), and the U.S. Council of Economic Advisers (CEA 2004). Though the idea of GDP-indexed debt has so far been implemented to a limited extent,[2] it received new impetus after the wave of financial and debt crises in a number of developing countries in the 1990s. There has been a revival of interest in instruments that could reduce developing countries' cyclical vulnerability. In particular, GDP-indexed bonds have attracted discussion in recent years, since a variant of this instrument has played a role in Argentina's debt restructuring following the collapse of convertibility at the end of 2001.

In the simplest terms, GDP-indexed bonds pay an interest coupon based on the issuing country's rate of growth. An example would be a country with a trend growth rate of 3 percent a year and an ability to borrow on plain vanilla terms at 7 percent a year. Such a country might issue bonds

We thank Inge Kaul, Pedro Conceicao, and Ron Mendoza for insightful comments. We are also very grateful to Randall Dodd for his valuable suggestions.

that pay 1 percentage point above or below 7 percent for every 1 percent that its growth rate exceeded or fell short of 3 percent. Of course, the country would also pay an insurance premium, which most experts expect to be small. Whether the coupon yield needs to vary symmetrically, in line with the gap between actual and trend growth and on both the upside and the downside, is an open question. Given the requirement for many institutional investors to hold assets that pay a positive interest rate, there may also be a need for a floor below which the coupon rate cannot fall.

This chapter draws on an extensive survey of the literature, interviews with financial market participants, and the discussions in an expert group meeting (comprising market participants, government officials, and representatives from multilateral organizations) held at the United Nations, New York, on October 25, 2005 (UN 2005).[3] The chapter begins by outlining the benefits and recent experience with GDP-indexed bonds. It then looks at the concerns, issues, and obstacles from the viewpoint of investors and issuers. Finally, it suggests constructive next steps.

The Benefits of GDP-Indexed Bonds

The benefits of GDP-indexed bonds can be divided into gains for borrowing countries, gains for investors, and broader benefits to the global economy and financial system.

Gains for Borrowing Countries

GDP-indexed bonds provide two major benefits to developing-country borrowers: First, they stabilize government spending and limit the procyclicality of fiscal pressures by requiring smaller interest payments at times of slower growth—providing space for higher spending or lower taxes—and vice versa. This runs counter to the actual experience of developing countries, which are often forced to undertake fiscal retrenchment during periods of slow growth in order to maintain access to international capital markets. By allowing greater fiscal space during downturns, growth-indexed bonds can also be thought to disproportionately benefit the poor by reducing the need to cut social spending when growth slows. They could also curb excessively expansionary fiscal policy in times of rapid growth.

Second, by allowing debt service ratios to fall in times of slow or negative growth, GDP-indexed bonds reduce the likelihood of defaults and debt crises. Crises are extremely costly, both in terms of growth and production and in financial terms (Eichengreen 2004; Griffith-Jones and Gottschalk 2006). The extent of this benefit is of course determined by the share of debt that is indexed to GDP.

Simulations show that the gains for borrowers can be substantial. If half of Mexico's total government debt had consisted of GDP-indexed bonds, it would have saved about 1.6 percent of GDP in interest payments during the financial crisis in 1994/1995 (Borenzstein and Mauro 2004). These additional resources would have provided the government with space to avoid sharp spending cuts and maybe even provided some leeway for additional spending that may have mitigated some of the worst effects of the crisis. Countries experiencing volatile growth and high levels of indebtedness (such as Brazil and Turkey) should find GDP-indexed bonds particularly attractive. However, a potential problem is that the countries that might benefit most from these instruments may also find it difficult to issue the bonds at reasonable premiums, due to markets questioning the countries' economic and policy fundamentals. If GDP-indexed bonds are to be widely used, it would be better if they were first issued by countries with greater credibility. Two such groups of countries were identified in the United Nation's 2005 expert group meeting. The first comprised developed countries that may have an interest in issuing GDP-indexed bonds, for example, the European Monetary Union (EMU) countries.[4] The second group may be developing countries, such as Mexico or Chile, whose fundamentals are attractive to markets. The instrument may also be of interest to countries such as India, that are considering liberalizing further restrictions on overseas capital flows in order to attract greater volumes of private finance. For such countries, GDP-indexed bonds may be an attractive instrument that manages their risk as they gradually liberalize the capital account of the balance of payments (UN 2005).

Gains for Investors

Investors are likely to receive two main benefits from the introduction of GDP-indexed bonds. First, the bonds would provide an opportunity for investors to take a position on countries' future growth prospects; that is, they would offer investors equitylike exposure to a country. Though this is made possible to some degree through stock markets, such opportunities are often not representative of the economy as a whole. In this respect, the GDP-indexed bonds would also provide a diversification opportunity. One way this instrument would provide diversification benefits is by giving investors in countries or regions with low growth rates an opportunity to have a stake in countries or regions with higher growth rates (UN 2005). Moreover, since growth rates across developing countries tend to be uncorrelated to some extent, a portfolio including GDP-indexed bonds for several of these economies would have the benefits of diversification, thus increasing the ratio of returns to risks. Second, investors in GDP-indexed bonds would benefit from a lower frequency of defaults and financial crises, which often result in costly litigation and renegotiation and sometimes in outright large losses.

Of course, it is important to differentiate between the various categories of investors (discussed later in this chapter). Some types of investors may find this instrument more attractive than others. For example, pension funds in some countries could find this instrument attractive. In Italy, private pension funds benchmark their returns against the public pension system, which is indexed to the growth of GDP. Thus, an instrument whose return is linked to domestic growth would be attractive. Similarly, domestic pension funds in emerging markets may be interested in purchasing growth-indexed securities issued by their governments (especially if there is a local currency variant). At the expert group meeting, an investor suggested potential interest in the instrument among pension funds in developing countries such as Mexico and Chile (UN 2005).

Broader Benefits to the Global Economy and Financial System

On a broader level, GDP-indexed bonds can be viewed as desirable vehicles for international risk-sharing[5] and as a way of avoiding the disruptions arising from formal default. They can be said to have the characteristics of a public good in that they generate systemic benefits over and above those accruing to individual investors and countries. For example, by reducing the likelihood of a default by the borrowing country, these instruments would benefit not just their holders but also the broader categories of investors, including those who hold plain vanilla bonds. In addition, improvements in GDP reporting necessitated by the introduction of growth-linked bonds should also benefit the wider universe of investors. Similarly, the benefits for countries of a lesser likelihood of financial crises extend to those that may be affected by contagion and also the advanced economies and multilateral institutions that may have to finance bailout packages. As elaborated below, these externalities provide an additional compelling explanation of why it is not sufficient to expect markets to develop these instruments on their own; rather, there exists a justification for the international community to pool resources and coordinate to achieve such an end.

Recent Argentine Experience with GDP-Indexed Bonds

Though GDP-indexed bonds have not yet been issued on a large scale, a number of countries (such as Bulgaria, Bosnia and Herzegovina, and Costa Rica) have issued them as part of their Brady restructurings.[6] However, in general these instruments were not well designed and had mixed success. For instance, in Bulgaria, the bonds were callable, which allowed the government to buy back the bonds when growth exceeded the nominated threshold rather than pay an additional premium. Moreover, the bonds did not specify what measure of GDP should be used to calculate the threshold and, even more seriously, whether nominal or real GDP should be used (CEA 2004). Given these design problems, the past experience with GDP-indexed bonds does not provide much information as to how they would perform if their structure was better thought out.

The possibility of a market being created for GDP-indexed bonds from developing countries may have been significantly enhanced by the introduction of a GDP-linked warrant into the Argentine debt restructuring package. Initially Argentina's creditors (and the financial markets more generally) seemed to disregard the offer by the Argentine government of the GDP warrant or argued that it had little value. However, the position of creditors in the middle of a negotiation can probably be best understood in the context of bargaining or game theory. It is in their interest to downplay the value of any offer by the debtor, especially in the context of a tough negotiation, such as the Argentine one. However, according to some observers, more creditors may have participated in the Argentine debt restructuring because of the offer of the warrants; thus, on the margin, the warrants may have helped the successful outcome of the Argentine offer. As a result of the efforts of some investment houses and—above all—of very rapid growth in the Argentine economy, which increases the potential value of these warrants, interest in Argentina's GDP warrants has increased significantly and its price has been rising.[7]

If Argentina continues on average to grow quite rapidly and services the warrants at a fairly significant rate, this may turn out to be somewhat costly for Argentina in terms of higher debt servicing (though this will occur only in times of fairly high growth, when it can be argued the country can presumably afford higher debt servicing). However, though potentially costly for Argentina, such a scenario could help create a GDP-linked bond market. To the extent that the instrument of GDP-linked bonds is a desirable financial innovation that benefits debtors and creditors, Argentina will have done the international community a favor by issuing these warrants and servicing them.

The GDP-linked unit (or warrant) is attached to every restructured Argentine bond, and its payments are linked to the growth of the economy. Payments will be made if the following three conditions are met simultaneously in any particular year between 2006 and 2035:

- Real GDP is at a higher level than the base GDP.

- Real growth of GDP versus the previous year is greater than the growth implied by base GDP (from 2015 the base growth rate is flat at 3 percent; before then, somewhat higher growth rates are assumed).

- The total payment cap has not been reached. This payment cap is denominated in the currency of the warrant and will not exceed 0.48 cents per unit of currency of the warrant.

When the three conditions are met, the government will pay 5 percent of the difference between the actual growth and the base-case growth of GDP during the relevant year. Given the lags in publishing GDP data, the payment relating to GDP performance in a given year is not actually paid until December 15 of the following year. The warrant is not callable; that is, even if the Argentine government buys back the debt, it still has to service the warrant.

The warrant was detached from the underlying bonds (bonds that result from the debt restructuring) 180 days after the issue date (end of November 2005). After that, the warrant had an individual trading price. As a consequence, the Argentine warrant can be defined as a detachable option.

The fact that Argentina has been growing very rapidly puts this growth well above the baseline growth. High, early growth increases the value of the warrant, because it puts the level of GDP above the baseline early, which increases the chance that one of the conditions will continue to be met in the future, as the level of GDP is more likely to stay above the baseline; more immediately, early payments have more value due to high discount rates for future payments.[8] As a result, the price of the warrants has gone up.

Initially, the market for warrant forwards was not very liquid, with an estimated scale of about $5 billion, which is relatively small in relation to the total level of warrants that will be issued. Reportedly, these warrant forwards were mainly traded by hedge funds and index funds, though potentially they could be very attractive for pension funds, given their potential upside.

Analysts hold different views on whether measurement of future real GDP could be problematic. Several analysts argue that investors are not at all concerned about this subject. Others argue that there are possible risks in underestimating GDP. These concerns are particularly linked to the GDP deflator. However, overall it seems increasingly difficult to manipulate GDP data, given that a number of international institutions (including the United Nations and the International Monetary Fund [IMF]) are checking for consistency of data and improving national and international standards for measuring GDP (UN 2005). Moreover, the IMF's International Standards and Codes policies include improvements in data and data reporting, which should help address any remaining data problems.

There are also some problems in the way the Argentine warrants were designed, which can offer lessons for the design of similar instruments—or of GDP-linked bonds—in the future. One of the first lessons, highlighted by investors at the recent experts meeting, was the warrants' apparent complexity (UN 2005). This may have contributed to the significant initial underpricing of the warrants. However, there was also an apparent failure by market participants to grasp the potential value of these warrants at the time they were incorporated into the debt restructuring package. A second problem is that the design could reportedly lead to fairly large debt servicing payments, at a time when the Argentine economy would be growing only slightly above the baseline growth. More careful construction of such instruments therefore seems essential. Further research is required on this issue.

Concerns, Issues, and Obstacles

The second section of this chapter referred to the benefits of GDP-indexed bonds for countries and investors, as well as the systemwide externalities that they are likely to generate. At the same time, there are issues and concerns, both at a general level and, more specifically, for both investors and issuers. These are dealt with below.

Some General Issues and Concerns

One potential problem is moral hazard. It has been argued that, by increasing debt repayments in case GDP growth is higher than normal, such bonds might reduce debtors' incentives to grow. This concern is exaggerated, as it is hard to imagine that politicians would ever want to limit growth. Moreover, it implies that this instrument is applicable for those countries that have the requisite policy credibility, strong institutions, and established systems of public accountability for economic performance.

There is also the issue of whether GDP is a good variable on which to index these instruments. Commodity-linked bonds can also play a role in reducing country vulnerabilities and stabilizing budgets and have the advantage, over indexing to GDP, that the sovereign usually has no control over commodity prices. Indexing to commodity prices has a longer and more established history. It also has existing derivatives to help in pricing, and the linking of payments is easier because commodity prices are widely known and their reporting does not lag by months. However, countries whose economies are substantially linked to changes in commodity prices tend to be low income (and unlikely to be able to issue GDP-linked bonds in any case). Many developing countries also have diversified production and exports with no natural commodity price to link to bond payments. Linking bond payments to GDP would in comparison allow countries to insure against a wider range of risks. Other alternative variables to index against may be exports or industrial production. However, GDP is the most comprehensive and widely accepted measure of a country's national income, and having a standard variable against which to index the bonds of different countries is crucial.[9]

Finally, if the benefits of GDP-indexed bonds can be significant, as suggested above, why have financial markets not adopted them yet? One point to stress at the outset is that the systemwide benefits provided by these instruments are greater than those realized by individual investors. Hence, there are externalities that do not enter the considerations of individual financial institutions. Other factors that dissuade beneficial financial innovation from taking place include the fact that the markets for new and complex instruments may be illiquid and are difficult for investors to price. There is therefore a need for a concerted effort to achieve and ensure critical mass so as to attain market liquidity. Related to this are coordination problems, whereby a large number of borrowers have to issue a new instrument in order for investors to be able to diversify risk. Other obstacles include the "novelty" premium charged by investors for new products they are uncertain about (that may serve to dissuade issuers), and the need for standardization to ensure that all instruments have similar features and payment standards (which is especially important to create a liquid secondary market).

Investors' Concerns

This section examines the potential obstacles, both real and perceived, to a wider introduction of GDP-indexed bonds. Three main concerns, in particular, stand out: uncertainty about potential misreporting of GDP data, uncertainty about sufficient liquidity of GDP-linked bonds, and concerns regarding the difficulties in pricing GDP-linked bonds.

Accurate Reporting of GDP Growth Data

Not only is this a relatively important concern for market participants and investors; it is also one that international institutions and national governments can do much to overcome. The concern can be decomposed into (1) inaccuracies in measurement of relevant variables, such as nominal GDP, and GDP deflator, and (2) deliberate tampering by debtor country authorities, with an aim to lower debt servicing.

As regards general inaccuracies, it can be legitimately argued that national income accounting is by now a fairly standard procedure. Existing deficiencies in statistical agencies could be overcome or ameliorated by technical assistance from international institutions. Given current efforts to increase transparency and improve quality of statistics, this is an area in which the international community could clearly help. Furthermore, clear definitions of relevant variables could be carefully addressed in the bond contract. It is encouraging that many borrowing countries, including emerging ones, overcame similar concerns about the measurement of inflation, resulting in successful issuance of inflation-indexed bonds.

The second concern, about deliberate tampering with GDP data to reduce debt service payments, seems quite unlikely. Furthermore, the idea that governments would deliberately reduce growth to reduce debt service seems absurd, as Williamson (2005) points out. It is indeed high GDP growth, rather than low growth, that is considered a success politically, and it is a major help in getting governments reelected. Higher growth also encourages higher investment by both domestic and foreign investors, again a desirable outcome for any politician. Finally, underreporting of growth would increase the cost of issuing new debt, an undesirable effect for any government. Therefore, the incentives for deliberate underreporting of growth would seem to be very weak. In any case, measures to improve GDP statistics, increase the independence of the statistical agencies, or increase the role of outside agencies should give an extra level of confidence to investors. These may therefore be important to introduce for the success of GDP-linked bonds.

An even more technical problem is how to deal with GDP revisions and possible methodological changes. It is interesting that such revisions have been reported to be smaller in developing than in developed countries (CEA 2004). Furthermore, over the long period during which a bond will be serviced, yearly revisions of GDP might actually even themselves out, with a relatively small impact on a cumulative basis. In any case, the existing literature proposes clear ways in which remaining concerns on data revisions could be overcome. The key is to specify ex ante in the debt contract a clear method for dealing with revisions (Borenzstein and Mauro 2004). The easiest way seems to be to ignore data revisions after a certain date; the coupon payment would be made at a fixed date (set so enough time would have passed for quite precise statistics to be available). If there was a major change in methodology of data calculation, governments could be required to keep separate GDP series calculated with the old methodology until the bonds mature. In an alternative solution, an outside agency could guarantee that the changes would not affect bond payments, as in the case of U.K. inflation-indexed bonds (CEA 2004).

Sufficient Liquidity and Scale

The other major concern of investors and market participants is that of uncertainty about future liquidity of GDP-indexed bonds. This clearly relates to scale of transactions. According to Borenzstein and Mauro (2004), it would be difficult to develop a market for this type of bond in a gradual way. Sufficient liquidity is important not only for investors, so these instruments can be actively traded, but also for issuers, as higher liquidity could reduce the required risk premium. Greater liquidity would help reduce the novelty premium, which a first issuer may face. A higher premium over that for a standard bond instrument could discourage countries from issuing GDP-linked bonds.

Indeed, small initial issues by individual countries would not be very attractive, especially as they would not reduce significantly the probability of a crisis. The most likely way in which such a market can begin to be created is through successful introduction of GDP-linked bonds in a major debt restructuring. This is why the large interest in the Argentine warrant, which has a very significant scale, offers great potential for the creation of such a market, especially by fostering investor interest. The hope would be that other countries would follow, perhaps with large one-off swaps, not necessarily in the context of debt servicing difficulties.

An even more attractive possibility for the development of a GDP-linked bond market is that several governments (preferably both developed and developing) start issuing these bonds more or less simultaneously. Support and encouragement from international organizations, such as the IMF, the World Bank, the regional development banks, or the United Nations, could be very helpful to overcome coordination problems.

Pricing

A third concern is about the pricing difficulty. GDP-linked bonds are more difficult to price than standard bonds, though they do not seem to be more difficult to price than emerging market equities, or the derivatives created in 2002 by Goldman Sachs in the United States and Deutsche Bank in Europe (Shiller 2005a).[10] Difficulties may partly relate to somewhat limited availability and quality of market-based forecasts of GDP growth. However, the development of a growth-indexed bond market should lead to an improvement on these fronts. At the experts meeting, it was pointed out that the simpler the structure of the instrument, the easier it would be to price. This has proved to be the case with inflation-indexed securities such as Treasury Inflation-Protected Securities (TIPS), which despite being skeptically viewed by market participants when first introduced in the late 1990s have been issued in large quantities and have overcome initial pricing problems (UN 2005). In this regard, there have also been many successful experiences with inflation-indexed securities in Latin America, which in several aspects provide a useful precedent for GDP-linked securities.

At the experts meeting, investors claimed that the premium they would expect to pay to purchase these bonds would depend on price discovery and the bid-offer spread. To overcome pricing difficulties, according to an investor, it is important to establish "comparables"; that is, there needs to be a range of exactly comparable GDP-linked bonds issued by different countries. This will enable investors to make comparisons, undertake arbitrage, and facilitate price discovery. Markets like to price comparability. It would be particularly valuable if countries with very good ratings, such as Mexico or Chile, were the first to issue these types of bonds in good times. It was also pointed out at the meeting that certain derivatives could support the price discovery process and that multilateral development banks can undertake transactions in derivative form that facilitate price setting.[11] It was suggested that an adequate way would be to swap a nominal bond and GDP-indexed bonds, even for small amounts (less than $20 million). This would give the price for at least small amounts of bond issuance, thus providing a first benchmark for countries willing to issue bigger amounts (UN 2005).

More generally, there may be a need to help address investors' concerns about the possible complexity of pricing these instruments by assisting with the development of pricing models for new instruments such as GDP-linked bonds. Market participants, international organizations, and academic researchers could be involved in such an exercise.

Investors would require a premium, because the yield on GDP-indexed bonds is more variable than on the fixed-rate plain vanilla bonds. An important issue therefore is whether—particularly initially—the premium that market participants would wish to charge (for other than plain vanilla bonds) would not be higher than what issuers would be willing to pay. Further research is required on how this hurdle could be overcome. An important consideration to be included in the pricing is the very low correlation between growth in developed and developing countries, which is far lower than correlation among developed countries even in times of crises (Griffith-Jones, Segoviano, and Spratt 2004; Shiller 2005b). This consideration also applies to stock market prices and bond spreads. Therefore, investing in instruments that reflect growth in developing countries could yield considerable diversification benefits and thus lower the premium charged due to variability of interest payments on GDP-linked bonds.

Other Concerns

A minor concern for investors could be the callability of bonds. This would imply that, when countries grew faster (as Bulgaria reportedly did), they could buy back the GDP-indexed bonds, thereby depriving investors of the upside benefits. This issue could be easily dealt with by specifying in the bond contract that the bonds would be noncallable.

Different Potential Investors

An important issue to consider is the types of investors that are and could be interested in GDP-linked bonds. Some initial clues are given by the fact that hedge funds have expressed most interest in the trade for Argentine warrants. However, there also seems a clear case for pension funds to have an interest in such an instrument, which could give them a stake in the upside of growth in developing countries, with all the accompanying benefits of international diversification. Perhaps efforts are needed to make these benefits explicit to institutional investors.

Another interesting issue is whether mainly fixed-income investors will provide the majority of demand for such instruments. Indeed, a case could be made that GDP-linked bonds could also be of interest to equity investors, since the risk associated with these instruments is similar to equity risk. At the experts meeting, a number of participants also noted that GDP-indexed bonds are neither pure equity instruments nor pure debt instruments. One participant thus suggested thinking more creatively about who the consumers of GDP-indexed bonds might be. It was pointed out that an entirely new set of investors—breaking from the traditional mold of bond and equity investors and hedge funds—might be interested in this type of investment (UN 2005).

Issuer Interest

The benefits of GDP-indexed bonds for issuing countries have been outlined above, but these need to be set alongside the costs. Two potential problems for issuers have been outlined in the literature:

One, long-term benefits versus short-term costs may sit uncomfortably with the political cycle. It typically takes years for unsustainable debt positions to emerge, and the proposed indexation is likely to apply only to relatively long-term bonds, with an original maturity of about five years or more. Against this, countries will have to pay a premium over the cost of standard debt. Given short political horizons, it has been argued that some governments could be unwilling to pay a premium to issue indexed bonds that might make life easier for their successors several years down the road.

Two, lags in the provision of GDP data may not be in sequence with the economic cycle. The advantages of GDP-indexed bonds, especially in playing the role of automatic stabilizers for borrowing countries, depend on the extent to which the indexed portion of the coupon payments reflects the true state of the economic cycle. If the GDP data become available with a long lag, savings on interest payments could materialize at a time when the economy might already be rebounding; this could present the risk that the impact would be pro-cyclical.

However, these concerns may be overplayed. Worries over lags in the provision of GDP figures may be limited by the high autocorrelation of GDP series and in countries where quarterly data are published. Though the incentives relating to the political cycle are a more serious issue, a number of countries have indicated a genuine interest in issuing GDP-indexed bonds at forums such as the Rio Group and the Summit of the Americas. As mentioned above, the more important issue may concern the size of the premium arising from pricing difficulties. While the literature suggests that the additional cost in terms of a premium is unlikely to be very large,[12] there is a need for further research in this area.

Consideration may also be given to ways of ensuring flexible payment arrangements that allow more breathing space for borrowers during bad times. For instance, one suggestion at the experts meeting was for coupon payments to remain fixed and the amortization schedule to be adjusted instead. Countries would postpone part or all of their debt payments during economic downturns; they would then make up by prepaying during economic upswings. A historical precedent was set by the United Kingdom when it borrowed from the United States in the 1940s. The loan was negotiated by J. M. Keynes and included "bisque clauses" specifying that payments would be stopped when certain events occurred (UN 2005).

Additional Suggestions for Overcoming Obstacles

In addition to the ideas that have been mentioned above on ways to make GDP-linked bonds a more attractive instrument for both investors and issuers, the following proposals may also deserve further examination.

First, multilateral or regional development banks could play a very active role as "market makers" for GDP-linked bonds,[13] and their involvement could help address concerns regarding liquidity and scale of transactions in these securities. These institutions could begin by developing a portfolio of loans, the repayments on which could be indexed to the growth rate of the debtor country. Once the institutions have a portfolio of such loans to different developing countries, they could securitize them and sell them on the international capital markets. Such a portfolio of loans could be particularly attractive for private investors, as it would offer them the opportunity of taking a position on the growth prospects of a number of developing economies simultaneously. Given the low correlation among these countries' growth rates, the return-risk ratio would be higher. As correlations tend to be lower at the global level, the World Bank may be best placed to do such securitization. Moreover, the expertise developed by the World Bank as market maker for the sale of carbon credits under the Kyoto Protocol could provide a basis for these activities.

Second, an alternative modality for this instrument is to provide a sweetener that would only vary on the upside, that is, paying only higher returns when growth is higher than expected. The investor would benefit from an equitylike instrument in upside periods. The benefit for the issuing country is that spreads would be lower than on plain vanilla bonds in normal or bad times; only in good times would the countries have to service more debt. Therefore such bonds could open up some space, albeit limited, for countercyclical fiscal policies due to the lower cost of the debt. Introducing such a sweetener could help entice investor interest in the early stages and ultimately provide a platform from which to develop a market for more symmetrical GDP-linked bonds. There are similarities with the Argentine warrant, but this instrument would be offered in so-called normal times.

Third, there have also been proposals for multilateral development banks to provide a form of partial guarantee to investors covering initial sales of GDP-linked bonds. The main problem, however, is that such guarantees could further complicate the pricing of this instrument and as such were not viewed favorably by some investors at the expert meeting. Another disadvantage of a guaranteed first bond is that it does not provide a benchmark for future issues that may not be covered by a guarantee (Schroder et al. 2004). Despite these problems, the feasibility of a guarantee may vary from case to case and needs to be examined in the country context.

Policy Implications and Next Steps

The preceding analysis suggests that the introduction of GDP-indexed bonds would represent a win-win situation, benefiting both issuer countries and investors. Moreover, GDP-indexed bonds should also be considered a public good that would benefit the global economic and financial system at large. At the same time, for reasons mentioned earlier, markets are unlikely to develop these instruments on their own. A natural tension is also likely to exist in the short term between the size of the premium that issuers are prepared to pay and that which investors expect. If a market develops, however, and these securities can be issued by a wider range of countries, including those that are not in distress, this tension should disappear as expected premiums come down. In fact, investors can change their minds about an instrument once it is demonstrated in the market. For example, as pointed out in the experts meeting, the introduction of TIPS was viewed skeptically by market participants when they were first introduced in 1997, but this has been overcome, and thus far the U.S. Treasury has issued approximately $100 billion of TIPS (UN 2005).

For these reasons, a case can be made for international public action to help develop GDP-indexed bonds. There also is a need to implement the steps suggested below, some of which would require collaboration among the main stakeholders—that is, interested governments, multilateral development banks, and the private sector:

1. Undertake research on the criteria for pricing GDP-indexed bonds and on the development of pricing models. Additional research could also be undertaken on the expected benefits of these instruments for different countries. Finally, there is a need to consider the design of these instruments and methods of flexible payment arrangements for countries.

2. Investigate possibilities for coordinated issuance to jump-start a market in GDP-indexed bonds. Coordinated actions by a number of borrowers to issue GDP-linked bonds could overcome the problems of critical mass and illiquidity. Having a number of countries issuing these instruments simultaneously would also help establish the comparability needed to ease pricing and enhance the diversification benefits for investors. It has been suggested that one or several advanced industrialized countries could issue these instruments first. This could have some positive effects for those countries. Furthermore, this would have a demonstration

effect and make it easier for developing countries to issue similar instruments. The precedent of introducing collective action clauses into bond contracts, done first by developed countries and later followed by developing countries, would seem to indicate that such demonstration effects can be very effective for financial innovation. Alternatively, groups of developing countries (for example, the Rio Group) could undertake issuance, in a coordinated manner, probably with support from international institutions.

3. Explore how international financial institutions could use this instrument. Regional development banks (such as the Inter-American Development Bank) or the World Bank, as well as the International Development Association, could consider lending through loans whose repayment would be indexed to GDP growth (Tabova 2005). This on its own could help create a precedent for the establishment of a GDP-indexed private bond market for developing countries. Moreover, consideration should also be given to a proposal made at the experts meeting for these institutions to go a step further and securitize these loans and sell them on the capital markets. Such a move would entail the World Bank and regional development banks carving out a new role for themselves.

4. Examine sources of creative partnerships between public and private sectors. In addition to the above ideas regarding the roles that multilateral development banks and governments could play in creating a market for GDP-linked bonds, there also is the possibility of public-private collaboration in jump-starting a market for these instruments. It might be interesting to draw lessons from the approach taken in the development of collective action clauses, wherein governments and private sector groups collaborated; the G-10 major industrial countries and the Institute of International Finance played an important role, notably in drafting model clauses and initiating discussions on how best to design them, as well as in spurring on a number of countries to take the lead in using the instrument.

5. Undertake initiatives to improve the reliability, accuracy, and timeliness of GDP data. An issue that needs to be further explored is the feasibility and need of having an outside agency verifying a country's GDP statistics. Other important actions include technical assistance from donors

and multilateral organizations to improve the quality of GDP statistics in issuer countries and also to strengthen the effectiveness and independence of national statistical agencies.

6. Prepare a draft GDP-linked bond contract. A sample contract could clarify how to address concerns relating to data revisions, the link between growth and interest payments, and specific problems that have occurred in the past such as governments calling back their bonds when growth was higher than expected (CEA 2004). Such a contract would also ensure standardization and emphasize simplicity and would draw on a code of best practices. It could be useful to have a model, with variants and wording options, to discuss with both potential investors and issuers.

Notes

1. Shiller proposed to create "macro markets" for GDP-linked securities, which were to be perpetual claims on a fraction of a country's GDP.

2. Some small countries, such as Bosnia and Herzegovina, Bulgaria, and Costa Rica have issued bonds as part of their Brady restructurings that included clauses or warrants that increased their payments if GDP reached a certain level.

3. Also see the United Nations Web site at http://www.un.org/esa/ffd/GDP-indexed%20Bonds.

4. GDP-indexed bonds may be particularly attractive for EMU countries because the "Stability and Growth Pact" tends to render their fiscal policies procyclical. Particularly relevant for European countries, these policies could include those in which pensions are indexed against GDP growth, such as Italy. Moreover, these countries may find it easier to issue and sell these bonds to investors due to their more comprehensive and reliable statistics on GDP and its components.

5. Several studies show that there are large unrealized gains from international risk-sharing (Borenzstein and Mauro 2004).

6. These included clauses or warrants that increased payments if GDP reached a certain threshold (CEA 2004).

7. See, for example, Credit Suisse First Boston Emerging Markets Sovereign Strategy, September 22, 2005.

8. It is calculated that if Argentina grows at the rates forecast for 2005 and 2006, more than 20 percent of the current market price of the warrant would be recovered just with payments for those two years.

9. It has been pointed out that for some developing countries, export and industrial production data might be more reliable than GDP figures (Borenzstein and Mauro 2004). Of course, in some cases, gross national product may be a better measure of welfare and, where appropriate and feasible, it could also be considered as a benchmark.

10. These derivative markets create options on macroeconomic variables. Although not directly tied to GDP, these macroeconomic variables are correlated to GDP.

11. This would be consistent with the envisaged role for multilateral development banks to act as market makers for GDP-indexed bonds. In this sense, it can be argued that there is an important role for public institutions to create markets that benefit development.

12. Calculations made using the Capital Asset Pricing Model suggest that the risk premium on GDP-indexed bonds issued by developing countries would likely be small. It could be higher for the initial transactions owing to the likely lack of liquidity, the novelty of these instruments, and any pricing difficulties. However, the cost required to compensate investors for the volatility of interest payments should, according to the literature, be minimal, since growth in emerging markets has a very small correlation with global equity markets and with growth in developed countries (Borenzstein and Mauro 2004; CEA 2004).

13. José Antonio Ocampo deserves credit for this interesting suggestion.

References

Borenzstein, Eduardo, and Paolo Mauro. 2004. "The Case for GDP-indexed Bonds." *Economic Policy* 19 (38): 166–216.

CEA (Council of Economic Advisers). 2004. "GDP-Indexed Bonds: A Primer." CEA, Washington, DC. http://www.whitehouse.gov/cea/growth-indexed-bonds-white-paper.pdf.

Eichengreen, Barry. 2004. "Financial Instability." In *Global Crises, Global Solutions*, ed. Bjorn Lomborg. New York: Cambridge University Press.

Griffith-Jones, Stephany, and Ricardo Gottschalk. 2006. "Costs of Currency Crises and Benefits of International Financial Reform." http://www.stephanygj.net.

Griffith-Jones, Stephany, Miguel Segoviano, and Stephen Spratt. 2004. "CADs and Developing Countries: The Potential Impact of Diversification Effects on International Lending Patterns and Pro-cyclicality." http://www.stephanygj.net.

IMF (International Monetary Fund). 2004. "Sovereign Debt Structure for Crisis Prevention." Background paper, IMF, Washington, DC. http://www.imf.org/external/np/res/docs/2004/070204.pdf.

Schroder, Michael, Friedrich Heinemann, Susanne Kruse, and Matthias Meitner. 2004. "GDP-Linked Bonds as a Financing Tool for Developing Countries and

Emerging Markets." Discussion Paper 04-64, ZEW Centre for European Economic Research, Mannheim. ftp://ftp.zew.de/pub/zew-docs/dp/dp0464.pdf.

Shiller, Robert. 1993. *Macro Markets: Creating Institutions for Managing Society's Largest Economic Risks*. New York: Oxford University Press.

———. 2005a. "In Favor of Growth-Linked Bonds." *The Indian Express*, March 10.

———. 2005b. "Macro Markets: Managing Risks to National Economies." In *The New Public Finance, Responding to Global Challenges,* ed. Inge Kaul and Pedro Conceicao. New York: Oxford University Press.

Tabova, Alexandra. 2005. "On the Feasibility and Desirability of GDP-Indexed Concessional Lending." GRADE Discussion Paper 9. Available from Group of Research and Analysis on Government, University of Trento, Italy. http://www-econo.economia.unitn.it/new/pubblicazioni/papers/9_05_tabova.pdf.

United Nations. 2005. "Report on the Brainstorming Meeting on 'GDP-Indexed Bonds: Making It Happen.'" Financing for Development Office and United Nations Development Program, New York.

Williamson, John. 2005. *Curbing the Boom-Bust Cycle: Stabilizing Capital Flows to Emerging Markets*. Washington, DC: Institute for International Economics.

CHAPTER 5

Shadow Sovereign Ratings for Unrated Developing Countries

Dilip Ratha, Prabal De, and Sanket Mohapatra

The credit rating issued by major international rating agencies such as Fitch Ratings (Fitch), Moody's Investors Service, and Standard & Poor's (S&P) is a key variable affecting a sovereign's or a firm's access to capital markets. Risk ratings not only affect investment decisions in the international bond and loan markets, but they also affect allocation of foreign direct investment (FDI) and portfolio equity flows. The allocation of performance-based official aid is also increasingly being linked to sovereign ratings.[1]

The foreign currency rating of the sovereign—which has the authority to seize foreign exchange earnings, impose exchange restrictions, fix exchange rates, and even expropriate private assets—typically acts as a ceiling for the foreign currency rating of subsovereign entities (Beers and Cavanaugh 2006; Fitch Ratings 1998; Lehmann 2004; Truglia and Cailleteau 2006). Even when the sovereign is not issuing bonds, a sovereign rating provides a benchmark for capital market activities of the private sec-

This research was carried out when Prabal De was a summer intern at the World Bank. We are grateful to Alan Gelb, Suhas Ketkar, and Vikram Nehru for extensive discussion, and to David Garlow, Luis Luis, Greg Sutton, the participants at World Bank seminars organized respectively by the Financial Policy and Country Creditworthiness Department, South Asia Chief Economist's Office, the Debt Department, Development Prospects Group, and the Kennedy School of Government, for useful comments and suggestion. Thanks to Zhimei Xu for excellent research assistance.

tor. "The rating process, as well as the rating itself, can operate as a power-ful force for good governance, sound market-oriented growth, and the enforcement of the rule of law. From a business perspective, sovereign credit ratings serve as a baseline for evaluating the economic environment surrounding investment possibilities and as a benchmark for investors to distinguish among markets, which provides valuable information and a basis for evaluating risk" (U.S. Department of State 2006).

It is worth noting, however, that as of today, 70 developing countries—mostly poor—and 12 high-income countries do not have a rating from a major rating agency.[2] Of the 86 developing countries that have been rated, the rating was established in 2004 or earlier for 15 countries. A few coun-tries do not need a rating, as they do not need to borrow. Most of the unrated countries, however, do need external credit and resort to relation-ship-based borrowing from commercial banks, or sell equity to foreign direct investors. Because of their ongoing relationship with the borrowers, banks can monitor the latter's willingness and ability to repay debt. Bond investors, on the other hand, rely heavily on standard indicators such as credit ratings to monitor the borrower. The cost of borrowing from inter-national capital markets is inversely related to the sovereign rating. For a $100 million, seven-year bond in 2005, the launch spread would rise from 27 basis points for an A- bond to 577 basis points for a CCC+ bond (box 5.1). There is a sharp jump in spreads (of 91 basis points in 2005) at the investment-grade threshold.[3]

When arm's-length monitoring of investment projects is difficult, non-bank investors either do not invest, or take direct control of the invest-ment project via FDI. Also, the cost of financing FDI projects is affected by sovereign risk ratings. In 2005, FDI constituted 85 percent of private capi-tal flows in the unrated countries, compared with 26 percent in the BBB-rated developing countries (figure 5.1).[4]

Several factors influence a country's reluctance or inability to get rated. Countries are constantly reminded of the risks of currency and term mis-match associated with market-based foreign currency debt, and the possi-bility of sudden reversal of investor sentiment (Calvo and Reinhart 2000; Panizza, Eichengreen, and Hausmann 2005). The information required for the rating process can be complex and not readily available in many coun-tries.[5] The institutional and legal environment governing property rights and sale of securities may be absent or weak, prompting reluctance on the part of politicians to get publicly judged by the rating analysts. The fact that

FIGURE 5.1

Composition of Private Capital Flows in Rated and Unrated Countries, 2005

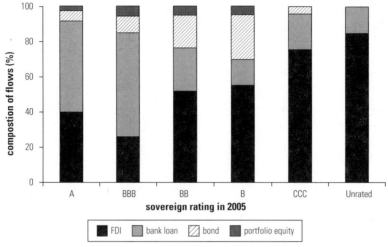

Source: World Bank 2006.

a country has to request a rating, and has to pay a fee for it, but has no say over the final rating outcome can also be discouraging.[6] Also Basel capital adequacy regulations that assign a lower risk weight (100 percent) to unrated entities than to those rated below BB− (150 percent) may discourage borrowing entities from getting rated.

Having no rating, however, may have worse consequences than having a low rating. Unrated countries are often perceived by creditors as riskier than they are, riskier even than very high-default-risk countries. In 2002, the U.S. Department of State's Bureau of African Affairs decided to fund a project to help African nations get an initial sovereign credit rating (U.S. Department of State 2006). Also, the United Nations Development Programme (UNDP) recently partnered with Standard & Poor's to rate eight African countries during 2003–06 (Standard & Poor's 2006). Interestingly, the newly established ratings under these two initiatives did not fall at the bottom of the rating spectrum. Of the 10 newly rated African countries, one was rated BB-, the rest were rated in B categories, and none was rated C.

This chapter hopes to make a modest contribution to these efforts by estimating a model of sovereign ratings for rated developing countries using readily available variables, and then attempting to predict sovereign ratings for the unrated developing countries.

BOX 5.1

Sovereign Spreads Are Inversely Related to Sovereign Ratings

The logarithm of spreads can be modeled as a function of sovereign ratings, a dummy that takes the value 1 if a country is considered investment grade, debt issue size, and maturity (Cantor and Packer 1996; Eichengreen and Mody 2000; Kamin and von Kleist 1999):

$$\text{Log(Spread)} = \alpha + \beta_1(\textit{Investment-grade dummy}) + \beta_2(\textit{Sovereign rating}) + \beta_3(\textit{Log(Issue size)}) + \beta_4(\textit{Maturity}) + \textit{error}$$

This model seems to work well in explaining the launch spreads of emerging-market sovereign bonds issued during 2003–05 (see figure). All the coefficients have the expected sign and, except for issue size, are statistically significant at 5 percent. The adjusted R-squared ranges from 0.74 in 2003 to 0.88 in 2005 (see table).

Relationship between Sovereign Ratings and Launch Spreads

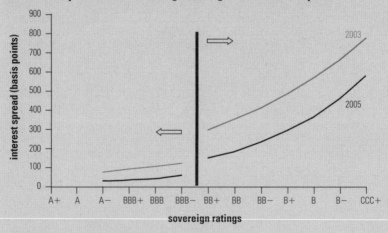

Sources: Bondware, Standard & Poor's, and authors' calculations.

Note: $100 million sovereign bond issue with a seven-year tenor. See figure 6.5 for the latest version of the figure for the relationship between sovereign ratings and launch spreads.

Regression Results: Relationship between Launch Spread and Sovereign Rating

Dependent variable: Log(launch spread)	2003	2005
Investment-grade dummy	−0.69**	−0.76*
	(0.33)	(0.38)
S&P sovereign rating (numeric equivalent)	0.16***	0.23***
	(0.05)	(0.05)
Log(issue size)	0.04	0.05
	(0.13)	(0.08)
Maturity (years)	0.02*	0.03***
	(0.01)	(0.01)
Number of observations	37	42
Adjusted R-squared	0.74	0.88

Source: Authors' calculations.

Note: White robust standard errors are reported below coefficient estimates.

* significant at 10%; ** significant at 5%; *** significant at 1%.

The plan of the chapter is as follows. The next section presents some stylized facts about sovereign ratings. It shows that ratings by different agencies are highly correlated with a correlation coefficient of 0.97 or higher. It also shows that ratings for individual countries tend to be sticky over time, a fact that brought criticism to the rating industry in the aftermath of the Asian crisis (Ferri, Liu, and Stiglitz 1999). The chapter then develops the rating prediction model, drawing on the existing literature. It also discusses the results on predicted or shadow sovereign ratings for the unrated countries. The concluding section summarizes the results and discusses how poor country entities could improve their borrowing terms through financial structuring or leveraging of official aid.

Some Stylized Facts about Sovereign Credit Ratings

Sovereign credit ratings in some form have been in existence for nearly a century. The major rating agencies—Standard & Poor's and Moody's—

started rating sovereign Yankee bonds in the early 20th century. By 1929, ratings of 21 countries had been done by Poor's Publishing, the predecessor to Standard & Poor's, and even included several of today's emerging markets, for example, Argentina, Colombia, and Uruguay (Bhatia 2002). Moody's started rating debt instruments in 1919, and within the next decade had rated bonds issued by about 50 governments (Cantor and Packer 1995). However, demand for ratings declined during the Great Depression, and most ratings were suspended in the period following World War II. Rating activity revived briefly in the postwar period but declined again in the late 1960s with the introduction of the Interest Equalization Tax (IET), a 15 percent levy on the interest from cross-border lending in the United States (Bhatia 2002). Rating activity for sovereigns resumed from the mid-1970s onward, with the withdrawal of the IET in 1974. In 1980, there were eight high-income countries that were rated by one or the other of the three leading rating agencies, that is, Moody's, Standard & Poor's, and Fitch. By the late 1980s, almost all the high-income Organisation for Economic Co-operation and Development countries had been rated.

Sovereign credit ratings for the developing countries (as currently defined by the World Bank) began in the late 1980s, after the debt crisis (figure 5.2). The number of rated countries increased significantly during the emerging market phenomena of the 1990s. By December 2006, 131 countries—45 high-income and 86 developing countries—were rated by one or more of the three premier agencies.

Sovereign ratings issued by different agencies tend to be highly correlated. The bivariate correlation coefficient between the ratings of the three agencies as of December 2006 ranged from 0.97 to 0.99 (figure 5.3). The ratings are exactly the same across the three agencies for most AAA-rated countries. For most developing countries, the ratings are similar across the three agencies, usually within one to two notches of one another. The differences (if any) are typically due to the different timings of ratings.

An examination of rating changes over time reveals "stickiness," or persistence over time (figure 5.4), reflecting the fact that rerating does not occur with any regularity, but only when a country requests it (and pays for it), or when some significant, unforeseen event prompts the rating agencies to revisit a rating. Changes to ratings announced by different

FIGURE 5.2

Evolution of Sovereign Credit Ratings, 1980–2006

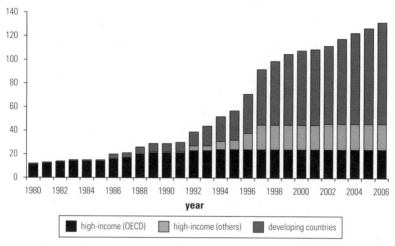

Sources: Standard & Poor's, Moody's, Fitch Ratings, and authors' calculations.

agencies also tend to be similar in direction and magnitude. A rating upgrade (or downgrade) by one agency is typically followed by a similar change by the others, usually with a lag. Rating agencies came under criticism for failing to predict the Asian crisis, and then for downgrading the countries after the crisis, which further deepened the crisis (Ferri, Liu, and Stiglitz 1999; Reinhart 2002b). Indeed, ratings were not downgraded by Moody's ahead of, or after, the financial crisis in Mexico in 1994–95, or in Turkey in 2000 (figure 5.4).

In developed countries, a firm's credit risk typically accounts for a large part of the information content of its ratings. In developing countries, however, the sovereign rating exerts significant influence on the ratings of firms and banks located in the country.[7] Nearly three-quarters of subsovereign issues that were rated by Standard & Poor's during 1993–2005 were rated equal to or lower than the sovereign rating (figure 5.5). Of these, almost half had exactly the same rating as the sovereign. A small number of subsovereign issues did pierce the sovereign foreign-currency rating ceiling, but these issues were mostly by firms in the oil and gas sector (e.g., Pemex, PDVSA, Petronas), or they were structured transactions backed by some form of collateral (such as export receivables and diversified payment rights).

FIGURE 5.3
Correlation of Sovereign Ratings by Different Agencies

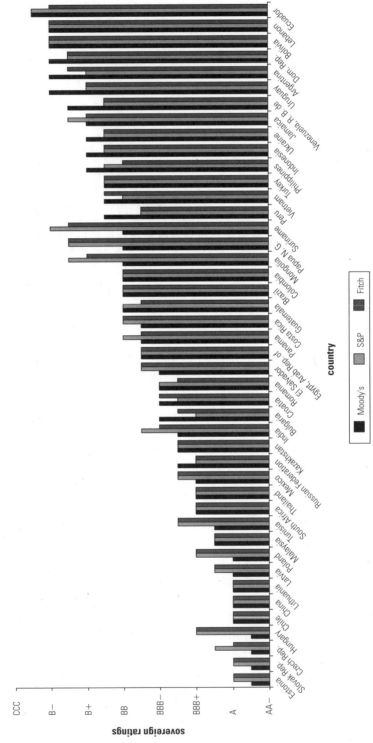

Sources: Standard and Poor's, Moody's, and Fitch Ratings.

Note: The figure shows ratings as of December 6, 2006, for developing countries rated by all three rating agencies. The correlation coefficient ranges between 0.97 and 0.99.

FIGURE 5.4

Evolution of Sovereign Credit Ratings in Selected Countries, 1986–2006

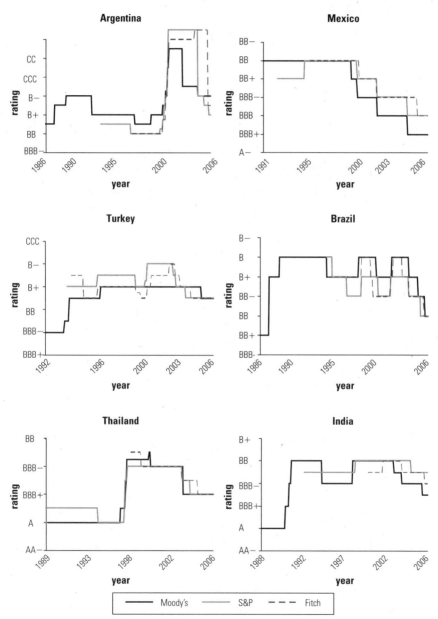

Sources: Standard & Poor's, Moody's, Fitch Ratings, and authors' calculations.

Note: A higher number indicates higher risk and lower letter rating.

FIGURE 5.5
Subsovereign Foreign Currency Debt Issues in Developing Countries Rated by S&P, 1993–2005

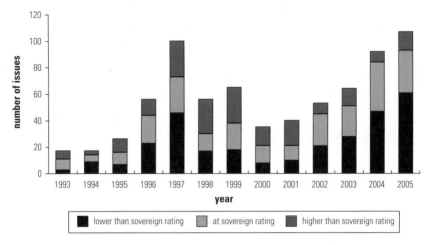

Sources: Bondware and authors' calculations.

Note: The sample excludes debt issued by supranationals, governments, provinces, and local authorities. It includes only debt issued in currencies of high-income OECD countries; it excludes cases where the sovereign is in default.

Prediction of Sovereign Credit Ratings

The care, rigor, and judgment that go into the sovereign rating process cannot be replaced by any mechanical models. But obtaining ratings from the major agencies for the 70 or so unrated countries would require considerable time and resources. The objective of this section, therefore, is more modest: to attempt to develop an econometric model using readily available variables to generate some preliminary, indicative ratings for the 70 or so unrated countries. The results may be interpreted as a rough indicator of what the actual rating might look like if the country were to get rated by a rating agency.

Rating agencies, owing to their business practice, do not officially disclose the precise models used for their rating methodologies. A common practice among rating agencies is to assign qualitative scores to several criteria and then arrive at a weighted average score. Beers and Cavanaugh (2006) provide an excellent explanation of the criteria used by Standard & Poor's. They list 44 variables grouped under nine categories—political risk, income and economic structure, economic growth prospects, fiscal flexibility, general government debt burden, off-budget and contingent liabilities, monetary flexibility, external liquidity, and public sector external debt burden. Similar criteria are also used by Moody's and by Fitch (Fitch Ratings 1998; Truglia and Cailleteau 2006). Both the scoring and the weights used to arrive at the final average rating are influenced by subjective judgment of the rating analysts. Understandably, many analysts believe that country risk ratings should not be determined by mechanical models.

Nevertheless, many researchers have found that the ratings by major agencies are largely explained by a handful of macroeconomic variables (see table 5.1 for a summary of this literature). Lee (1993) estimated a linear regression model with panel data for 40 developing countries for 1979–87 using growth, inflation, growth volatility, international interest rates, industrial countries' growth rates, debt-to-exports ratio, and dummies for geographical location as explanatory variables for ratings. In an often-cited article, Cantor and Packer (1996) used a cross-sectional regression model of sovereign credit ratings as a function of per capita income, GDP growth, inflation, fiscal balance and external balance, external debt, default history, and an indicator for the level of economic development. This study used a cross-section of high-income and developing countries. Rowland (2005) estimated a similar model using pooled time-series and cross-section data to identify the determinants of sovereign ratings and spreads. Ferri, Liu, and Stiglitz (1999) and Mora (2006) used a similar model to examine whether ratings were pro-cyclical during the Asian crisis by comparing predicted with actual ratings. Reinhart, Rogoff, and Savastano (2003) estimated similar cross-section and panel regression models for evaluating debt intolerance, the duress that many emerging-market countries experience at debt levels that would seem manageable by industrial country standards.

Sutton (2005) used an instrumental variable estimation to tackle the potential reverse causality that runs from ratings to debt burdens. He found little evidence of reverse causality and concluded that ordinary least squares may be the most appropriate technique. Related literature has examined the determinants of actual debt defaults and debt distress (Berg and Sachs 1988; Kraay and Nehru 2006; Manasse, Roubini, and Schimmelpfennig 2003). This literature also has found that a small set of variables (growth, external debt, and policy performance) explain the likelihood of debt distress and defaults.[8]

A common finding from this rich set of papers is that sovereign ratings can be explained to a significant extent by a handful of rather easily available macroeconomic variables. For this chapter, the steps taken to develop a model for predicting sovereign ratings proceeded as follows: (1) Estimate the sovereign ratings for the rated developing countries as a function of macroeconomic variables, rule of law, debt and international reserves, and macroeconomic volatility, as identified in the literature. (2) Test the predictive power of this model using within-sample prediction. Step two also exploited the high correlation across ratings assigned by the three rating agencies to test whether the predicted rating for one agency is similar to the actual ratings by other agencies. (3) Use the econometric model to predict ratings for developing countries that did not have a rating as of end-2006.

TABLE 5.1
Literature on Model-Based Determinants of Ratings

Source	Basis of analysis
Lee (1993)	Dependent variable: sovereign rating (log of the Institutional Investor rating) Explanatory variables: per capita GDP growth, inflation, international interest rates, industrial countries' growth rate, variance of per capita GDP growth, debt-to-exports ratio, dummies for geographical location, dummy for highly indebted country, and dummy for major borrower Number of observations: 360 Adjusted R-squared: 0.70 Pooled cross-section and time series of 40 developing countries for 9 years (1979–87)
Cantor and Packer (1996)	Dependent variable: sovereign rating (Moody's and Standard & Poor's), spread Explanatory variables: per capita income, GDP growth, inflation, fiscal balance and external balance, external debt-to-GDP ratio, default history (dummy for whether a country defaulted since 1970), and an indicator for the level of economic development (dummy for industrialized country) Number of observations: 49 Adjusted R-squared: 0.91 for Moody's, 0.93 for Standard & Poor's Cross-section of 27 high-income and 22 developing countries in 1995
Ferri, Liu, and Stiglitz (1999)	Dependent variable: sovereign rating (Moody's) Explanatory variables: GDP per capita, real GDP growth, inflation rate, budget deficit, current account balance, an indicator for debt-sustainability (short-term debt and current account balance as a ratio of foreign exchange reserves), and an indicator for the level of economic development (dummy for industrialized country) Number of observations: not applicable R-squared: 0.30–0.33 Pooled cross-section and time series of 6 high-income and 11 developing countries for 10 years (1989–98)

Literature on Model-Based Determinants of Ratings

Source	Basis of analysis
Reinhart, Rogoff, and Savastano (2003)	Dependent variable: sovereign rating (Institutional Investor rating) Explanatory variables: percentage of 12-month periods of inflation at or above 40 percent since 1948, percentage of years in a state of default or restructuring since 1824, number of years since last default or restructuring, external debt-to-GDP ratio (1970–2000 average), and a dummy for countries with high ratings Number of observations: 53 for cross-section, 769–1,030 for panel Adjusted R-squared: 0.74–0.79 for cross-section, 0.78–0.91 for panel regression Cross-section and panel regressions for 53 industrialized and developing countries for 1979–2000
Rowland and Torres (2004)	Dependent variable: sovereign rating (Institutional Investor rating), spread Explanatory variables: GDP growth rate, inflation rate, external debt-to-GDP ratio, external debt-to-exports ratio, debt service as a share of GDP, the level of international reserves as a share of GDP, the openness of the economy (exports and imports as share of GDP), and a dummy that takes value of 1 for the years in which a country is in default Number of observations: 225 R-squared: 0.62 Pooled cross-section and time series of 15 emerging market (developing) countries for 1987–2001
Rowland (2005)	Dependent variable: sovereign rating (Moody's, Standard & Poor's, Institutional Investor rating), spread Explanatory variables: GDP per capita, GDP growth rate, inflation rate, external debt-to-GDP ratio, debt-service ratio (ratio of external debt service to current account receivables), level of international reserves as a share of GDP, and openness of the economy (exports and imports as share of GDP) Number of observations: 49 Adjusted R-squared: 0.58 for Moody's, 0.69 for Standard & Poor's Pooled time-series and cross-section data
Sutton (2005)	Dependent variable: sovereign rating (average of Moody's and Standard & Poor's) Explanatory variables: Corruption index, international reserves, ratio of short-term bank claims to total claims, external debt-to-exports ratio, external debt-to-GDP ratio, years since resolution of last default, and a dummy for whether the country was admitted to the EU Number of observations: 32 R-squared: 0.87 Cross-section of 32 developing countries in 2004
Mora (2006)	Dependent variable: sovereign rating (average of Moody's and Standard & Poor's) Explanatory variables: GDP per capita (PPP), GDP growth, inflation rate, budget balance (% of GDP), current account balance (% of GDP), ratio of external debt to exports of goods and services, an indicator for the level of economic development (dummy for OECD), dummies for default on bonds and bank debt, and lagged spread Number of observations: 705 R-squared: 0.58–0.68 Pooled cross-section and time series of 88 countries for 1986–2001

Source: Authors' compilation.

Regression Model

As in the literature—notably Cantor and Packer (1996) and Sutton (2005)—this analysis postulated a simple linear regression model in the data of the following form:

$$\text{Sovereign rating} = \alpha + \beta_1(\log \text{ of GNI per capita}) + \beta_2(\text{GDP growth rate}) + \beta_3(\text{Debt/Exports}) + \beta_4(\text{Reserves/(Imports+short-term debt)}) + \beta_5(\text{Growth volatility}) + \beta_6(\text{Inflation}) + \beta_7 (\text{Rule of law}) + \text{error} \tag{1}$$

Gross national income (GNI) per capita, measured at the current market price, is a proxy for the level of development of a country. The ratio of total reserves to the sum of import and short-term debt obligations is a liquidity indicator (originally proposed by Greenspan-Guidotti). In the analysis, a higher value of these variables indicates reduced risk of a default on external obligations. Growth volatility refers to five-year standard deviation of the GDP growth rate.[9] The rule-of-law variable is taken from a widely used data set produced and updated by Kaufmann, Kraay, and Mastruzzi (2006). This variable, constructed as a function of various governance indicators, such as enforcement of property rights and accountability of the government, takes a value between −2.5 and +2.5, with higher values indicating better governance. (The world average for this variable is zero.) This variable was also used by Kraay and Nehru (2006).

The analysis also tried fiscal balance as an explanatory variable in the regressions. However, as in Cantor and Packer (1996) and Rowland (2005), this variable was not statistically significant. This may be due to data problems: the definition of the public sector and the reporting standards for fiscal deficit vary greatly from one country to another. To some extent, the fiscal balance is indirectly reflected in the regression through the other variables such as growth, inflation, and external debt.[10]

In this analysis, the dependent variable was the numeric equivalent of the sovereign long-term foreign currency rating from one of the three major agencies—Moody's, Standard & Poor's, and Fitch Ratings. The sovereign ratings issued by the three rating agencies were converted to a numeric scale, with 1 denoting the highest rating (corresponding to AAA for Standard & Poor's and Fitch, and to Aaa for Moody's) to 21 being lowest (C for all three agencies).[11] Table 5.2 shows the correspondence in the ratings between the three rating agencies. Cases of sovereign default or selective default were excluded in the regression analysis, since it is difficult to assign a specific numeric rating to such extreme credit events. Although default or selective default appears to be just another step down the road of getting a rating downgrade, assigning a specific value to such an event would run the risk of ignoring the degree of distress (e.g., a temporary liquidity crisis versus a systemic crisis).

Because a higher value of the dependent variable indicates a higher level of country risk, the correct sign for the coefficients of GNI per capita, GDP growth rate, reserve ratio, and rule of law was negative, whereas the sign of the coefficients of debt-to-exports ratio, growth volatility, and inflation was positive.

TABLE 5.2
Ratings—Conversion from Letter to Numeric Scale

	Standard & Poor's	Fitch	Moody's	Numeric grade
Investment grade				
Highest credit quality	AAA	AAA	Aaa	1
Very high credit quality	AA+	AA+	Aa1	2
	AA	AA	Aa2	3
	AA−	AA−	Aa3	4
High credit quality	A+	A+	A1	5
	A	A	A2	6
	A−	A−	A3	7
Good credit quality	BBB+	BBB+	Baa1	8
	BBB	BBB	Baa2	9
	BBB−	BBB−	Baa3	10
Speculative grade				
Speculative	BB+	BB+	Ba1	11
	BB	BB	Ba2	12
	BB−	BB−	Ba3	13
Highly speculative	B+	B+	B1	14
	B	B	B2	15
	B−	B−	B3	16
High default risk	CCC+	CCC+	Caa1	17
	CCC	CCC	Caa2	18
	CCC−	CCC−	Caa3	19
Very high default risk	CC	CC	Ca	20
	C	C	C	21

Sources: Standard & Poor's, Moody's, and Fitch Ratings.

The following sections report results for four specifications of the model summarized in equation (1):

1. Dependent variable is the rating as of end-2006; explanatory variables for 2005.

2. Dated model: dependent variable is the rating as of end-2006, but if the rating was established in year t, then for that observation, use explanatory variables for year $t-1$.

3. Dated pooled model to test whether a first-time rating by an agency systematically differs from its subsequent ratings.

4. Dated model to test whether a first-time rating by an agency is systematically affected by an existing rating from another agency.

The motivation for these different specifications and results are discussed below. After specification 2, results of model validation using within-sample prediction are reported and, separately, cross-comparison of a forecasted rating from one agency with an actual rating by another agency.

Specification 1: Dependent variable is the rating as of end-2006; explanatory variables for 2005
The first specification models the ratings as of end-2006 as a function of (lagged) explanatory variables for 2005. The analysis used ordinary least squares for a cross-section of latest available ratings, following the literature on modeling sovereign credit ratings (Cantor and Packer 1996; Sutton 2005). However, some of the latest available ratings were established several years back and have not changed in the meantime.[12] To exclude these outdated ratings, the analysis used ratings that were established between the beginning of 2003 and end-2006. This period covers most of the sample for the three rating agencies. Lagged values of the explanatory variables were used instead of contemporaneous values in order to limit possible reverse causality from ratings to explanatory variables. For example, the current sovereign rating may plausibly influence the risk premium and willingness of investors to hold foreign currency liabilities of the country. The results are reported in table 5.3.

All of the explanatory variables (except inflation) used for the analysis have the expected sign and are statistically significant at 5 percent across the three rating agencies. A higher GDP growth rate, a summary indicator of the performance of the economy, is associated with a better rating. Because ratings are on a negative numeric scale (with AAA equivalent to 1, AA+ to 2 and so on), a negative relationship between an explanatory variable and the numeric rating implies that higher values of the explanatory variable are associated with better credit ratings. This is also true for the GNI per capita, the reserve ratio, and the rule of law—higher values should be associated with lower numeric ratings and better letter rating. The coefficients associated with GNI per capita, the reserve ratio, and the rule-of-law variables have the expected negative signs. On the other hand, external debt (as a share of GDP) and the volatility of GDP growth are associated with a lower letter rating (and hence the positive sign). The coefficient of inflation is positive (as expected) but not significant. Given the cross-sectional nature of the regression, the R-squared presented in table 5.3 is adjusted for the degrees of freedom.

To get a better fit, the analysis excluded some outliers in the above regressions (Belize and Kazakhstan in the Moody's regressions; Belize,

TABLE 5.3
Regression Results Using 2005 Explanatory Variables for Ratings in December 2006

Dependent variable: sovereign rating	Standard & Poor's	Moody's	Fitch
GDP growth	−0.50***	−0.43***	−0.29***
	(0.07)	(0.09)	(0.09)
Log of GNI per capita	−1.63***	−2.17***	−1.49***
	(0.24)	(0.47)	(0.22)
Ratio of reserves to import and short-term debt	−4.23***	−4.41***	−3.76***
	(1.03)	(1.15)	(0.98)
Ratio of external debt to exports	0.57**	0.92***	0.82***
	(0.22)	(0.31)	(0.14)
GDP volatility (5-year standard deviation)	0.63***	0.76***	0.49***
	(0.10)	(0.14)	(0.10)
Rule of law	−1.77***	−2.15***	−1.95***
	(0.45)	(0.71)	(0.43)
Inflation		0.05	
		(0.08)	
Observations	55	47	60
Adjusted R-squared	0.81	0.82	0.81

Source: Authors' calculations.

Note: White robust standard errors are reported below coefficient estimates.

** significant at 5%; *** significant at 1%.

Grenada, Madagascar, and Uruguay in the S&P regressions; and Lebanon and the Islamic Republic of Iran in the Fitch regressions). The adjusted R-squared was lower when these outliers were included (for example, 0.76 versus 0.82 in the Moody's regressions), but the signs and significance of the explanatory variables were unchanged.[13]

It is plausible that some of the coefficients may be inconsistent and causality may be confounded in this regression because of the potential presence of reverse causality from ratings to some of the explanatory variables. In other words, income per capita or external debt may itself depend on ratings. There are two reasons why this did not present serious difficulties for this analysis. First, this is a cross-sectional study that deliberately used lagged data for all the independent variables, instead of contemporaneous values. Second, the purpose of the regression model was to use it as a best linear predictor of ratings, rather than for testing a hypothesis. In a cross-section, this method gives reasonably good results.

Specification 2: Dated model: dependent variable as of end-2006; but if the rating was established in year t, then use explanatory variables for year t−1
The regression model in the previous specification assumed that the latest available rating in end-2006 reflects the prevailing view of the rating agency, that is, that the macroeconomic and political situation has not improved (deteriorated) sufficiently to warrant an upgrade (downgrade) between the date the rating was established and end-2006. However, a rating established a few years back may not have changed for other reasons; one likely reason is that the country may not have requested or paid for a rating. Since it is not possible to distinguish between the two with the available information, the model used a more robust specification. Instead, it used lagged "dated" explanatory variables relative to the year in which the latest available rating was established.[14] For example, the latest available rating by Standard & Poor's for Estonia was for 2004 and used 2003 control variables. For the latest ratings that were established in 2006, the 2005 control variables still apply. As before, outliers were excluded to improve the fit of the prediction model. The results are reported in table 5.4.

The signs of the explanatory variables in table 5.4 are in the expected direction and are significant at the 10 percent level or better. The additional variable that is now significant is inflation, with higher inflation being correlated with worse ratings. All these variables together explain about 80 percent of the variation in ratings for the dated regression sam-

TABLE 5.4
Regression Results Using Dated Explanatory Variables for Latest Ratings as of December 2006

Dependent variable: sovereign rating	Standard & Poor's	Moody's	Fitch
GDP growth	−0.47***	−0.03	−0.19*
	(0.08)	(0.09)	(0.10)
Log of GNI per capita	−1.41***	−0.69*	−1.34***
	(0.29)	(0.35)	(0.26)
Ratio of reserves to import and short-term debt	−3.41***	−2.21***	−4.16***
	(0.87)	(0.65)	(0.92)
Ratio of external debt to exports	0.68***	1.68***	0.77***
	(0.24)	(0.25)	(0.23)
GDP volatility (5-year standard deviation)	0.37***	0.06	0.38***
	(0.10)	(0.12)	(0.09)
Rule of law	−2.60***	−2.68***	−2.20***
	(0.43)	(0.60)	(0.41)
Inflation		0.17***	
		(0.04)	
Observations	54	45	60
Adjusted R-squared	0.78	0.82	0.80

Source: Authors' calculation.

Note: White robust standard errors are reported below coefficient estimates.

* significant at 10%; *** significant at 1%.

ple. With such high explanatory power, it is not surprising that the predicted ratings are the same or close to the actual ratings for a large number of countries in the sample (see annex table 5A.1). The results presented in table 5.4 are used as the benchmark model for predicting ratings for unrated countries.

Model Validation Using Within-Sample Predictions

The next step was to use the fitted model to predict the value of the dependent variable. This step consisted of three models, one for each agency. Before proceeding to prediction, the validity of each model was checked using a variety of methods. Model validation involves using the available sample to verify that the model would give reasonable predictions. Using a model for the latest rating as of end-2005, the analysis predicted ratings for 2006 and compared these with the actual ratings assigned in 2006. This within-sample forecasting allowed a comparison of the actual ratings with the ratings predicted by the model. The regression results for ratings as of end-2005 are qualitatively very similar to the results reported in table 5.4 above, confirming that the model is indeed very stable.[15]

Figure 5.6 compares the ratings established in 2006 by Standard & Poor's with the predicted ratings using explanatory variables for 2005. The predicted ratings for 2006 are within one to two notches of the actual rating for most of the countries that have a rating. The small variation around actual ratings can be attributed to two factors. First, several of these developing countries have not been rated for some time and were therefore not part of the regression sample (the latest available rating for these was established before 2003). Second, the model captures economic and governance variables and the average relationship of these variables with the sovereign rating. The explanatory variables in the model may not adequately capture some events, for example, a military coup and nationalization of some crucial export sector such as oil. Based on these within-sample forecasts, the conclusion is that the benchmark prediction model (Specification 2) is reasonably good at predicting the sovereign rating for most developing countries.

FIGURE 5.6

Comparison of Actual S&P Ratings Established in 2006 with Predicted Ratings

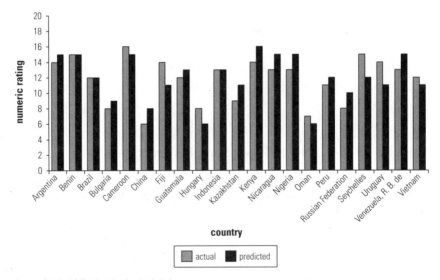

Sources: Standard & Poor's and authors' calculations.

Note: A higher numeric rating indicates higher risk and lower letter rating. (See table 5.2 for conversion from letter to numeric scale.)

Model Validation Using Cross-Comparison between Agency Ratings

To validate the models used, the analysis also exploited the fact that several countries are rated by one of the agencies but not by the others. In such cases, the predicted rating from one of the rating models can be compared with the actual rating by another agency. For example, Lesotho is rated BB− by Fitch, but it is not rated by Standard & Poor's and Moody's. The predicted rating for Lesotho, using the model estimated for S&P ratings, is also found to be BB−. Similarly, Uganda is rated B by Fitch, within one notch of the predicted rating of B− using the Standard & Poor's model. Figure 5.7 compares sovereign ratings established by Fitch in 2005–06 with the predicted rating from Moody's and Standard & Poor's for countries that were not rated by one or the other agency by end-2006. The average predicted rating from the Moody's and S&P models was used when both actual ratings were unavailable. The model seems to perform reasonably well in terms of emulating the actual rating of countries rated by Fitch.[16]

FIGURE 5.7

Comparison of Actual Fitch Ratings at End-2006 with Predicted Ratings from the Other Two Agencies

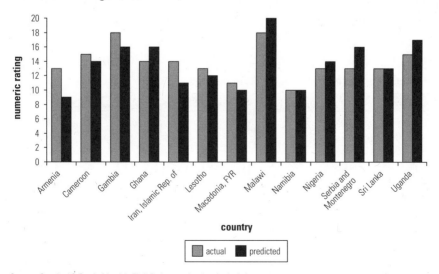

Sources: Standard & Poor's, Moody's, Fitch Ratings, and authors' calculations.

Note: A higher numeric rating indicates higher risk and lower letter rating. (See table 5.2 for conversion from letter to numeric scale.)

Modeling of New Ratings and the Very First Rating

The analysis carried out two final regressions for sovereign ratings. The interest is in what a new rating for a country would look like if there is no existing rating by all three agencies, and when there is an existing rating by one agency.

Specification 3: Dated pooled model to test whether a first-time rating by an agency systematically differs from its subsequent ratings

To test whether the sovereign rating varies systematically between a new rating by an agency and a subsequent rating by the same agency, the analysis used a regression model similar to the dated model specification for the entire pooled sample of all available ratings, with a dummy for the very first rating by the agency as an additional explanatory variable. The International Country Risk Guide (ICRG) composite index was used as an explanatory variable instead of the rule of law since the latter was not available for the period prior to 1996. The results are reported in table 5.5.

The explanatory variables have the expected signs and are statistically significant. The coefficient for the very first rating is negative in all three cases, but significant only in the case of Fitch. The first rating tends to be somewhat more optimistic than subsequent ratings, perhaps because countries choose to get rated when they are doing relatively well. It may also imply that rating agencies oblige new customers with a better first rating.

TABLE 5.5

Pooled Regression Results: On New Ratings

Dependent variable: sovereign rating	Standard & Poor's	Moody's	Fitch
GDP growth (3-year moving average, %)	−0.23***	−0.29***	−0.08 **
Log of GNI per capita	−0.66***	−0.77***	−0.51***
ICRG composite index	−.20***	−0.14***	−0.18**
Ratio of reserves to import and short-term debt	−1.01***	−0.64***	−1.67***
Ratio of external debt to exports	0.66***	0.67***	0.96***
GDP volatility (5-year standard deviation)	0.17***	0.18***	0.29***
Dummy for first rating	−0.39	−0.19	−1.55**
Observations	520	514	374
Adjusted R-squared	0.65	0.62	0.68

Source: Authors' calculation.

Note: White robust standard errors suppressed.

** significant at 5%; *** significant at 1%.

Specification 4: Dated model to test whether a first-time rating by an agency is systematically affected by an existing rating from another agency

The final specification considers the case when there is an existing rating by another agency when a rating agency rates a country for the very first time. The very first rating used a regression model similar to the dated specification, with the existing rating by another agency as an additional explanatory variable. The results reported in table 5.6 show that the first rating assigned by an agency is highly influenced by the existing rating assigned by its competitors. Indeed, this factor appears more important than the standard set of explanatory variables used in our models (which presumably are already reflected in the existing rating, according to the results of specification 3 above). These results again underscore that ratings by the three major agencies tend to be highly correlated.

Predictions for Unrated Developing Countries

The benchmark model in table 5.4 was used to predict ratings for the unrated developing countries. The range of predicted ratings generated by the three separate models is reported in table 5.7.

From these results, many countries appear to be more creditworthy than previously believed. It is rather striking to see that the predicted ratings for the unrated countries do not all lie at the bottom end of the rating spectrum

TABLE 5.6

Regression Results: On Very First Rating

Dependent variable: sovereign rating	Standard & Poor's	Moody's	Fitch
GDP growth (3-year MA %)	−0.85*	−0.15	0.15**
Log of GNI per capita	−0.15	0.38	0.39
Rule of law	0.48	−0.06	−0.08*
Ratio of reserves to import and short-term debt	−0.56**	0.2	−1.7**
Ratio of external debt to exports	0.19	0.28	0.06
GDP volatility (5-year standard deviation)	0.08	−0.16*	0.01
Existing rating (by another agency)	0.76***	0.91***	0.87***
Observations	36	28	38
Adjusted R-squared	0.89	0.90	0.92

Source: Authors' calculation.

Note: White robust standard errors suppressed.

* significant at 10%; ** significant at 5%; *** significant at 1%.

but are spread over a wide range (figure 5.8). Of the 55 unrated countries for which the analysis generated predicted ratings, only 14 were rated CC or lower; 8 were above investment grade, 18 were in the B to BB category, and 15 were in the CCC category.[17] The countries just below the investment grade but at or above CCC are comparable to many emerging market countries with regular market access. For example, the shadow rating for Standard & Poor's for Bangladesh in the analysis is a range from B− to B, which puts it in a similar bracket as emerging market countries such as Bolivia and Uruguay. There are several other unrated developing countries (e.g., Belarus, Cambodia, Chad, Dominica, Equatorial Guinea, Tajikistan, and the Republic of Yemen) with shadow ratings in the B category or above.

Even though the model-based shadow ratings may not capture all possible elements of country risk, a natural question that arises is: what variables included in the model explain what percentage of a country's predicted rating? As an illustration, annex table 5A.2 shows the contribution of each explanatory variable to the predicted rating using the benchmark model for Standard & Poor's (table 5.4). The predictions are based on the latest information as of end-2005, to ensure the broadest possible sample.

The results focus first on the countries with predicted S&P ratings in the investment-grade category. Some of their success is due to factors such as past wealth and high oil prices that may not be sustainable over the long

FIGURE 5.8
Distribution of Predicted Ratings

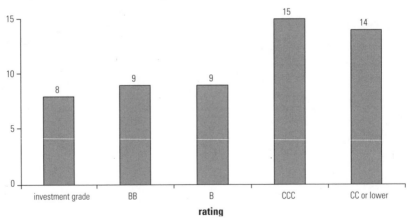

Source: Authors' calculations.

Note: The distribution is based on the lowest predicted rating in table 5.7.

run. For example, Kiribati's AAA rating is mostly due to extraordinarily high reserves accumulated from a trust fund, the Revenue Equalization Reserve Fund of some $600 million that was established from earlier phosphate mining revenues (Graham 2005). Algeria, Equatorial Guinea, Libya, and the Syrian Arab Republic are all oil exporters and consequently have very strong foreign exchange reserve positions and low levels of external debt relative to exports. Furthermore, Algeria's, Equatorial Guinea's, and Libya's oil wealth puts them in the middle- or upper-middle-income categories among developing countries. Others, such as the island nations St. Kitts and Nevis, St. Lucia, and St. Vincent and the Grenadines have high ratings, primarily owing to their high incomes from offshore banking and tourism. Bhutan, a lower-middle-income country, has an investment-grade rating due to a strong reserve position, above-average growth, and good governance (a high rule-of-law indicator), although with a debt ratio close to the average for unrated countries.

At the lower end of the spectrum are countries such as Burundi, the Central African Republic, Eritrea, Liberia, São Tomé and Principe, and Zimbabwe, whose predicted S&P numeric ratings puts them out-of-range on the S&P letter rating scale. All of these countries are poor, with per capita GNI ranging from $130 to $340 in 2005, with high debt ratios, poor governance, and low (or negative) GDP growth. These negative factors contribute to very low shadow ratings.

Countries in the middle that have a sub-investment-grade shadow rating for Standard & Poor's but are at least in the B category (from Vanuatu down to the Lao People's Democratic Republic) are usually characterized by higher GDP growth, lower debt ratio, lower GDP volatility, and better governance compared with the sample of all unrated countries. These countries are not uniformly good performers in all respects. For example, several (Lao PDR, Mauritania, Samoa, Tanzania, and Tonga) had significantly higher external debt ratios than the average in 2005. However, some of their positive attributes ameliorate this to some extent—high GDP growth in Lao PDR, Mauritania, and Tanzania; and relatively high GNI per capita and good governance in Samoa and Tonga. Similarly, Bangladesh had low external reserves relative to imports and short-term debt in 2005 and relatively poor governance, but it did well in terms of growth and macroeconomic stability.

The predicted ratings of four countries are shown as out of range in table 5.7, to indicate that they are riskier than a C rating. These countries are conventionally perceived as extremely risky. Indeed, all these countries are considered at high risk of debt distress ("red light" countries) by the International Development Association (IDA 2006b).[18] However, whether they are below default status is not clear, because it is not clear what numeric value can be assigned to default level. Therefore, default cases are excluded from this regression analysis.

TABLE 5.7

Predicted Ratings for Unrated Developing Countries

Country	Predicted rating range	Rated countries in the same range
Albania**	BB to BB+	Brazil, Colombia, El Salvador
Algeria	A to AA	Chile, China, Estonia
Angola	CCC+ to B+	Argentina, Ecuador, Uruguay
Bangladesh	B− to B	Bolivia, Dominican Republic, Jamaica
Belarus**	BB− to BB+	El Salvador, Indonesia, Philippines
Bhutan	BBB− to BBB+	Poland, South Africa, Thailand
Burundi	*	—
Cambodia**	B+	Argentina, Georgia, Pakistan
Central African Republic	C or lower	—
Chad	B− to B+	Argentina, Bolivia, Uruguay
Comoros	CC to CCC+	Belize, Ecuador
Congo, Dem. Rep. of	C or lower	—
Congo, Rep. of	CCC+ to B−	Bolivia, Cameroon, Paraguay
Côte d'Ivoire	CCC− to CCC+	Ecuador
Djibouti	B to B+	Argentina, Georgia, Uruguay
Dominica	BB+ to BBB	India, Mexico, Romania
Equatorial Guinea	BB+ to BBB−	El Salvador, India, Peru
Eritrea	*	—
Ethiopia	CCC−	—
Gabon**	BB+ to BBB	Mexico, Peru, Romania
Guinea	CCC or lower	—
Guinea-Bissau	C to CC	—
Guyana	CCC+ to B	Bolivia, Ecuador, Dominican Republic
Haiti	C to CCC−	—
Kiribati	AAA	—
Kyrgyz Republic	CCC+ to B−	Bolivia, Lebanon, Paraguay
Lao PDR	CCC− to B−	Bolivia, Ecuador, Paraguay
Liberia	*	—
Libya	AA to AAA	—
Maldives	BB+ to BBB	Croatia, India, Mexico
Marshall Islands	B− to B+	Bolivia, Pakistan, Uruguay
Mauritania	CCC to B	Bolivia, Dominican Republic, Paraguay
Myanmar	CCC−	—

Predicted Ratings for Unrated Developing Countries

Country	Predicted rating range	Rated countries in the same range
Nepal	CCC+ to B	Bolivia, Dominican Republic, Paraguay
Niger	CCC− to CCC	—
Rwanda	CC or lower	—
Samoa	CCC+ to BB−	Philippines, Turkey, Ukraine
São Tomé and Principe	*	—
Sierra Leone	CCC−	—
Solomon Islands	B− to B+	Pakistan, Sri Lanka, Uruguay
St. Kitts and Nevis	BBB+ to A−	Czech Republic, Malaysia, Thailand
St. Lucia	BBB to BBB+	Mexico, South Africa, Thailand
St. Vincent & the Grenadines**	BBB to BBB+	Mexico, South Africa, Thailand
Sudan	CCC or lower	—
Swaziland	BB− to BB	Brazil, Colombia, Turkey
Syrian Arab Rep.	A− to A+	Chile, China, Czech Republic
Tajikistan	B to B+	Argentina, Georgia, Uruguay
Tanzania	CCC+ to B+	Argentina, Bolivia, Pakistan
Togo	CCC to CCC+	Ecuador
Tonga	B+ to BB+	Brazil, Colombia, Indonesia
Uzbekistan	B to BB−	Argentina, Indonesia, Philippines
Vanuatu	BB+ to BBB+	Peru, Russian Federation, Thailand
Yemen, Republic of	BB− to BB	Colombia, Costa Rica, Guatemala
Zambia	CCC+ or lower	Ecuador
Zimbabwe	CC or lower	—

Source: Authors' calculations.

Note: — = not available. The model-based ratings presented here should be treated as indicative; they are clearly not a substitute for the broader and deeper analysis, and qualitative judgment, employed by experienced rating analysts. The predicted ratings range is based on predictions for the benchmark models for Standard & Poor's, Moody's, and Fitch. Dated explanatory variables were used for predicting ratings for 2006. These shadow ratings are not predictions for future rating changes. For that, one would need forecasts for the explanatory variables. See table 6.5 for shadow ratings for unrated countries in Sub-Saharan Africa as of December 2007.

* When the predicted rating was above 21 in the numeric scale, it was classified as out of range.

** Rated—exactly or closely aligned with the prediction here—since the preparation of this table.

The regression analysis used outstanding external debt instead of the net present value of external debt. In the case of countries that have received debt relief under the Heavily Indebted Poor Countries Initiative or the Multilateral Debt Relief Initiative, the net present value of future repayments may be lower than the stock of outstanding debt. Such countries may be more creditworthy than predicted by this model.[19] The rating agencies have been slow to upgrade such countries, taking the view that debt relief may be a one-time-only event with transitory effects.

It is worth reiterating that model-based predictions reported here can only be a rough guide, but not a substitute for rigorous and forward-looking analysis by seasoned analysts. First, the data used here are past data, rather than forecasts for the explanatory variables, in order to include the largest possible sample of unrated countries. Second, the shadow ratings may not capture political factors that are not fully captured in the rule-of-law index, for example, war or civil conflict. Budget deficit, which has been cited in the literature as an important explanatory variable, was not used because of the lack of consistent and comparable information, such as varying definitions of, for example, central government versus general government. Since the objective was to generate predictions for the broadest sample of countries possible, only variables that were available on a comparable basis for the largest possible set of countries were used. This exercise does not explicitly account for why countries do not get rated, which is an area of future research. Even with these important caveats, the above results show that unrated countries are not necessarily at the bottom of the ratings spectrum and that many of them are more creditworthy than previously believed.

Summary of Results and Policy Implications

Sovereign ratings from major rating agencies affect the access of sovereign and subsovereign entities to international capital markets. In addition to raising debt in capital markets, ratings are useful for the Basel II capital-adequacy norms for commercial banks. Foreign direct investment and portfolio investors typically use sovereign ratings to gain an aggregate view of the risk of investing in a particular country. For a developing country, the sovereign rating can provide a benchmark for the cost and size of potential debt issuance. Even aid allocations from multilateral agencies (e.g., IDA) and bilateral donors (e.g., the U.S. Millennium Challenge Account) are affected by sovereign creditworthiness criteria.

This chapter has tried to develop an econometric model for explaining sovereign ratings assigned to developing countries by the three major rating agencies. The ultimate purpose is to predict shadow ratings for the 70 or so unrated countries.

The main findings can be summarized as follows: First, the model works very well in explaining sovereign credit ratings. Within-sample forecasts—for example, using the ratings sample until 2005 to predict 2006 ratings—are usually within one to two notches of the actual sovereign ratings for rated developing countries.

Second, the ratings by the three agencies are highly correlated. The bivariate correlation ranges from 0.97 to 0.99.

Third, the model-based rating predictions show that many unrated countries would be likely to have higher ratings than currently believed, and many would be in a similar range as the so-called emerging markets. This finding is robust to a variety of specifications. Also, this finding contradicts the conventional wisdom that countries that lack a sovereign rating are at the bottom of the ratings spectrum.

Finally, spreads rise exponentially as the credit rating deteriorates, registering a sharp rise at the investment-grade threshold. For a $100 million, seven-year bond in 2005, the launch spread would rise from 55 basis points for a BBB− rating, then rise sharply to 146 basis points as the rating falls below the investment-grade threshold to BB+ before reaching a high of 577 basis points for a CCC+ rating. The large shift of 91 basis points at the investment-grade threshold likely reflects the limitations or regulations that prevent institutional investors from buying sub–investment grade. An implication is that if a country or borrowing entity were to obtain an investment-grade rating, the investor base would widen considerably.

The shadow rating for a country can provide a sense of where the country would lie on the credit rating spectrum if it were to be rated. The model-based shadow ratings can provide a benchmark for evaluating unrated countries, as well as rated countries that have not been rated for some time and might have improved sufficiently in the meantime to deserve an upgrade (or downgrade, in some cases).

As shown in box 5.1, for developing countries with sovereign ratings that are below investment grade, the sovereign ceiling often acts as a binding constraint, which limits market access and keeps borrowing costs high for subsovereign entities located in these countries. Preliminary results indicate that, after controlling for global liquidity conditions and country and firm-specific factors, a developing country's sovereign credit rating explains some 64 percent of the variation in ratings of subsovereign entities located in its jurisdiction.

Poor countries can use a variety of structuring mechanisms to raise their creditworthiness, pierce the sovereign ceiling, and establish market access. A country's spread savings as a result of improving ratings from B to BBB would be in the range of 320–450 basis points. The knowledge of this relationship can be helpful for bilateral and multilateral donors interested in setting up guarantees and other financial structures to reduce project risks and mobilize private financing. According to Gelb, Ramachandran, and Turner (2006), World Bank and IDA guarantees of $2.9 billion have been able to catalyze private capital of $12 billion for large infrastructure projects.[20] An official grant can be used as a first-loss reserve, for example, which can substantially improve the credit rating of the project.

A financing structure that raises the rating of a project to investment grade can attract a larger pool of investors (e.g., pension funds) that face limitations on buying non-investment-grade securities. In poor countries that have recently received debt relief and where there are concerns regarding nonconcessional borrowing, these mechanisms can be used mainly for private sector development projects. By lowering borrowing costs and lengthening maturities, these structures can in turn increase net resource flows to poor countries. These mechanisms can complement existing efforts to improve aid effectiveness (Gelb and Sundberg 2006).

Similarly, foreign currency inflows (of remittances, tourism revenue, and export receivables) can be leveraged to improve foreign currency ratings. Any improvement in sovereign rating is likely to translate into an improvement in the rating of subsovereign borrowers whose foreign currency borrowing is typically subject to the sovereign rating ceiling. Future foreign currency inflows can then be used as collateral by private sector entities, banks, and other financial intermediaries to improve their own ratings, allowing them to pierce the sovereign rating ceiling and issue bonds at lower interest spreads and longer tenor (Ketkar and Ratha 2004–2005). Several banks in developing countries—such as Brazil, Mexico, and Turkey and, in more recent years, the Arab Republic of Egypt, Jamaica, and Kazakhstan—have been able to raise cheaper and longer-term financing from international capital markets using securitization of future remittance flows (Ratha 2006).

That many unrated poor countries may be more creditworthy than currently believed provides hope for a private sector–to–private sector alternative for financing poverty reduction and other Millennium Development Goals in these countries. Future research should examine how sovereign ratings influence the ratings of subsovereign entities; what kind of financing structures can help poor countries access international capital markets; and what regulatory preconditions are necessary for such financial structures to succeed in poor countries.

ANNEX TABLE 5A.1
Actual and Predicted Ratings for Rated Developing Countries

| Country | Actual rating | | | Predicted rating range |
	Standard & Poor's	Moody's	Fitch	
Argentina	B+ (Oct-06)	B3 (Jun-05)	B (Aug-06)	B− to BB
Armenia	—	Baa3 (Jul-06)	BB− (Jun-06)	BB+ to BBB
Azerbaijan	—	Baa2 (Sep-06)	BB (Nov-04)	BB− to BBB−
Barbados	BBB+ (Aug-04)	Baa2 (Feb-00)	—	A
Belize	CC (Aug-06)	Caa3 (Oct-05)	—	*
Benin	B (Sep-06)	—	B (Sep-04)	CCC+ to B
Bolivia	B− (Oct-03)	B3 (Apr-03)	B- (Jun-05)	B+ to BB−
Bosnia and Herzegovina	—	B2 (May-06)	—	BB− to BB
Botswana	A (Apr-01)	Aa3 (May-06)	—	AA to AAA
Brazil	BB (Feb-06)	Ba2 (Aug-06)	BB (Jun-06)	BB to BB+
Bulgaria	BBB+ (Oct-06)	Baa3 (Mar-06)	BBB (Aug-05)	BBB−
Burkina Faso	B (Mar-04)	—	—	CCC to B-
Cameroon	B− (May-06)	—	B (Jun-06)	B to B+
Cape Verde	—	—	B+ (Aug-03)	BB+
Chile	A (Jan-04)	A2 (Jul-06)	A (Mar-05)	A to A+
China	A (Jul-06)	A2 (Oct-03)	A (Oct-05)	BBB+ to A
Colombia	BB (May-00)	Ba2 (Aug-99)	BB (May-04)	BB to BB+
Costa Rica	BB (Jul-97)	Ba1 (May-97)	BB (Apr-03)	BBB to BBB+
Croatia	BBB (Dec-04)	Baa3 (Jan-97)	BBB− (Jul-05)	BBB− to BBB
Czech Republic	A− (Nov-98)	A1 (Nov-02)	A (Aug-05)	A− to A
Dominican Republic	B (Jun-05)	B3 (Jan-04)	B (May-06)	B+ to BB
Ecuador	CCC+ (Oct-05)	Caa1 (Feb-04)	B− (Aug-05)	BB− to BB−
Egypt, Arab Rep. of	BB+ (May-02)	Ba1 (Jul-01)	BB+ (Dec-04)	BBB− to BBB
El Salvador	BB+ (Apr-99)	Baa3 (Dec-03)	BB+ (Jan-05)	BB− to BB
Estonia	A (Nov-04)	A1 (Nov-02)	A (Jul-04)	A to A+
Fiji	B+ (Nov-06)	Ba1 (May-06)	—	BB+ to BBB
Gambia, The	—	—	CCC (Dec-05)	B− to B−
Georgia	B+ (Dec-05)	—	—	BB− to BB
Ghana	B+ (Sep-03)	—	B+ (Mar-05)	B− to BB−
Grenada	B− (Nov-05)	—	—	*
Guatemala	BB (Jul-06)	Ba2 (Aug-97)	BB+ (Feb-06)	BB− to BB
Honduras	—	Ba3 (May-06)	—	B to BB−
Hungary	BBB+ (Jun-06)	A1 (Nov-02)	BBB+ (Dec-05)	BBB+ to A−
India	BB+ (Feb-05)	Baa2 (May-06)	BBB− (Aug-06)	BBB- to BBB
Indonesia	BB− (Jul-06)	B1 (May-06)	BB− (Jan-05)	B+ to BB−
Iran, Islamic Rep. of	—	—	B+ (Apr-06)	*
Jamaica	B (Jul-03)	B1 (May-03)	B+ (Aug-06)	B+ to BB+
Jordan	BB (Jul-03)	Baa3 (May-06)	—	BBB to BBB+
Kazakhstan	BBB (Nov-06)	Baa2 (Jun-06)	BBB (Dec-05)	*

(Table continues on the following page.)

ANNEX TABLE 5A.1 (continued)
Actual and Predicted Ratings for Rated Developing Countries

| Country | Actual rating | | | Predicted rating range |
	Standard & Poor's	Moody's	Fitch	
Kenya	B+ (Sep-06)	—	—	B– to B
Latvia	A– (Jul-04)	A2 (Nov-02)	A– (Aug-05)	BBB to A
Lebanon	B– (Apr-02)	B3 (Mar-05)	B– (Nov-05)	*
Lesotho	—	—	BB– (Nov-05)	BB- to BB+
Lithuania	A (Dec-05)	A2 (Sep-06)	A (Oct-06)	A– to A
Macedonia, FYR	BB+ (Aug-05)	—	BB+ (Dec-05)	BB to BBB–
Madagascar	B (May-04)	—	—	*
Malawi	—	—	CCC (Dec-05)	CC or lower
Malaysia	A– (Oct-03)	A3 (Dec-04)	A– (Nov-04)	A– to A
Mali	B (May-04)	—	B– (Apr-04)	B to B
Mauritius	—	Baa1 (May-06)	—	A–
Mexico	BBB (Jan-05)	Baa1 (Jan-05)	BBB (Dec-05)	BB+ to BBB–
Moldova	—	Caa1 (May-03)	B- (Feb-03)	B+ to BB
Mongolia	B (Dec-99)	Ba2 (May-06)	B+ (Jul-05)	BB– to BB
Morocco	BB+ (Aug-05)	Ba1 (Jul-99)	—	BBB– to BBB
Mozambique	B (Jul-04)	—	B (Jul-03)	B– to B
Namibia	—	—	BBB– (Dec-05)	BB+ to BBB
Nicaragua	BB– (Feb-06)	B3 (May-06)	—	CCC+ to B
Nigeria	BB– (Feb-06)	—	BB– (Jan-06)	B+ to BB–
Oman	A– (Sep-06)	A1 (Oct-06)	—	A– to A+
Pakistan	B+ (Nov-04)	B1 (Nov-06)	—	B to B+
Panama	BB (Nov-01)	Ba1 (Jan-97)	BB+ (Dec-03)	BB+ to BB+
Papua New Guinea	B (Aug-01)	Ba2 (May-06)	B (Jul-03)	B– to BB
Paraguay	B– (Jul-04)	B3 (May-06)	—	B to B+
Peru	BB+ (Nov-06)	Ba3 (Jul-99)	BB+ (Aug-06)	BB to BB+
Philippines	BB– (Jan-05)	B1 (Feb-05)	BB (Jul-05)	BB– to BB
Poland	BBB+ (May-00)	A2 (Nov-02)	BBB+ (Mar-05)	BBB+
Romania	BBB– (Sep-05)	Baa3 (Oct-06)	BBB (Aug-06)	BBB
Russian Federation	BBB+ (Sep-06)	Baa2 (Oct-05)	BBB+ (Jul-06)	BB to BBB+
Senegal	B+ (Dec-00)	—	—	B to B+
Serbia and Montenegro	BB– (Jul-05)	—	BB– (May-05)	B– to BB
Seychelles	B (Sep-06)	—	—	BB– to BBB+
Slovak Republic	A (Dec-05)	A1 (Oct-06)	A (Oct-05)	A–
South Africa	BBB+ (Aug-05)	Baa1 (Jan-05)	BBB+ (Aug-05)	BBB+
Sri Lanka	B+ (Dec-05)	—	BB– (Dec-05)	BB– to BB
Suriname	B– (Aug-04)	Ba2 (May-06)	B (Jun-04)	BB+ to BBB–
Thailand	BBB+ (Aug-04)	Baa1 (Nov-03)	BBB+ (May-05)	BBB to BBB+
Trinidad and Tobago	A– (Jul-05)	Baa1 (Jul-06)	—	BBB+ to A
Tunisia	BBB (Mar-00)	A3 (May-06)	BBB (May-01)	BBB– to BBB
Turkey	BB– (Aug-04)	Ba3 (Dec-05)	BB– (Dec-05)	BB+ to BBB–

Actual and Predicted Ratings for Rated Developing Countries

| Country | Actual rating | | | Predicted rating range |
	Standard & Poor's	Moody's	Fitch	
Turkmenistan	—	B1 (May-06)	CCC− (May-01)	BB to A
Uganda	—	—	B (Mar-05)	CCC to B−
Ukraine	BB− (May-05)	B1 (Nov-03)	BB− (Jun-05)	BB to BB+
Uruguay	B+ (Sep-06)	B3 (Jul-02)	B+ (Mar-05)	*
Venezuela, R. B. de	BB− (Feb-06)	B2 (Sep-04)	BB− (Nov-05)	BB−
Vietnam	BB (Sep-06)	Ba3 (Jul-05)	BB− (Nov-03)	BB

Source: Authors' calculations.

Note: — = not available. The actual ratings are the latest available as of December 6, 2006. The dates when the ratings were established are shown in parentheses. The model-based ratings should be treated as indicative; they are clearly not a substitute for the broader and deeper analysis, and for qualitative judgment, employed by experienced rating analysts. The predicted ratings range is based on predictions for the benchmark models for Standard & Poor's, Moody's, and Fitch. Dated explanatory variables were used for predicting ratings for 2006. Note that these shadow ratings are not predictions for future rating changes. For that, one would need forecasts for the explanatory variables. See table 6.4 for actual and predicted ratings for rated Sub-Saharan African countries as of December 2007.

* Outliers excluded from prediction model.

ANNEX TABLE 5A.2

Contribution of Explanatory Variables to Predicted S&P Ratings for Unrated Countries

Country	Predicted rating using S&P regression[b]	Explanatory variables as of end-2005					
		GDP growth	GNI per capita	Ratio of reserves to import & short-term debt	Ratio of external debt to exports	GDP volatility (5-yr std. dev.)	Rule of law
Albania	BB	5.7	2,580	0.3	0.8	1.5	−0.8
Algeria	AA−	5.9	2,730	2.3	0.6	1.7	−0.7
Angola	B+	9.8	1,350	0.2	0.6	5.7	−1.3
Bangladesh	B	5.7	470	0.2	1.9	0.7	−0.9
Belarus	BB+	9.2	2,760	0.1	0.3	2.9	−1
Bhutan	BBB+	6.8	870	1.0	2.6	1.1	0.5
Burundi	*	1.5	100	0.3	22.4	2.5	−1.2
Cambodia	B+	7.3	380	0.3	0.6	1.1	−1.1
Cen. Afr. Rep.	*	−1.4	350	0.6	6.5	4.0	−1.3
Chad	B+	16.7	400	0.1	0.5	9.4	−1.2
Comoros	CCC	2.3	640	0.4	5.0	0.3	−1
Congo, Dem. Rep. of	C	6.4	120	0.1	4.0	3.7	−1.4
Congo, Rep. of	CCC+	4.5	950	0.3	1.5	3.0	−1.8
Côte d'Ivoire	CCC−	−0.1	840	0.2	2.0	1.4	−1.5
Djibouti	B	3.1	1,020	0.2	1.7	0.5	−0.9
Dominica	BB+	1.7	3,790	0.2	1.5	3.6	0.7
Equatorial Guinea	BBB−	10.2	6,205	0.6	0	6.5	−1.3
Eritrea	*	3.6	220	0	8.2	3.3	−0.8
Ethiopia	CCC−	6.0	160	0.3	3.4	6.4	−0.8
Gabon	BB+	2.1	5,010	0.2	0.2	1.1	−0.5
Guinea	CCC−	2.3	370	0.1	3.4	1.2	−1.1
Guinea-Bissau	C	2.1	180	0.5	4.4	4.1	21.3
Guyana	CCC+	−0.6	1,010	0.3	1.7	2.1	−0.8
Haiti	CC	−0.3	450	0.1	2.2	1.5	−1.6
Kiribati	AAA	0.4	1,390	5.3	2.1	2.7	0.8
Kyrgyz Republic	CCC+	4.5	440	0.4	2.2	3.8	−1.1
Lao PDR	B−	6.5	440	0.3	3.7	0.5	−1.1
Liberia	*	−7.8	130	0	5.9	15.7	−1.6
Libya	AAA	5.7	5,530	3.2	0.2	2.4	−0.7
Maldives	BB+	4.6	2,390	0.2	1.1	5.1	0.3
Marshall Islands	B	1.9	2,930	0	3.6	2.0	−0.3
Mauritania	B	6.2	560	0.2	3.7	1.9	−0.5
Myanmar	CCC−	7.3	219	0.2	2.0	4.7	−1.6
Nepal	CCC+	3.0	270	0.7	3.1	2.3	−0.8
Niger	CCC	3.3	240	0.3	3.4	2.7	−0.8
Rwanda	C	3.3	230	0.6	7.4	3.2	−1
Samoa	BB−	3.6	2,090	0.1	6.7	2.0	1.1

		Contribution to rating[a]			
GDP growth	Log of GNI per capita	Ratio of reserves to[·] import & short-term debt	Ratio of external debt to exports	GDP volatility (5-yr std. dev.)	Rule of law
−0.7	−1.7	0.6	−1.5	−0.5	0.3
−0.8	−1.8	−6.1	−1.7	−0.5	0
−2.6	−0.8	1.2	−1.7	1.0	1.5
−0.7	0.7	1.1	−0.7	−0.8	0.4
−2.4	−1.8	1.5	−1.9	0	0.8
−1.2	−0.2	−1.6	−0.3	−0.7	−3.2
1.3	2.9	0.6	13.1	−0.2	1.2
−1.4	1.0	0.9	−1.6	−0.7	1.1
2.6	1.1	−0.1	2.3	0.4	1.5
−5.9	0.9	1.4	−1.7	2.4	1.3
0.9	0.2	0.4	1.3	−1.0	0.6
−1.0	2.6	1.6	0.7	0.3	1.8
−0.2	−0.3	0.9	−1.0	0	2.7
2.0	−0.1	1.1	−0.7	−0.6	2.0
0.5	−0.4	1.1	−0.9	−0.9	0.4
1.2	−2.3	1.0	−1.0	0.2	−3.6
−2.8	−3.0	−0.3	−2.0	1.3	1.6
0.3	1.7	1.6	3.5	0.1	0.2
−0.8	2.2	0.8	0.2	1.3	0.1
1.0	−2.7	1.0	−1.9	−0.7	−0.6
0.9	1.0	1.3	0.3	−0.7	1.0
1.0	2.0	0.1	1.0	0.4	1.6
2.3	−0.4	0.9	−0.9	−0.3	0.2
2.1	0.7	1.5	−0.5	−0.5	2.4
1.8	−0.9	−16.4	−0.6	−0.1	−3.8
−0.1	0.8	0.3	−0.6	0.3	0.9
−1.1	0.8	0.9	0.5	−0.9	1.1
5.6	2.5	1.7	1.9	4.7	2.3
−0.7	−2.8	−9.2	−1.9	−0.2	0
−0.2	−1.6	1.1	−1.3	0.8	−2.7
1.1	−1.9	1.7	0.4	−0.4	−1.2
−1.0	0.4	0.9	0.4	−0.4	−0.5
−1.4	1.7	1.0	−0.7	0.7	2.2
0.5	1.5	−0.7	0	−0.3	0.2
0.4	1.6	0.7	0.3	−0.1	0.3
0.4	1.7	−0.3	3.0	0.1	0.7
0.3	−1.4	1.3	2.5	−0.4	−4.7

(Table continues on the following page.)

ANNEX TABLE 5A.2 (continued)
Contribution of Explanatory Variables to Predicted S&P Ratings for Unrated Countries

Country	Predicted rating using S&P regression[b]	GDP growth	GNI per capita	Ratio of reserves to import & short-term debt	Ratio of external debt to exports	GDP volatility (5-yr std. dev.)	Rule of law
São Tomé and Principe	*	3.6	390	0.3	11.4	0.4	−0.6
Sierra Leone	CCC−	8.0	220	0.3	2.4	8.7	−1.1
Solomon Islands	B−	5.2	590	0.5	1.3	6.4	−0.9
St. Kitts and Nevis	A−	4.5	8,210	0.2	1.3	2.0	0.8
St. Lucia	BBB	3.9	4,800	0.2	1.1	3.7	0.8
St. Vincent	BBB	5.1	3,590	0.1	1.4	2.6	0.8
Sudan	CCC	6.3	640	0.3	4.9	1.1	−1.5
Swaziland	BB−	2.1	2,280	0.1	0.3	0.5	−0.8
Syrian Arab Rep.	A−	3.2	1,380	1.9	0.5	1.6	−0.4
Tajikistan	B+	9.4	330	0.1	1.0	1.3	−1.0
Tanzania	B+	6.9	340	0.6	3.5	0.4	−0.5
Togo	CCC	2.8	350	0.2	2.2	1.6	−1.1
Tonga	BB	2.3	2,190	0.4	3.9	0.5	0.5
Uzbekistan	BB−	6.3	510	0.8	0.9	1.8	−1.3
Vanuatu	BB+	4.1	1,600	0.3	0.6	4.7	0.5
Yemen, Republic of	BB	6.5	600	1.2	1.7	3.7	−1.1
Zambia	CCC+	5.2	490	0.3	6.4	0.8	−0.6
Zimbabwe	*	−7.2	340	0	1.0	3.0	−1.5

Source: Authors' calculations using the S&P model in benchmark specification 2.

a. Deviation from mean rating of B; a negative number indicates a better-than-average rating.

b. The shadow ratings for 2006 reported here are predictions from the benchmark model for Standard & Poor's using dated explanatory variables described in table 5.4. These model-based ratings should be treated as indicative; they are clearly not a substitute for the broader and deeper analysis, and qualitative judgment, employed by experienced rating analysts.

* When the predicted rating was above 21 in the numeric scale, it was classified as out of range.

		Contribution to rating[a]			
GDP growth	Log of GNI per capita	Ratio of reserves to import & short-term debt	Ratio of external debt to exports	GDP volatility (5-yr std. dev.)	Rule of law
0.3	0.9	0.6	5.7	−0.9	−0.2
−1.8	1.7	0.7	−0.4	2.1	1.1
−0.5	0.4	−0.1	−1.2	1.3	0.5
−0.1	−3.4	1.0	−1.2	−0.3	−4
0.2	−2.6	1.1	−1.3	0.3	−4
−0.4	−2.2	1.3	−1.1	−0.1	−4.0
−1.0	0.2	0.6	1.3	−0.7	2.0
1.0	−1.6	1.4	−1.9	−0.9	0.1
0.5	−0.8	−4.9	−1.7	−0.5	−0.8
−2.5	1.2	1.4	−1.4	−0.6	0.7
−1.3	1.1	−0.2	0.3	−0.9	−0.6
0.6	1.1	1.1	−0.6	−0.5	0.9
0.9	−1.5	0.6	0.6	−0.9	−3.0
−1.0	0.6	−1.0	−1.5	−0.4	1.5
0.1	−1.1	0.6	−1.7	0.6	−3.2
−1.1	0.3	−2.5	−0.9	0.3	1.0
−0.5	0.6	0.8	2.3	−0.8	−0.2
5.4	1.1	1.7	−1.4	0	2.0

Notes

1. See International Development Association (2006a and 2006b). Kaminsky and Schmukler (2002) provide evidence of the influence of sovereign ratings on portfolio equity returns. See also Reinhart (2002a); Claessens and Embrechts (2002); and Ferri, Liu, and Majnoni (2001).

2. Many countries are rated by export credit agencies, insurance agencies, and international banks. But these ratings are tailored for internal use in these institutions and meant for specific purposes such as short-term trade credit. They may not be useful for risk evaluation by general institutional investors.

3. This sharp jump reflects the limitations or regulations that prevent institutional investors from buying sub–investment grade. Knowing where a country lies on the credit spectrum can give some idea about the cost of capital. For poor countries that are rated below investment grade, an improvement in rating (via financial structuring or proper accounting of hard currency flows such as remittances) could result in significant spread savings, in the range of 300–700 basis points, depending on the initial rating and global credit market conditions.

4. Hausmann and Fernández-Arias (2001) argued that a higher share of FDI—and a correspondingly lower share of private debt flows—may be an indicator of poorly functioning markets, inadequate institutions, and high risks. The authors found a higher FDI share in countries that are poorer, riskier, more closed, more volatile, less financially developed, and with weaker institutions and more natural resources. Loungani and Razin (2001) reported a similar negative relationship between Moody's country ratings and FDI share.

5. For example, Fitch's questionnaire for government officials includes 128 questions in 14 categories (ranging from demographic and educational factors to trade and foreign investment policy), all of which require supporting documentation, past data for five years, and two-year-ahead forecasts (Fitch Ratings 1998).

6. The rating process is initiated by a sovereign (or subsovereign) entity. After the signing of the initial contract with a rating agency, which also involves a fee, the rating agency sends out a detailed questionnaire to the entity. Analysts from the rating agency visit the entity and collect information about the institutional, economic, and political environment. The rating committee comprising these and other analysts compares the entity being rated against other entities and decide a rating. If the borrowing entity does not agree with the rating, it could request reconsideration, but the rating committee may or may not alter its rating decision. At the final stage, the borrowing entity may request that the rating not be published. Otherwise, the rating is made available publicly to potential investors.

7. Ferri (2003) and Ferri, Liu, and Majnoni (2001) provide evidence on the close relationship between the sovereign rating and firm-level credit ratings in developing countries. See also Lehmann (2004).

8. Since most of the unrated countries (for which this chapter predicts ratings) are also low-income countries, this chapter has some similarities with Kraay and Nehru (2006). However, the current calculations employ a continuous numeric scale for ratings and exclude cases of default in the regressions, unlike the use of a 0–1 dummy for debt distress used in Kraay and Nehru.

9. For the empirical analysis, data for most of the right-hand-side variables are taken from the World Bank's *World Development Indicators* database and the IMF's *World Economic Outlook* database. Data on short-term and long-term claims are collected from the Bank of International Settlements.

10. The analysis also considered including default history, which has been found to be a significant explanatory variable in several studies (Cantor and Packer 1996; Reinhart, Rogoff, and Savastano 2003; Sutton 2005). However, the data on default history is not well defined or does not exist for unrated countries, which typically have no cross-border bond financing, and where the data on international bank lending tends to be incomplete. Since the purpose of this analysis was to predict sovereign rating for unrated developing countries, right-hand-side variables that are readily available from standard data sources were included for both rated and unrated countries.

11. This conversion rule is the converse of the one mostly used in the literature (see Cantor and Packer 1996). Since the ultimate objective of this analysis is to project ratings for poor countries, the rating spectrum downward was left open.

12. For example, Cuba's "Caa1" rating from Moody's was established in 1999.

13. Belize was downgraded from CC to Selective Default by Standard & Poor's in December 2006 following the announcement of a debt restructuring. It was subsequently upgraded to B in February 2007 after the completion of the restructuring. The predicted shadow rating for Belize is in the range of BB− to BB+. Similarly, Grenada had been rated as being in Selective Default in early 2005 and was upgraded back to B− by the end of 2006. Another outlier is Lebanon, where the rating is affected by a high level of debt but does not adequately account for large remittances from the Lebanese diaspora (World Bank 2005a, chapter 4).

14. The latest rating contains the most valid information about the macroeconomic and political fundamentals of a country in the year it was established. Therefore, the information content in the "dated" explanatory variable would be the highest.

15. These results are too long to present in this chapter. They are available from the authors upon request.

16. Across-agency comparisons of Standard & Poor's and Moody's ratings are qualitatively similar.

17. This distribution is based on the lowest of the predicted ratings from the three rating models. If the highest rating were used instead, the ratings would be even more striking: as many as 13 countries would be above investment grade, 7 would be BB, 15 would be B, and 11 would be CCC.

18. There are 40 unrated International Development Association (IDA) countries for which the analysis predicted shadow ratings. Of these, countries with a shadow rating below CCC- are classified as being at high risk of debt distress ("red light") by IDA methodology, which is based on Kraay and Nehru (2006).
19. The "free-rider" problem created by debt relief may be less of a concern when outstanding debt is used instead of net present value.
20. See Klein (1997) and World Bank (2005b) for the key features of World Bank partial risk and credit guarantees. Similar credit enhancements using official aid have been used to mobilize private resources for a diverse range of programs, for example, charter schools in the United States, with leverage ratios as high as 10–15 times the grant (see http://www.ed.gov/programs/charter facilities/2005awards).

References

Beers, David, and Marie Cavanaugh. 2006. "Sovereign Credit Ratings: A Primer." *RatingsDirect.* Standard &Poor's, New York. September. http://www2.standard andpoors.com/spf/pdf/fixedincome/KR_sovereign_APrimer_Eng.pdf.

Berg, Andrew, and Jeffrey Sachs. 1988. "The Debt Crisis: Structural Explanations of Country Performance." *Journal of Development Economics* 29: 271–306.

Bhatia, Ashok V. 2002. "Sovereign Credit Ratings Methodology: An Evaluation." Working Paper 02/170, International Monetary Fund, Washington, DC.

Calvo, Guillermo A., and Carmen M. Reinhart. 2000. "When Capital Inflows Come to a Sudden Stop: Consequences and Policy Options." In *Key Issues in Reform of the International Monetary and Financial System,* ed. Peter Kenen and Alexandre Swoboda, 175–201. Washington, DC: International Monetary Fund.

Cantor, Richard, and Frank Packer. 1995. "Sovereign Credit Ratings." *Current Issues in Economics and Finance* 1 (3). Federal Reserve Bank of New York. http://www .ny.frb.org/research/current_issues/ci1-3.html.

———. 1996. "Determinants and Impact of Sovereign Credit Ratings." *Economic Policy Review* 2 (2). Federal Reserve Bank of New York. http://www.ny.frb.org/ research/epr/96v02n2/9610cant.html.

Claessens, Stijn, and Geert Embrechts. 2002. "Basel II, Sovereign Ratings and Transfer Risk: External versus Internal Ratings." Presented at the conference "Basel II: An Economic Assessment," Bank for International Settlements, Basel, May 17–18.

Eichengreen, Barry, and Ashoka Mody. 2000. "What Explains Changing Spreads on Emerging Market Debt?" In *Capital Flows and the Emerging Economies: Theories, Evidence, and Controversies,* ed. Sebastian Edwards. Chicago: University of Chicago Press.

Ferri, Giovanni. 2003. "How Do Global Credit-Rating Agencies Rate Firms from Developing Countries?" *Asian Economic Papers* 2 (3): 30–56.

Ferri, Giovanni, Li-Gang Liu, and Giovanni Majnoni. 2001. "The Role of Rating Agency Assessments in Less Developed Countries: Impact of the Proposed Basel Guidelines." *Journal of Banking and Finance* 25: 115–25.

Ferri, Giovanni, Li-Gang Liu, and Joseph E. Stiglitz. 1999. "Are Credit Ratings Pro-cyclical? Evidence from East Asian Countries?" *Economic Notes* 28 (3): 335–55.

Fitch Ratings. 1998. "Sovereign Rating Methodology." Fitch Ratings, New York. Available at U.S Department of State Web site, http://www.state.gov.

Gelb, Alan, Vijaya Ramachandran, and Ginger Turner. 2006. "Stimulating Growth and Investment in Africa—from Macro to Micro Reforms." Paper prepared for the second African Economic Conference on "Opportunities and Challenges of Development for Africa in the Global Arena, Tunis, November 22–24.

Gelb, Alan, and Mark Sundberg. 2006. "Making Aid Work." *Finance and Development* 43 (4). International Monetary Fund, Washington, DC.

Graham, Benjamin. 2005. "Trust Funds in the Pacific: Their Role and Future." *Pacific Studies Series.* Asian Development Bank, Manila.

Hausmann, Ricardo, and Eduardo Fernández-Arias. 2001. "Foreign Direct Investment: Good Cholesterol?" In *Foreign Direct Investment Versus Other Flows to Latin America,* ed. Jorge Braga de Macedo and Enrique V. Iglesias. Paris: Organisation for Economic Co-operation and Development.

IDA (International Development Association). 2006a. "Assessing Implementation of IDA14 Grants Framework." World Bank, Washington, DC.

———. 2006b. "Debt Dynamics and Financing Terms: A Forward-Looking Approach to IDA Grant Eligibility." World Bank, Washington, DC.

Kamin, Steven B., and Karsten von Kleist. 1999. "The Evolution and Determinants of Emerging Market Credit Spreads in the 1990s." Working Paper 68, Bank for International Settlements, Basel.

Kaminsky, Graciela, and Sergio Schmukler. 2002. "Emerging Market Instability: Do Sovereign Ratings Affect Country Risk and Stock Returns?" *World Bank Economic Review* 16 (2): 171–90.

Kaufmann, Daniel, Aart Kraay, and Massimo Mastruzzi. 2006. "Governance Matters V: Aggregate and Individual Governance Indicators for 1996–2005." Policy Research Working Paper 4012, World Bank, Washington, DC.

Ketkar, Suhas, and Dilip Ratha. 2004–2005. "Recent Advances in Future-Flow Securitization." *The Financier* 11/12.

Klein, Michael. 1997. "Managing Guarantee Programs in Support of Infrastructure Investment." Policy Research Working Paper 1812, World Bank, Washington, DC.

Kraay, Aart, and Vikram Nehru. 2006. "When Is External Debt Sustainable?" *World Bank Economic Review* 20 (3): 341–65.

Lee, Suk Hun. 1993. "Are the Credit Ratings Assigned by Bankers Based on the Willingness of LDC Borrowers to Repay?" *Journal of Development Economics* 40: 349–59.

Lehmann, Alexander. 2004. "Sovereign Credit Ratings and Private Capital Flows to Low-Income Countries." *African Development Review* 16 (2).

Loungani, Prakash, and Assaf Razin. 2001. "How Beneficial Is Foreign Direct Investment for Developing Countries?" *Finance and Development* 38 (2). International Monetary Fund, Washington, DC.

Manasse, Paolo, Nouriel Roubini, and Axel Schimmelpfennig. 2003. "Predicting Sovereign Debt Crises," Working Paper 03/221, International Monetary Fund, Washington, DC.

Mora, Nada. 2006. "Sovereign Credit Ratings: Guilty beyond Reasonable Doubt?" *Journal of Banking and Finance* 30 (7): 2041–62.

Panizza, Ugo, Barry Eichengreen, and Ricardo Hausmann. 2005. "The Mystery of Original Sin." In *Other People's Money: Debt Denomination and Financial Instability in Emerging-Market Economies,* ed. Barry Eichengreen and Ricardo Hausmann. Chicago: University of Chicago Press.

Ratha, Dilip. 2006. "Leveraging Remittances for International Capital Market Access." Mimeo. Development Prospects Group, World Bank, Washington, DC.

Reinhart, Carmen M. 2002a. "Sovereign Credit Ratings Before and After Financial Crises." In *Ratings, Rating Agencies and the Global Financial System,* ed. Richard Levich, Carmen M. Reinhart, and Giovanni Majnoni. New York: Kluwer Academic Press.

———. 2002b. "Credit Ratings, Default, and Financial Crises: Evidence from Emerging Markets." *World Bank Economic Review* 16 (2): 151–70.

Reinhart, Carmen M., Kenneth S. Rogoff, and Miguel A. Savastano. 2003. "Debt Intolerance." *Brookings Papers on Economic Activity* 1: 1–74.

Rowland, Peter. 2005. "Determinants of Spread, Credit Ratings and Creditworthiness for Emerging Market Sovereign Debt: A Follow-Up Study Using Pooled Data Analysis." Mimeo. Banco de la República, Bogota.

Rowland, Peter, and Jose L. Torres. 2004. "Determinants of Spread and Creditworthiness for Emerging Market Sovereign Debt: A Panel Data Study." Mimeo. Banco de la República, Bogota.

Standard & Poor's. 2006. *Sovereign Ratings in Africa.* New York: Standard & Poor's.

Sutton, Gregory. 2005. "Potentially Endogenous Borrowing and Developing Country Sovereign Credit Ratings." Financial Stability Institute Occasional Paper 5, Bank for International Settlements, Basel.

Truglia, Vincent, and Pierre Cailleteau. 2006. "A Guide to Moody's Sovereign Ratings." *Special Comment*. Moody's Investors Service, New York.

U.S. Department of State. 2006. "Sovereign Credit Ratings for Sub-Saharan Africa." Bureau of African Affairs, U.S Department of State. http://www.state .gov/p/af/rt/scr/.

World Bank. 2005a. *Global Economic Prospects 2006: Economic Implications of Remittances and Migration*. Washington, DC: World Bank.

———. 2005b. "The World Bank Guarantees: Overview and Key Features." Mimeo. World Bank, Washington, DC.

———. 2006. *Global Development Finance*. Washington, DC: World Bank.

CHAPTER 6

Beyond Aid: New Sources and Innovative Mechanisms for Financing Development in Sub-Saharan Africa

Dilip Ratha, Sanket Mohapatra, and Sonia Plaza

Official aid alone will not be adequate for funding efforts to accelerate economic growth and alleviate poverty and other Millennium Development Goals (MDGs) in Africa. Ultimately the private sector will need to be the engine of growth and employment generation, and official aid efforts must catalyze innovative financing solutions for the private sector. It is important to stress that financing MDGs would require increasing the investment rate above the domestic saving rate, and bridging the financing gap with additional financing from abroad.[1]

This chapter examines the level and composition of resource flows to Sub-Saharan Africa: foreign direct investment (FDI), portfolio debt and equity flows, bank lending, official aid flows, capital flight, and personal and institutional remittances. Recognizing that South Africa is expectedly the largest economy and the most dominant destination of private flows, the analysis focuses on the rest of Sub-Saharan Africa wherever appropriate.[2] The chapter then examines some new or overlooked sources of financing, such as diaspora bonds and remittances, and some innovative

Our special thanks go to Uri Dadush for his constructive comments on an earlier draft. We would like to thank Jorge Araujo, Delfin Go, Douglas Hostland, and Michael Fuchs for useful comments and suggestions, and to Zhimei Xu for research assistance. Financial support from the World Bank Research Support Budget and the Africa Region Chief Economist is gratefully acknowledged.

mechanisms such as future-flow securitization and partial guarantees provided by multilateral agencies for raising additional cross-border financing in the private sector. In passing, the chapter also briefly discusses recent initiatives, such as the Global Alliance for Vaccines and Immunization (GAVI) and the International Finance Facility for Immunisation (IFFIm), that use innovative methods to front-load future financing commitments from bilateral donors in order to introduce more predictability in aid flows.[3]

Resource flows to Sub-Saharan Africa have increased since 2000, a welcome reversal of the declining or flat trend seen during the 1990s. Official development assistance (ODA) to the region, excluding South Africa, increased from $11.7 billion in 2000 to $37.5 billion in 2006; FDI increased from $5.8 billion to an estimated $17.2 billion in 2006,[4] while net private bond and bank lending flows decreased from $−0.7 billion to an estimated $−2.5 billion during the same period.[5] Capital outflows from the region have also started reversing in recent years. Workers' remittances to Sub-Saharan Africa more than doubled, from $4.6 billion in 2000 to $10.3 billion in 2006, and institutional remittances increased from $2.9 billion in 2000 to $6.3 billion in 2006. New donors and investors (for example, China and India) have increased their presence in the region.

The picture is less rosy, however, when Sub-Saharan Africa is compared with the other developing regions. Sub-Saharan Africa continues to depend on official aid for its external financing needs. In 2006, ODA was more than two-and-a-half times the size of private flows received by Sub-Saharan Africa, excluding South Africa. The recent increase in ODA appears to be driven by debt relief provided through the Heavily Indebted Poor Countries (HIPC) Initiative and the Multilateral Debt Relief Initiative (IBRD 2007).[6] According to the International Bank for Reconstruction and Development (IBRD 2007), debt relief represented close to 70 percent of the increase in bilateral ODA to Sub-Saharan Africa between 2001 and 2005. The relatively small FDI flows to the region went mostly to enclave investments in oil-exporting countries.[7] Portfolio bond and equity flows were almost nonexistent outside South Africa. Private debt flows were small and predominantly relationship-based commercial bank lending,[8] and even these flows were mostly short-term in tenor. Less than half the countries in the region have a sovereign rating from the major credit rating agencies. Of those that are rated, most have below-investment-grade ratings. Capital outflows appear to be smaller than in the previous decade, but the stock of flight capital from the region remains high. Migrant remittances appear to be increasing, but much of the flows are believed to be unrecorded as they bypass formal financial channels. In short, there is little room for complacency; efforts to explore new sources and innovative mechanisms for financing development in the region must continue.

This chapter suggests several new instruments for improving Sub-Saharan African countries' access to capital. The analysis of country creditworthiness suggests that many countries in the region appear to be more creditworthy than previously believed. Establishing sovereign rating benchmarks and credit enhancement through guarantee instruments provided by multilateral aid agencies would facilitate market access. Creative financial structuring, such as the IFFIm, can help front-load aid commitments, although they may not result in additional financing in the long run. Preliminary estimates suggest that Sub-Saharan African countries can potentially raise $1 billion to $3 billion by reducing the cost of international migrant remittances, $5 billion to $10 billion by issuing diaspora bonds, and $17 billion by securitizing future remittances and other future receivables.

African countries, however, need to be cautious when resorting to market-based debt. It is essential that the borrowing space created by debt relief be used prudently, and not used to borrow excessively at commercial terms (IBRD 2007). "Free riding" by commercial and bilateral creditors can even lead to another round of excessive accumulation of debt.[9] Countries should also monitor and manage short-term external debt (especially those intermediated by domestic banks) to avoid currency and maturity mismatch between assets and liabilities and potential liquidity crisis (Dadush, Dasgupta, and Ratha 2000). Short-term capital flows can reverse rapidly, with potentially destabilizing effects on the financial markets.

The chapter is structured as follows. The following section analyzes trends in resource flows to Sub-Saharan Africa relative to other developing regions. The next section highlights some new sources and innovative mechanisms for development financing in the region. The final section concludes with a summary of findings and some recommendations for the way forward.

Trends in Financial Flows to Sub-Saharan Africa

In one of the largest expansions in private capital flows to developing countries in recent decades, private medium- and long-term capital flows more than tripled in size from $195 billion in 2000 to $670 billion in 2006. This period also saw significant diversification in the composition of private flows to developing countries (for FDI, portfolio bond, and equity flows; bank lending; and derivative instruments). Official development assistance nearly doubled, from $54 billion to $104 billion, and migrant remittances more than doubled, from $85 billion in 2000 to $221 billion in 2006.

Official aid flows to Sub-Saharan Africa also rose, from $12.2 billion in 2000 to $38.2 billion (or 37 percent of ODA to developing countries) in 2006. Private resource flows to Sub-Saharan Africa (other than FDI), however, have risen at a slower pace compared with other developing regions, and the region's share of private capital flows to developing regions has remained small and undiversified (table 6.1).

FDI to Sub-Saharan African countries other than South Africa rose from $5.8 billion in 2000 to an estimated $17.2 billion in 2006, making FDI the second-largest source of external finance. However, a large part of FDI in the region is concentrated in enclave investments in a few resource-rich countries. Portfolio equity flows to Sub-Saharan Africa increased from $4.2 billion in 2000 to an estimated $15.1 billion in 2006, but almost all of these flows ($15 billion) went to South Africa. Debt flows were mostly short-term bank credit secured by trade receivables—medium- and long-term bank lending was concentrated in Angola and South Africa, and international bond issuance was concentrated in South Africa until 2006.

Sub-Saharan Africa excluding South Africa received a minuscule 2.2 percent of medium- and long-term flows received by developing countries. Medium- and long-term private capital flows to Sub-Saharan Africa excluding South Africa increased from $5.1 billion in 2000 to an estimated $14.8 billion during 2006. Private flows to South Africa alone were significantly larger throughout this period (table 6.1). The low- and middle-income Sub-Saharan African countries excluding South Africa and a few commodity exporters have benefited little from the surge in private debt and portfolio equity flows to developing countries (figure 6.1).

Official aid continues to be the dominant source of external finance for Sub-Saharan Africa

Compared with other regions, Sub-Saharan African countries rely heavily on official aid flows. At $38.2 billion, official development assistance is the largest source of external financing for Sub-Saharan African countries,

TABLE 6.1

Financial Flows to Sub-Saharan Africa and Other Developing Countries, 1990–2006

(US$ billions)

	1990	1995	2000	2005	2006 estimate	Growth rate, 2000–06 (%)
Sub-Saharan Africa excluding South Africa						
Official flows						
ODA[a]	17.0	17.4	11.7	30.1	37.5	220
Official debt	4.3	3.5	0.7	−0.7	−2.5	..
Private medium- and long-term flows	0.8	3.9	5.1	12.4	14.8	189
FDI	1.3	3.3	5.8	10.8	17.2	197
Portfolio equity	0.0	0.1	0.0	0.2	0.1	..
Bond	0.0	0.2	−0.2	0.0	−1.4	..
Bank lending	−0.5	0.3	−0.5	1.4	−1.1	..
Private short-term debt	2.3	1.1	−1.4	1.0	4.6	.:
Migrants' remittances[b]	1.7	3.1	4.3	8.7	9.6	124
Institutional remittances	1.4	2.3	2.9	5.4	6.2	117.
Capital outflows	3.2	5.3	6.3	7.5	3.6	..
South Africa						
Official flows						
ODA[a]	0.0	0.4	0.5	0.7	0.7	47
Official debt	0.0	0.0	0.1	0.1	0.0	..
Private medium- and long-term flows	0.3	4.0	6.2	17.4	16.1	160
FDI	−0.1	1.2	1.0	6.5	−0.1	..
Portfolio equity	0.4	2.9	4.2	7.2	15.0	257
Bond	0.0	0.7	1.2	1.3	1.6	32
Bank lending	0.0	−0.8	−0.2	2.4	−0.4	..
Private short-term debt	0.0	1.9	0.3	1.8	5.6	1,940
Migrants' remittances[b]	0.1	0.1	0.3	0.7	0.7	114
Institutional remittances	0.1	0.0	0.0	0.1	0.1	..
Capital outflows	0.2	4.1	3.3	2.5	10.5	214
Other developing regions						
Official flows						
ODA[a]	37.3	41.0	41.5	76.1	65.7	58
Official debt	19.8	35.4	−6.6	−69.9	−13.8	..
Private medium- and long-term flows	30.9	158.9	183.3	465.5	639.2	249
Private short-term debt	11.5	54.1	−5.3	86.8	84.1	..
Migrants' remittances[b]	29.2	54.3	79.9	181.9	211.0	164
Institutional remittances	15.7	14.0	26.9	58.1	63.0	134
Capital outflows	34.6	79.9	163.3	364.7	545.4	234

Source: Authors' calculations using the Global Development Finance database, March 2008.

Note: .. = negligible.

a. Development Assistance Committee donors only.

b. Migrants' remittances are the sum of workers' remittances, compensation of employees, and migrants' transfers (World Bank 2005).

FIGURE 6.1

Resource Flows to Sub-Saharan Africa Remain Less Diversified Than Flows to Other Developing Regions

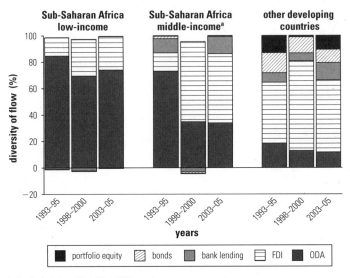

Source: Authors' calculations; World Bank 2007a.

a. Sub-Saharan Africa excluding South Africa.

both in dollar amounts and as a share of GDP. In 2006, official aid to Sub-Saharan African countries other than South Africa was $37.5 billion, or 8.2 percent of GDP, compared with 1 percent for all developing countries. Medium- and long-term private capital flows were only about 40 percent of official flows in Sub-Saharan African countries other than South Africa, and they were almost 10 times the amount of official aid flows in other developing regions (figure 6.1).

Aid flows to Sub-Saharan Africa declined until the late 1990s but have increased again in recent years. Official aid to Sub-Saharan African countries other than South Africa declined between 1995 and 2000, from $17.4 billion to $11.7 billion, but it has increased again in recent years with a substantial scaling up of aid. However, debt relief under the HIPC Initiative and the MDRI and exceptional debt relief provided by Paris Club creditors to Nigeria in 2005–06 have contributed a large share of this increase in official flows (IBRD 2007; World Bank 2007a). According to IBRD, debt relief represented close to 70 percent of the increase in bilateral ODA to Sub-Saharan Africa between 2001 and 2005.[10] Net official debt flows have declined dramatically in recent years (from 1.5 percent of GDP in the early 1990s to 0.3 percent of GDP in 2000–05 for Sub-Saharan African countries for which data were available in 2005) because debt relief under the HIPC Initiative and MDRI has reduced debt stocks and the stream of future repayments for many Sub-Saharan African countries.[11]

Although developed countries have pledged to substantially increase aid flows to Sub-Saharan Africa over the next decade, recent pledges for scaling up aid have not yet materialized for many donor countries. Excluding the exceptional debt relief to Nigeria, real ODA flows to Sub-Saharan Africa fell in 2005 and stagnated in 2006 (IBRD 2007).[12] The promised doubling of aid to Africa by 2010 seems unlikely at the current rates of growth. The lack of predictability of future aid is a cause for concern, in addition to the duplication of activities among donors and misalignment of the donor community's priorities with the country's development objectives.

A new group of aid donors—comprising Brazil, China, India, Lebanon, and Saudi Arabia—has emerged on the African scene. In January 2006, the Chinese government issued an official paper on China's Africa policy, and at the November 2006 China-Africa Summit, China promised to double its aid to Africa by 2009.[13] The old relationship between India and Africa is now being refocused to deepen economic collaboration in the areas of trade, technology, and training. Under the Indian Technical and Economic Cooperation Program, India spent more than $1 billion on aid assistance, including training, deputation of experts, and implementation of projects.

With traditional donors still failing to live up to their aid commitments, assistance from new donors could fill some of the funding gap in Sub-Saharan Africa. However, China's and India's approaches of delinking aid from political and economic reforms have raised concerns among traditional donors. These new emerging donors could cause traditional aid institutions to lower their own standards regarding governance and environmental issues, among others, given that China and India have not been involved in the debates on aid effectiveness. In the future, the new aid givers could participate in the global donor system.[14]

FDI flows to Sub-Saharan Africa were comparable to other regions, but appear to be mostly in enclave sectors

Foreign direct investment to Sub-Saharan African countries reached an estimated $17.1 billion in 2006, becoming the second largest source of external financing for the region. Low-income Sub-Saharan African countries received virtually all medium- and long-term private capital flows in the form of FDI. The region's improved macroeconomic management and growth performance, the commodity price boom, and debt relief have resulted in more investor interest. FDI to Sub-Saharan African countries excluding South Africa more than doubled after 2000, reaching an estimated $17.2 billion in 2006. Although the amount received by Sub-Saharan Africa is tiny compared with the total FDI flows to developing countries, it is equivalent to 2.4 percent as a share of GDP, comparable to the share of foreign direct investment in the GDP of other developing regions.

However, FDI flows to Sub-Saharan Africa appear to be concentrated in enclave sectors such as oil and natural resources (McDonald, Treichel, and Weisfeld 2006; World Bank 2007a). FDI flows to oil-exporting and commodities-exporting countries were larger than in other countries in the region from 1990 onward (figure 6.2). Oil exporters received nearly 70 percent of FDI going to Sub-Saharan African countries other than South Africa in 2005. Net FDI inflows to four major oil-producing countries in Sub-Saharan Africa—Angola, Equatorial Guinea, Nigeria, and Sudan—alone were estimated at $10 billion in 2006, half of all FDI to low-income countries in 2006 (World Bank 2007a). Non-resource-intensive countries other than South Africa recorded rising but substantially lower inflows.

FIGURE 6.2

FDI Flows Are Larger in Oil-Exporting Countries in Sub-Saharan Africa

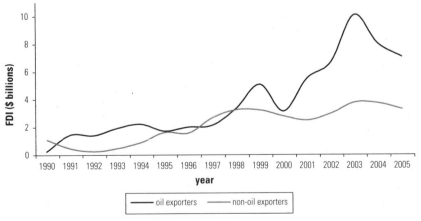

Source: Authors' calculations, *Global Development Finance* database, September 2007.
Note: Excludes South Africa.

Private debt flows to Sub-Saharan Africa are small and short-term

Debt flows to Sub-Saharan African countries are small compared with other developing regions. Countries other than South Africa received an estimated –$0.6 billion annually during 2005–06 in private medium- and long-term debt flows, and $2.8 billion in short-term debt flows (usually in the form of trade credits) during 2005–06, almost half of all short-term debt flows to the region. The high share of short-term debt in private debt flows reflects the high risk of lending on unsecured terms and at longer maturities to Sub-Saharan African firms. These short-term flows were relatively volatile and carry the risk of rapid reversal (see box 6.1).

Medium- and long-term flows were mostly bank lending to middle-income Sub-Saharan African countries. One middle-income oil-exporting country, Angola, appears to account for virtually all medium- and long-term bank lending to Sub-Saharan African countries other than South Africa in 2003–05. More recent data on syndicated loans from the Loanware database suggest that bank lending has grown since 2005, but mainly in resource-rich countries such as Angola, Liberia, Nigeria, and Zambia. Bond issuance in Sub-Saharan Africa was almost exclusively limited to South Africa until 2006. Low- and middle-income Sub-Saharan African countries other than South Africa received negligible amounts of bond financing from international markets. More recently, Ghana issued $750 million of international bonds in 2007, and several other Sub-Saharan African countries are considering international bond issues.[15]

Portfolio equity flows were almost absent in Sub-Saharan Africa excluding South Africa

Portfolio equity flows have increased since 1990 to an estimated $15.1 billion in 2006 and are now an important source of external finance for Sub-Saharan Africa. However, portfolio flows have gone almost exclusively to South Africa ($15 billion). When South Africa is excluded, portfolio equity flows are negligible in low- and middle-income Sub-Saharan African countries. Although South Africa has received more than $4 billion annually, on average, since 1995, other Sub-Saharan African countries together received less than $50 million annually during this period. Foreign investors appear to be averse to investing in Africa because of lack of infor-

BOX 6.1

Reliance on Short-Term Debt in Sub-Saharan Africa

Short-term debt comprises a large share of private debt flows to Sub-Saharan Africa.[a] Even as developing countries in other regions reduce their dependence on short-term debt, these flows continue to be a large and volatile component of private debt flows to Sub-Saharan Africa (see figure below). After a surge in private short-term debt flows to Sub-Saharan Africa during the mid-1990s, these flows turned negative from 1998 to 2002, after the Asian financial crisis. They have again increased in recent years as Sub-Saharan Africa's growth performance has improved. Since 1990, most private debt inflows into Sub-Saharan Africa have been short term.

Short-Term Debt Has Been a Large and Volatile Component of Private Debt Flows to Sub-Saharan Africa

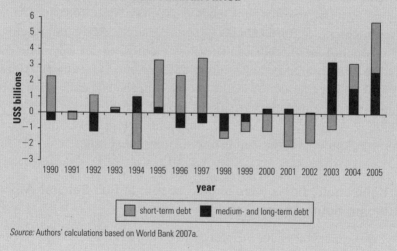

Source: Authors' calculations based on World Bank 2007a.

mation, severe risk perception, and the small size of the market that makes stocks relatively illiquid assets. One way to encourage greater private investment in these markets could be to tap into the diaspora outside Africa. Some of the initiatives being prepared by the diaspora are the formation of regional funds to be invested in companies listed on African stock markets.

The high share of short-term debt may be partly explained by the severe informational asymmetries and perceptions of risk of investing in Sub-Saharan Africa. Similar factors also account for the dominance of foreign direct investment in private capital flows to Sub-Saharan Africa and the small share of arm's-length financing through bond issuance and portfolio equity. In situations characterized by high risks, investors typically prefer to take direct control of their investment through FDI (Hausmann and Fernández-Arias 2001) or resort to relationship-based bank lending that is typically short term or can be secured by some tangible collateral, such as trade credits (see box 6.3).

A reliance on short-term debt can be risky for the receiving countries. Short-term debt tends to be pro-cyclical in developing countries, increasing when economic growth is cyclically faster and declining when growth rates falter (Dadush, Dasgupta, and Ratha 2000). Favorable conditions attract large inflows, encouraging potentially unsustainable levels of consumption and investment. Changes in risk perceptions, however, can lead to rapid reversals, imposing larger-than-necessary adjustment costs for the receiving countries.

a. Short-term international debt is defined as cross-border debt falling due within a year. The original maturity concept followed by World Bank (2002) is used here. The Bank for International Settlements, however, uses a "remaining maturity" concept—that is, all cross-border debt falling due within one year is counted as short-term debt, regardless of its original maturity (Dadush, Dasgupta, and Ratha 2000). Although conceptually different, the trends in the two are usually similar.

Personal and institutional remittances are a growing source of external financing for Sub-Saharan Africa

Recorded personal remittance inflows to Sub-Saharan Africa have increased steadily during the past decade, from $3.2 billion in 1995 to $9.3 billion in 2005 and to $10.3 billion in 2006. Most of this flow ($8.5 billion) in 2006 went to low-income Sub-Saharan African countries. Unrecorded flows through informal channels are believed to be even higher (World Bank 2005; Page and Plaza 2006).[16] In six Sub-Saharan African countries—Botswana, Côte d'Ivoire, Lesotho, Mauritius, Swaziland, and Togo— remittances were higher than ODA flows. In Lesotho, Mauritius, Swaziland, and Togo, remittances were also greater than foreign direct investment.

However, remittance flows to Sub-Saharan Africa have lagged behind other developing countries. Low-income countries received some $56 billion, or 3.5 percent of GDP, as remittances in 2006, whereas Sub-Saharan African countries other than South Africa received 2.1 percent. The relatively low share of recorded remittances to Sub-Saharan Africa is almost certainly attributable to a high share of informal transfers.

Institutional remittances, which include grants by U.S. and European foundations, were another category of resource flows that are large and growing steadily.[17] Institutional remittances to Sub-Saharan Africa increased from less than $2 billion in the early 1990s to $6.3 billion by 2006. As with personal remittances, most institutional remittances went to the poorest countries, with low-income Sub-Saharan African countries receiving $5 billion, or 1.6 percent of GDP, in 2005.

Private foundations, such as the Bill & Melinda Gates Foundation, are increasingly becoming important players in financing development. U.S. and European foundations provide some $4.4 billion in grants annually for international development (Sulla 2007). However, most of the international assistance from U.S. foundations is channeled through global funds such as GAVI, international institutions, and international nongovernmental organizations, and goes to emerging markets such as Brazil, China, India, Mexico, the Russian Federation, and South Africa, rather than the poorest countries in Sub-Saharan Africa, where grants from the International Development Association (IDA) continue to play a dominant role.[18] This may result partly from a lack of information and from difficulties in implementing projects in the poorest countries in Sub-Saharan Africa.

Institutional remittances have become increasingly important for financing the most pressing development needs of Sub-Saharan Africa, including those essential for reaching the Millennium Development Goals. However, some of the so-called vertical funds raise challenges because of their focus on specific issues, for example, diseases such as AIDS, tuberculosis, or malaria (see Sulla 2007 for recent trends and issues in grant giving by U.S. and European foundations). Multilateral institutions such as the IDA can help channel external assistance in a coordinated manner, provide support for broader sector-specific (education, health) strategies, and align these with Sub-Saharan African countries' own development priorities.

BOX 6.2

New Players in Sub-Saharan Africa

Emerging creditors such as China—and India on a smaller scale—have increased their financial involvement in Sub-Saharan Africa in the form of loans, grants, debt relief, and direct investment. Relevant data are not easily available, but China appears to be the largest of six new creditor nations. By May 2006, China had contributed $5.7 billion for more than 800 aid projects (IMF 2007). In the latest Beijing Summit of the Forum on China-African Cooperation in November 2006, China announced that it would provide $5 billion on preferential credits for the period 2007–09 ($3 billion in concessional loans and $2 billion for export buyer credits). Counting media reports only, Export-Import Bank of China provided $7 billion in the period 2004–06. In May 2007, Export-Import Bank of China stated that it planned to provide about $20 billion in infrastructure and trade financing to Africa over the next three years (*Financial Times* 2007a). China's investment in oil and textiles has rapidly spiked upward in Angola, Sudan, and Zimbabwe. With the support of the Export-Import Bank of China, Chinese companies have quickly become leaders in the development of roads, railroads, and major public buildings, as well as telecommunications on the African continent (Broadman et al. 2007). Chad and China just signed a $257 million economic package to finance several projects in the central African country, including telecommunications, a cement factory, and roads.

Chinese banks are also entering a new phase of involvement in Africa by developing partnerships with and buying equity stakes in African banks. The Industrial and Commercial Bank of China is acquiring 20 percent of South Africa's Standard Bank for about $5 billion (*Financial Times* 2007b). The two banks will jointly establish a global resources fund to invest in mining, metals, and oil and gas in emerging markets. China Development Bank

(*Box continues on the following page.*)

BOX 6.2 (continued)

has formed a partnership with Nigeria's United Bank for Africa to cooperate in financing energy and infrastructure projects in Nigeria and other West African countries (*Oxford Analytica* 2007).

China has offered debt forgiveness to 31 African countries, amounting to $1.27 billion since 2000, and more write-offs are expected. By mid-May 2007, China had signed debt forgiveness agreements with 11 of the 31 countries and expected to conclude agreements with the other 20 by the end of 2007 (Wang 2007).

China's nonconcessional loans to some countries have raised concerns that it may be free riding in countries that received debt relief under the MDRI and the HIPC programs (*Economist* 2007). According to some authors, however, the majority of the projects undertaken by China are in non-HIPC resource-rich countries, such as Angola, Nigeria, and Sudan (Goldstein et al. 2006). In those countries, these loans are part of China's FDI directed to strategic resource seeking.[a] A $5 billion China-Africa Development Fund has been created to support Chinese FDI in Africa.

a. China's and India's investments in Africa are examples of a broader South-South investment trend. Aykut and Ratha (2005) show that by the late 1990s, more than a third of FDI received by developing countries originated in other developing countries.

Capital outflows from Sub-Saharan Africa have decreased in recent years, but the stock of flight capital abroad remains high

Capital outflows from Sub-Saharan African countries averaged $8.1 billion annually from 1990 to 2005 (figure 6.3).[19] The cumulated stock of outflows from Sub-Saharan African countries was $178 billion in 2006, nearly 30 percent of GDP—down from a high of 51 percent of GDP in 2002. Capital outflows increased faster from middle-income and resource-rich Sub-Saharan African countries in the 1990s, reaching 59 percent of GDP in 2002 (figure 6.3).[20]

Several studies have identified a number of factors that encourage capital flight from Africa (see, for example, Ajayi 1997; Boyce and Ndikumana 2001; Collier, Hoeffler, and Pattillo 2001; Hermes, Lensink, and Murinde

FIGURE 6.3

Capital Outflows from Sub-Saharan Africa Have Declined Recently

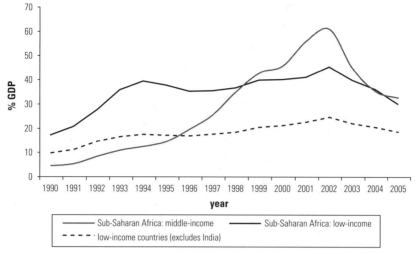

Source: Authors' calculations based on World Bank 2007a.

2002; Ndikumana and Boyce 2002; Powell, Ratha, and Mohapatra 2002; Salisu 2005; World Bank 2004). Some of the main determinants of capital flight include macroeconomic instability, political instability, external borrowing, risk-adjusted rates-of-return differentials, and financial development, among others. Consistent with the view of outflows as a portfolio diversification choice (Collier, Hoeffler, and Pattillo 2004), the stock of accumulated capital outflows appears to be negatively related to the country's performance rating, including corruption, economic management, and transparency (figure 6.4).

A reversal of capital flight appears to have occurred in the past few years. Improving macroeconomic fundamentals, better growth prospects, and an improving business environment have improved the risk-adjusted returns from investing domestically.

New Sources and Innovative Mechanisms for Financing Development in Sub-Saharan Africa

This section discusses some new or hitherto overlooked sources and some innovative structures for development financing in Sub-Saharan African

FIGURE 6.4

A Better Policy Environment Reduces Capital Outflows

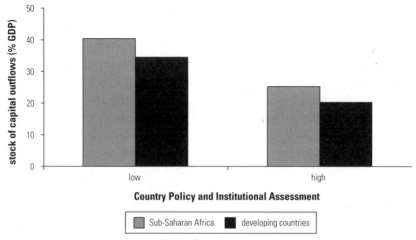

Source: Authors' calculations.

countries. First, the section discusses two new sources of financing: issuance of diaspora bonds and efforts to increase migrant remittances by reducing money transfer costs. The section then discusses some recent initiatives that involve innovative financial structures—multilateral guarantees that leverage official financing for mobilizing private capital and the IFFIm that front-loads aid commitments—before describing a more generalized financial structuring that allows private entities to issue debt backed by future remittances and other future-flow receivables. Finally, the section argues for establishing sovereign credit ratings for Sub-Saharan countries, because ratings are key to attracting private capital.

New Sources of Financing

Diaspora bonds

A diaspora bond is a debt instrument issued by a country—or, potentially, by a subsovereign entity or by a private corporation—to raise financing from its overseas diaspora. India and Israel have raised $11 billion and $25 billion, respectively, from their diaspora abroad (Ketkar and Ratha 2007). The diaspora usually have more information about their country of origin. These bonds often are issued in times of crisis and often at a "patriotic" discount. Unlike international investors, the diaspora tend to be less averse to convertibility risk because they are likely to have current and contingent liabilities in their home country. Furthermore, the diaspora usually have a strong desire to contribute to the development of their home country and are therefore more likely to purchase diaspora bonds (see table 6.2).

Table 6.2 shows estimates of the diaspora stocks of Sub-Saharan African countries and their annual savings. The stock of Sub-Saharan African diaspora is estimated to be about 16 million, with 5 million in high-income countries. Assuming that members of the Sub-Saharan African diaspora earn the average income of their host countries and save a fifth of their income, their annual savings would be more than $28 billion. Most of these savings would come from the migrants in the Organisation for Economic

TABLE 6.2
Potential Market for Diaspora Bonds

Country	Diaspora stocks (US$ thousands)	Potential diaspora savings (US$ billions)
South Africa	713	2.9
Nigeria	837	2.8
Kenya	427	1.7
Ghana	907	1.7
Ethiopia	446	1.6
Somalia	441	1.6
Senegal	463	1.3
Zimbabwe	761	1.0
Sudan	587	1.0
Angola	523	1.0
Congo, Dem. Rep. of	572	0.8
Cape Verde	181	0.7
Uganda	155	0.7
Mauritius	119	0.7
Cameroon	231	0.6
Mozambique	803	0.6
Madagascar	151	0.6
Tanzania	189	0.6
Eritrea	849	0.6
Mali	1,213	0.6
Other Sub-Saharan African countries	5,285	5.5
Total	**15,854**	**28.5**

Source: Authors' calculations.

Note: Diaspora stocks for 2005 include only identified migrants (from Ratha and Shaw 2007). Diaspora savings are calculated by assuming migrants earned the average per capita income of the host country and saved one-fifth of their income. Under the alternative scenario of African migrants earning half of the per capita income in the host countries and saving a fifth of their income, the potential annual saving of the African diaspora would be over $10 billion.

Co-operation and Development (OECD) countries, where a third of Sub-Saharan African diasporas are located, because of the larger income differentials. In an alternative scenario, if the Sub-Saharan African diaspora were assumed to earn half the average per capita income in the host countries and saved only 20 percent of their income, the annual savings of the African diaspora would still be over $10 billion. The bulk of this saving is currently invested outside Africa. African governments and private corporations can potentially tap into these resources by issuing diaspora bonds. Diaspora bonds can also provide an instrument for repatriation of Africa's flight capital, estimated at more than $170 billion (as discussed). Diaspora bonds could potentially raise $5 billion to $10 billion annually by tapping into the wealth of the African diaspora abroad and the flight capital held abroad by its residents.[21]

Though the size of the potential market for diaspora bonds is indeed impressive, it may be difficult for some unrated Sub-Saharan African countries that are characterized by high risks to issue diaspora bonds. Some of the constraints that Sub-Saharan African countries may face in issuing diaspora bonds include weak and nontransparent legal systems for contract enforcement; a lack of national banks and other institutions in destination countries, which can facilitate the marketing of these bonds; and a lack of clarity on regulations in the host countries that allow or constrain diaspora members from investing in these bonds (Chander 2001; Ketkar and Ratha 2007). However, because of recent debt relief initiatives and improving macroeconomic management, many Sub-Saharan African countries are in a better position to access private capital markets than at any other time in recent decades.

Reduced remittance costs

Reducing remittance costs would increase remittance flows to Sub-Saharan Africa. Among all regions, Sub-Saharan Africa is believed to have the highest share of remittances flowing through informal channels (Page and Plaza 2006).[22] This is partly because of the high cost of sending remittances in Sub-Saharan Africa. For example, the average cost of sending $200 from London to Lagos, Nigeria, in mid-2006 (including the foreign exchange premium) was 14.4 percent of the amount, and the cost from Cotonou, Benin, to Lagos was more than 17 percent (Ratha and Shaw 2007). Reducing remittance fees would increase the disposable income of remitters, encouraging them to remit large amounts and at greater frequencies. It would also encourage remittance senders to shift from informal to formal channels.

Estimating the additional remittance flows that would result from a decrease in remittance cost is complicated by several factors. For example, remittances sent for an immediate family emergency may not be responsive to costs. However, estimates based on surveys of Tongan migrants indicate the cost elasticity to be in the range of 0.22; that is, a 1 percent decrease in cost would increase remittances by 0.22 percent (Gibson, McKenzie, and Rohorua 2006). For example, halving remittance costs from the current high levels, from 14 percent to 7 percent for the London-Lagos corridor, would thus increase remittances by 11 percent. This change implies additional remittance flows of more than $1 billion every year. Assuming that the reduction in remittance cost also succeeds in bringing half the unrecorded remittances into formal channels, this would result in an increase of $2.5 billion in recorded remittance flows to Sub-Saharan Africa.

Remittance costs faced by poor migrants from Sub-Saharan African countries can be reduced by improving the access to banking for remittance senders and recipients and by strengthening competition in the remittance industry (Ratha 2007; World Bank 2005). Clarifying regulations related to anti–money laundering and countering the financing of terrorism and avoiding overregulation, such as requiring a full banking license for specialized money transfer operators, would facilitate the entry of new players. It would also encourage the adoption of more efficient technologies, such as the use of the Internet and mobile phone technology. Sharing payment platforms and nonexclusive partnerships between remittance service providers and existing postal and retail networks would help expand remittance services without requiring large fixed investments.

Innovative Structuring

Guarantees
World Bank and International Development Association partial risk guarantees of some $3 billion were successful in catalyzing $12 billion in private financing in 28 operations in developing countries during the last decade (Gelb, Ramachandran, and Turner 2006). These guarantees typically cover project financing in large infrastructure projects and other sectors with high social returns. World Bank guarantees include partial risk guarantees and partial credit guarantees that cover private debt for large

public projects (typically infrastructure). Although the partial risk guarantees typically cover the risk of nonperformance of sovereign contractual obligations, partial credit guarantees cover a much broader range of credit risks and are designed to lower the cost and extend the maturity of debt (Matsukawa and Habeck 2007).[23] Political risk guarantees issued by the Multilateral Investment Guarantee Agency have helped alleviate political and other risks in agribusiness, manufacturing, and tourism. The African Export-Import Bank and other agencies provide guarantees for trade credits (see box 6.3). There appears to be potential to increase the use of IDA guarantees beyond large infrastructure projects to small and medium enterprises.

BOX 6.3

Trade Finance as an Attractive Short-Term Financing Option

Trade finance is an attractive way of increasing short-term financing to risky African countries in the presence of asymmetric information. Firms operating in international markets require financing for the purchase of their imports and for the production of their exports. Many African firms, however, have no access to trade finance or instruments to support their operations because of information asymmetries and their perceived greater risk. Larger firms that have access to credit from importers, the banking system (typically from affiliates of European global banking corporations whose core business is often short-term trade finance), or other nonbank financial institutions often provide trade credit to their smaller suppliers, who in many cases have no access to credit.

In recent years, the export credit agencies of China and India have become increasingly prominent in promoting trade finance in Sub-Saharan Africa, not only for raw materials, commodities, and natural resources, but also for capital goods (machinery, equipment) and manufactured products. In 2006, the Export-Import Bank of India extended a $250 million line of credit to the Economic Community of West African States Bank for Investment and Development (EBID) to finance India's exports to the 15 member countries of EBID. The Indian bank has also previously extended trade financing to the Eastern and Southern African Trade and Development Bank (PTA Bank) for

$50 million to promote India's exports to 16 eastern and southern African countries. The Export-Import Bank of China is financing a larger set of activities—providing export credit, loans for construction contracts and investment projects (including energy and communication projects), and concessional loans and guarantees.

The World Bank is supporting an innovative project through its Regional Trade Facilitation Program to address the gaps in the private political and credit-risk insurance market for cross-border transactions involving African countries. The project is managed by the African Trade Insurance Agency (ATI), a multilateral agency set up by treaty, and brings together a group of countries in the southern and eastern African regions to develop a credible insurance mechanism. To date, ATI has facilitated $110.7 million in trade and investments in ATI member countries, using only $21.6 million of IDA resources—a gearing ratio of almost five to one in sectors that include mining (Zambia), housing (the Democratic Republic of Congo), flowers (Kenya), and telecommunications (Burundi and Uganda). Clients have indicated that without ATI's support, they might not have received the necessary financing.

Although trade finance can facilitate trade and economic linkages with Africa's major trading partners, Africa needs additional longer-term sources of external finance. Trade finance is typically short term and carries many risks associated with short-term debt (see box 6.1). The recent expansion of trade finance may also partly reflect the inability of Sub-Saharan African countries to obtain unsecured financing at longer maturities. Enhancing the scope and volume of trade finance can facilitate trade and improve regional economic cooperation, but additional external resource flows are required to finance the projects in infrastructure, manufacturing, education, and health that have high social returns and involve significantly longer time horizons.

The first-ever IDA partial risk guarantee in Sub-Saharan Africa—in 1999 for the Azito power project in Côte d'Ivoire—catalyzed private financing of $200 million while keeping IDA support to $30 million, or 15 percent of the project (World Bank 1999). IDA partial risk guarantees are being prepared for the 250-megawatt Bujagali hydropower project in

Uganda, a 50-megawatt hydropower project in Sierra Leone, and a project to increase power sector efficiency in Senegal (World Bank 2007c).

There is potential for extending the scope and reach of guarantees to use aid resources to catalyze large volumes of private financing in Sub-Saharan Africa beyond the traditional large infrastructure projects and beyond sovereign borrowers. Gelb, Ramachandran, and Turner (2006) suggest that guarantees should be available not only to foreign investors but also to domestic investors, including pension and insurance funds, to raise local currency financing. Guarantee facilities can be established to support several small projects in the same sector, similar to a "master trust" arrangement. Innovations include service guarantees that can protect investors against service failures, in areas such as power, customs, and licensing, that discourage private investment in Sub-Saharan African countries.

IFFIm, AMC, and other innovative structuring by public-private partnerships
Several international initiatives are under way for innovative development financing mechanisms. They include a search for new sources of financing, innovative ways of realizing future commitments, and innovative ways of using existing resources. The International Finance Facility for Immunisation is an innovative structuring mechanism for realizing future aid commitments to introduce more reliable and predictable aid flows for immunization programs and health system development for the Global Alliance for Vaccines and Immunization.[24] IFFIm raised $1 billion in 2006 and plans to raise $4 billion more during the next 10 years by securitizing—in other words, front-loading—future aid commitments from several donor countries (France, Italy, Norway, South Africa, Spain, Sweden, and the United Kingdom). The donor countries have signed legally binding agreements with the GAVI fund affiliate to provide future grants to IFFIm, which issues the bonds in international markets. IFFIm disburses the proceeds as required for GAVI-approved programs to procure needed vaccines and to strengthen the health systems of recipient countries. Future grant flows from donors are used to repay bondholders. The backing of highly creditworthy developed country donors has enabled IFFIm to issue AAA-rated bonds in international capital markets at competitive spreads.

Such a facility, however, faces several constraints, including the question of "additionality" (whether the countries that bought the bonds will reduce aid), high transaction costs, and the question of whether the coupon yield will be paid for by sovereign bond guarantors or subtracted from the proceeds.

The advance market commitment (AMC) for vaccines, launched in February 2007, is another innovative structuring mechanism that would complement the efforts of IFFIm by providing financial incentives to accelerate the development of vaccines important to developing countries. The donors provide up-front financing for the AMC, which negotiates with the pharmaceutical industry to provide a set level of funding in return for future supply at an agreed-upon price for the manufacturer that first develops the vaccine (GAVI and World Bank 2006). Canada, Italy, Norway, the Russian Federation, the United Kingdom, and the Gates Foundation have provided $1.5 billion for the pilot AMC to develop a vaccine for pneumococcal disease, which causes 1.9 million child deaths a year. The AMC is not expected to increase aid flows substantially to poor countries, but it brings together public and private donors in an innovative way to help meet the MDGs (IBRD 2007).[25]

Other public-private partnerships to generate new sources of innovative financing that are under consideration include a currency transaction levy, airline and environmental taxes, and private contributions.[26] Introducing a one-basis-point levy on currency transactions could yield over $16 billion in revenue annually, according to Hillman, Kapoor, and Spratt (2006). This variation of a Tobin tax, however, is not popular with the financial institutions, nor with countries that are major financial centers. Such taxes would cause friction in financial transactions and have cascading effects. Airline taxes are already being implemented in some countries (e.g., eight countries, including France, have raised $250 million in 2007), but there are questions as to whether these were new taxes (IBRD 2007).[27]

These public-private partnerships, however, rely on donor government efforts to mobilize financing and are subject to the same concerns about aid allocation, coordination, and effectiveness. These innovative projects are not designed for catalyzing private-to-private flows to developing countries from the international capital markets.

A new initiative by the World Bank Group—the Global Emerging Markets Local Currency (Gemloc) Bond Fund announced in October 2007—proposes to raise $5 billion from international capital markets to invest in local currency bond markets in developing countries.[28] The Gemloc public-private partnership will mobilize local currency–denominated resources for governments in selected emerging market countries, thereby eliminating the devaluation risk associated with foreign-currency borrowing. Corporate bonds will be included subsequently, but at least 70 percent of the proceeds of Gemloc would be invested in local currency bonds issued by sovereign and quasi-sovereign entities.

The creation of an independent and transparent benchmark index and "investability" rankings of countries' local currency bond markets are expected to facilitate external financing flows to emerging markets. Like portfolio equity flows, however, Gemloc is likely to favor middle-income countries with market access. Although Gemloc plans to include Kenya, Nigeria, and West African countries in a subsequent phase, most of the countries selected for the first phase (for example, Brazil, China, India, and South Africa) are countries with sovereign ratings in the BB or BBB categories. It is also not entirely clear whether Gemloc would result in additional funding or whether it might substitute portfolio equity flows.[29]

Future-flow securitization

Sub-Saharan African countries can potentially raise significant bond financing by using securitization of future flows, such as remittances, tourism receipts, and export receivables. Securitization of future hard-currency receivables is a potential means of improving Sub-Saharan African countries' access to international capital markets. In a typical future-flow transaction, the borrower pledges its future foreign-currency receivables— for example, oil, remittances, credit card receivables, and airline ticket receivables—as collateral to a special-purpose vehicle (Ketkar and Ratha 2001, 2005). The special-purpose vehicle issues the debt. By a legal arrangement between the borrowing entity and major international customers or correspondent banks, the future receivables are deposited directly in an offshore collection account managed by a trustee. The debt is serviced from this account, and excess collections are forwarded to the borrowing entity in the developing country.[30]

This future-flow securitization mitigates sovereign transfer and convertibility risks and allows the securities to be rated better than the sovereign credit rating. These securities are typically structured to obtain an investment-grade rating. For example, in the case of El Salvador, the remittance-backed securities were rated investment grade, two to four notches above the sub-investment-grade sovereign rating. The investment-grade rating makes these transactions attractive to a wider range of "buy-and-hold" investors (for example, insurance companies) that face limitations on buying sub–investment grade. As a result, the issuer can access international capital markets at a lower interest-rate spread and longer maturity. Moreover, by establishing a credit history for the borrower, these deals enhance the ability to obtain and reduce the costs of accessing capital markets in the future.[31]

The potential size of future-flow securitizations for various kinds of flows, including remittances, for Sub-Saharan Africa was estimated here based on the methodology of Ketkar and Ratha (2001, 2005) using an overcollateralization ratio of five to one and average flows in 2003–06. The calculations indicate that the potential future-flow securitization is $17 billion annually, with remittance securitization of about $800 million (table 6.3). These include only the securitization of remittances recorded in the balance of payments. The actual unrecorded remittances through formal and informal channels are estimated to be a multiple of that estimate in several countries (Page and Plaza 2006).

Remittances are a large and stable source of external financing that can be creatively leveraged for Sub-Saharan Africa's development goals. Remittances can improve capital market access of banks and governments in poor countries by improving ratings and securitization structures (Ratha 2006). Hard currency remittances, properly accounted for, can significantly

TABLE 6.3
Securitization Potential in Sub-Saharan Africa
(US$ billions)

	Sub-Saharan Africa		Low income		All developing	
	Receivable	Potential securiti- zation	Receivable	Potential securiti- zation	Receivable	Potential securiti- zation
Fuel exports	51.3	10.3	63.5	12.7	490.9	98.2
Agricultural raw materials exports	6.4	1.3	6.7	1.3	51.0	10.2
Ores and metals exports	16.4	3.3	11.8	2.4	129.9	26.0
Travel services	12.9	1.3	12.6	1.3	179.6	17.9
Remittances	8.4	0.8	45.2	4.5	179.4	17.9
Total	95.5	17.0	139.8	22.2	1,030.8	170.2

Sources: Authors' calculations using an overcollateralization ratio of 5:1. Data on exports are from the World Bank's World Development Indicators. Worker remittances, as defined in Ratha (2003), are calculated from the IMF's *Balance-of Payments Statistics Yearbook 2007.*

Note: Based on average for 2003–06.

improve a country's risk rating. It may even encourage many poor countries that are currently not rated to obtain a credit rating from major international rating agencies (see the following section for more discussion).

The African Export-Import Bank (Afreximbank) has been active in facilitating future-flow securitization since the late 1990s. In 1996, it coarranged the first ever future-flow securitization by a Sub-Saharan African country, a $40 million medium-term loan in favor of a development bank in Ghana backed by its Western Union remittance receivables (Afreximbank 2005; Rutten and Oramah 2006). The bank launched its Financial Future-Flow Prefinancing Programme in 2001 to expand the use of migrant remittances and other future flows—credit cards and checks, royalties arising from bilateral air-services agreements over flight fees, and so forth—as collateral to leverage external financing to fund agricultural and other projects in Sub-Saharan Africa. In 2001 Afreximbank arranged a $50 million remittance-backed syndicated note issuance facility in favor of a Nigerian entity using Moneygram receivables, and in 2004 it coarranged a $40 million remittance-backed syndicated term loan facility in favor of an Ethiopian bank using its Western Union receivables (Afreximbank 2005).

There are, however, several institutional constraints to future-flow securitization in Sub-Saharan Africa. A low level of domestic financial development; lack of banking relationships with banks abroad; and high fixed costs of legal, investment-banking, and credit-rating services, especially in poor countries with few large entities, make the use of these instruments especially difficult for Sub-Saharan countries. Absence of an appropriate legal infrastructure, weak protection of creditor rights (including inadequate or poorly enforced bankruptcy laws), and a volatile macroeconomic environment can also pose difficulties. In the case of remittance securitization, extensive use of informal channels in Sub-Saharan Africa can reduce the flows through the formal financial system and thereby the size of potential securitization.

Securitization by poor countries carries significant risks—currency devaluation and, in the case of flexible rate debt, unexpected increases in interest rates—that are associated with market-based foreign currency debt (World Bank 2005). Securitization of remittances (and other future flows) by public sector entities reduces the government's flexibility in managing its external payments and can conflict with the negative pledge provision included in multilateral agencies' loan and guarantee agreements, which prohibit the establishment of a priority for other debts over the multilateral debts.

Still, this asset class can provide useful access to international capital markets, especially during liquidity crises. Moreover, for many developing countries, securitization backed by future flows of receivables may be the only way to begin accessing such markets. Given the long lead times involved in such deals, however, issuers need to keep securitization deals in the pipeline and investors engaged during good times so that such deals remain accessible during crises.

Recovery of stolen assets

Another innovative way of using existing resources includes recovery of flight capital and stolen assets. The cross-border flow of the global proceeds from criminal activities, corruption, and tax evasion are estimated to be more than $1 trillion annually.[32] Some $20 billion to $40 billion in assets acquired by corrupt leaders of poor countries, mostly in Africa, are kept overseas. The World Bank and the United Nations Office on Drugs and Crime have launched the Stolen Assets Recovery initiative to help countries recover their stolen assets. This initiative will help countries establish institutions that can detect and deter illegal flows of funds, work with the OECD countries in ratifying the Convention against Corruption, and support and monitor the use of recovered funds for development activities. These recovered assets could provide financing for social programs and infrastructure.[33]

Positive effects of sovereign ratings on market access

Sovereign risk ratings not only affect investment decisions in the international bond and loan markets, they also affect allocation of FDI and portfolio equity flows (Ratha, De, and Mohapatra 2007). The allocation of performance-based official aid is also increasingly being linked to sovereign rating. The foreign currency rating of the sovereign typically acts as a ceiling for the foreign currency rating of subsovereign entities. Even when the sovereign is not issuing bonds, a sovereign rating provides a benchmark for the capital market activities of the private sector.

Borrowing costs rise exponentially with a lowering of the credit rating (figure 6.5). There is also a threshold effect when borrowing spreads jump up as the rating slides below the investment grade (Ratha, De, and Mohapatra 2007). A borrowing entity with a low credit rating, therefore, can significantly improve borrowing terms (that is, lower interest spread and increase maturity) by paying up-front for a better credit rating.

Only 21 Sub-Saharan African countries had been rated by a major international rating agency as of December 2007 (table 6.4).[34] The average rating of Sub-Saharan African countries remains low compared with other regions, restricting the access of their private sector to international capital. As noted in the previous section, private debt and equity flows to Sub-Saharan African countries were the lowest among all regions. Some authors have pointed to the existence of an "Africa premium"—equivalent to roughly two rating notches or 200 basis points—even for relatively better-performing countries with above-median growth and low aid dependence (Gelb, Ramachandran, and Turner 2006).

FIGURE 6.5
Launch Spreads Decline with an Increase in Sovereign Rating

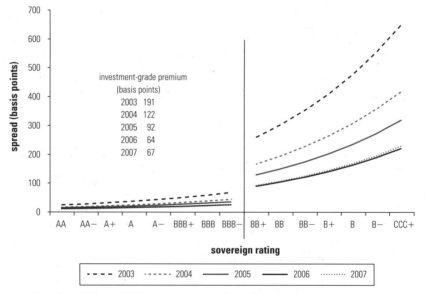

Source: Ratha, De, and Mohapatra (2007) based on Bondware and Standard & Poor's.

Note: Assuming a $100 million sovereign bond issue with a seven-year tenor. Borrowing costs have fallen steadily since 2003 with a slight reversal more recently, reflecting changes in the global liquidity situation. The investment-grade premium indicates the rise in spreads when the rating falls below BBB–. The relationship between sovereign ratings and spreads is based on the following regression:

log(launch spread) = 2.58 − 1.2 investment grade dummy + 0.15 sovereign rating + 0.23 log(issue size) + 0.03 maturity − 0.44 year 2004 dummy − 0.73 year 2005 dummy − 1.10 year 2006 dummy − 1.05 year 2007 dummy

$N = 200$; Adjusted $R^2 = 0.70$

All the coefficients were significant at 5 percent. A lower numeric value of the sovereign rating indicates a better rating.

At the subsovereign level, few firms in Sub-Saharan Africa outside of South Africa are rated by the three international rating agencies.[35] Several firms are highly creditworthy in local currency terms, but they are constrained by either an absent or low foreign currency sovereign rating.

Model-based estimates indicate that several unrated Sub-Saharan African countries would be rated higher than currently believed. Drawing on the well-established literature on the empirical determinants of sovereign ratings, Ratha, De, and Mohapatra (2007) found that the predicted or shadow sovereign ratings for several Sub-Saharan African countries that are currently unrated are in a similar range as some established emerging markets (table 6.5).[36]

Sub-Saharan African countries with large remittance inflows can leverage those inflows for raising the sovereign rating (Ratha 2006). Preliminary

TABLE 6.4
Rated Sub-Saharan African Countries, December 2007

Country	S&P		Moody's		Fitch		Predicted shadow rating[a]
	Rating	Date	Rating	Date	Rating	Date	
Botswana	A	Apr 2001	Aa3	May 2006			AA to AAA
South Africa	BBB+	Aug 2005	Baa1	Jan 2005	BBB+	Aug 2005	BBB to BBB+
Mauritius			Baa1	May 2006			BBB+ to A−
Namibia					BBB−	Dec 2005	BBB− to BBB
Lesotho					BB−	Nov 2005	BB to BB+
Gabon	BB−	Nov 2007			BB−	Oct 2007	BBB− to BBB
Nigeria	BB−	Feb 2006			BB−	Jan 2006	BB to BBB−
Cape Verde					B+	Aug 2003	BBB−
Ghana	B+	Sep 2003			B+	Sep 2007	BB− to BB
Kenya	B+	Sep 2006					B to B+
Senegal	B+	Dec 2000					BB to BB+
Seychelles	B	Sep 2006					BB to BBB−
Cameroon	B	Feb 2007			B	Jun 2006	BB− to BB
Benin	B	Sep 2006			B	Sep 2004	BB− to BB
Burkina Faso	B	Mar 2004					B to B+
Madagascar	B	May 2004					B to B+
Mozambique	B	Jul 2004			B	Jul 2003	B+ to BB−
Uganda					B	Mar 2005	BB−
Mali	B	May 2004			B−	Apr 2004	BB
Malawi					B−	Mar 2007	CCC+ to B
Gambia, The					CCC	Dec 2005	B+ to BB−

Sources: Ratings from Standard & Poor's, Moody's, and Fitch.

a. These shadow ratings are based on forecasts of explanatory variables for 2007 for the benchmark sovereign rating model of chapter 5.

estimates indicate that including remittances in the debt-to-exports ratio in creditworthiness assessments would result in an improvement in sovereign ratings by up to two notches (World Bank 2005). The securitization of future receivables, including trade payments and future remittances, can further improve the rating of the transaction, typically to investment grade (BBB). For example, the spread saving from improving ratings from B to BBB would be in the range of 320 to 450 basis points (figure 6.5).

Sub-Saharan African countries that received debt relief and improved their macroeconomic management appear to be better positioned to access international markets. Debt relief under the HIPC Initiative and under the MDRI has reduced the external debt-service obligations for 16 countries in Sub-Saharan Africa. Since mid-2005, private foreign investors have started acquiring government debt in local currencies in Sub-Saharan Africa (IMF 2006). Investors have been attracted by high yields relative to the per-

TABLE 6.5

Shadow Sovereign Ratings for Unrated Countries in Sub-Saharan Africa, December 2007

Country	Predicted shadow rating[a]	Rated countries in the same range
Equatorial Guinea	BBB– to BBB	India, Mexico, Romania
Angola	BB+	El Salvador, Peru
Swaziland	BB– to BB+	Brazil, Peru, Turkey
Zambia	BB– to BB	Brazil, Turkey
Tanzania	BB–	Turkey, Uruguay
Congo, Rep. of	B+ to BB–	Pakistan, Turkey
Niger	B– to B	Argentina, Bolivia, Paraguay
Rwanda	B– to B	Argentina, Bolivia, Paraguay
Togo	CCC+ to B–	Bolivia, Ecuador, Paraguay
Mauritania	CCC to B	Dominican Rep., Ecuador
Côte d'Ivoire	CCC to B	Dominican Rep., Ecuador
Sierra Leone	CCC to B	Ecuador, Pakistan
Ethiopia	CCC to CCC+	Ecuador
Sudan	CCC– to CCC+	Ecuador
Comoros	CCC– to CCC+	Ecuador
Congo, Dem. Rep. of	CCC– to CCC	Ecuador
Guinea	CC to CCC	Ecuador
Chad	C to CCC+	Ecuador
Guinea-Bissau	C to CC	
Zimbabwe	C or lower	

Sources: Ratings from Standard & Poor's, Moody's, and Fitch.

a. Shadow ratings use forecasts of explanatory variables for 2007 for the benchmark sovereign rating model of chapter 5.

ceived risk, better macroeconomic fundamentals, and diversification benefits (IMF 2006, 2007). Countries that have elicited the most investor interest are Botswana, Cameroon, Ghana, Kenya, Malawi, Nigeria, and Zambia. Also, Gabon, an oil-exporting middle-income African country, is preparing to raise $1 billion in international capital markets. Gabon was rated by Fitch in late October 2007 and by Standard & Poor's in November 2007.[37]

Conclusion

Both official and private flows to Sub-Saharan Africa have increased in recent years, a welcome reversal of the declining or flat trend seen during the 1990s. The picture is less rosy, however, when Sub-Saharan Africa is compared with the other developing regions, and more important, when it is compared with its enormous resource needs for growth, poverty reduction, and other Millennium Development Goals. Sub-Saharan Africa outside South Africa continues to depend on official aid. The recent increase in official development assistance appears to be driven by one-off debt relief provided through the HIPC Initiative and MDRI; the prospect for scaling up aid is not entirely certain.[38] FDI flows to the region are concentrated in enclave investments in oil-exporting countries. Portfolio bond and equity flows are negligible outside South Africa, although several African countries are considering bond issues in international markets. Private debt flows are small and dominated by relationship-based commercial bank lending, and even these flows are largely short-term in tenor. More than half of the countries in the region do not have a sovereign rating from the major credit rating agencies, and the few rated countries have sub-investment-grade ratings. Low or absent credit ratings impede not only sovereign but also private sector efforts to raise financing in the capital markets. Capital outflows appear to be smaller than in the previous decade, but the stock of flight capital from the region remains very high. Migrant remittances appear to be increasing, but a large part of the flows bypass formal financial channels.

In short, the development community has little choice but to continue to explore new sources of financing, innovative private sector–to–private sector solutions, and public-private partnerships to mobilize additional international financing. An analysis of country creditworthiness suggests that many countries in the region may be more creditworthy than previously believed. Establishing sovereign rating benchmarks and credit enhancement through guarantee instruments provided by multilateral aid agencies would facilitate market access. Creative financial structuring such as the International Finance Facility for Immunisation can help front-load aid commitments, although these may not result in additional financing in the long run. Preliminary estimates suggest that Sub-Saharan African countries can potentially raise $1 billion to $3 billion by reducing the cost of international migrant remittances, $5 billion to $10 billion by issuing diaspora bonds, and $17 billion by securitizing future remittances and other future receivables.

In raising financing using these means, African countries will face several challenges. Leveraging remittances for Sub-Saharan Africa's development will imply efforts to significantly improve both migration and remittances data. Remittances are private flows, and governments should not try to direct the use of remittances, nor should they think of them as a substitute for official aid. Instead, governments should try to reduce costs, increase flows through banking channels, and constructively leverage these flows to improve capital market access of banks and governments in poor countries by improving ratings and securitization structures.[39]

Efforts to attract private capital to Africa are constrained by shallow domestic financial markets, lack of securitization laws, a paucity of investment-grade firms and banks in local currency terms, and absence of national credit-rating agencies. African countries, however, need to be cautious when resorting to market-based debt. It is essential that the borrowing space created by debt relief be used prudently, and not be used to borrow excessively at commercial terms (IBRD 2007). Free riding by commercial and bilateral creditors can even lead to another round of excessive accumulation of debt. Countries should also monitor and manage short-term external debt (especially those intermediated by domestic banks) to avoid currency and maturity mismatch between assets and liabilities and a potential liquidity crisis (Dadush, Dasgupta, and Ratha 2000). Short-term capital flows can reverse rapidly, with potentially destabilizing effects on the financial markets.

The findings in this chapter suggest that Sub-Saharan African countries need to make external finance more broad based, attract a broader category of investors such as pension funds and institutional investors, and expand public-private partnerships to raise additional external financing.[40] Donors and international financial institutions can play an important role by providing guarantees, political risk insurance, help in establishing ratings, and advice on financial instruments such as securitization of remittances and other future-flow receivables. Accessing private capital markets in a responsible manner will require a sound contractual environment as well as credible monetary, fiscal, and exchange-rate policies.

Notes

1. Local borrowing by one investor would lower the availability of capital for another borrower, a point often overlooked in the literature.
2. From 2000 to 2005, almost all portfolio flows went to South Africa. In contrast, the rest of Sub-Saharan Africa received the bulk of official development assistance and remittances.
3. Some of the other initiatives under consideration, although in a more preliminary form, include an international airline tax and a levy on international currency transactions; see discussions of the Second and Third Plenary Meetings of the Leading Group on Solidarity Levies to Fund Development (http://www.innovativefinance-oslo.no and http://www.innovativefinance .go.kr). See also Kaul and Le Goulven (2003), Technical Group on Innovative Financing Mechanisms (2004), and United Nations (2006).
4. Although the amount received by Sub-Saharan Africa is tiny compared with the total FDI flows to developing countries, as a share of GDP it is equivalent to 2.4 percent, comparable to the share of FDI in the GDP of other developing regions.
5. There is a reporting lag in the transfer items of the balance-of-payments statistics. Data on official debt flows were unavailable for 2006 as of March 2008.
6. Aid effectiveness is hampered by coordination difficulties among donors and by a lack of absorptive capacity among borrowers in the region (see Gelb, Ramachandran, and Turner 2006; IBRD 2006; World Bank 2006).
7. Oil exporters in Sub-Saharan Africa comprise nine low- and middle-income countries (Angola, Cameroon, Chad, the Democratic Republic of Congo, the Republic of Congo, Equatorial Guinea, Gabon, Nigeria, and Sudan) with a combined gross domestic product of $255 billion or 37 percent of Sub-Saharan Africa's gross domestic product in 2006.
8. Only one middle-income oil-exporting Sub-Saharan African country, Angola, accounted for virtually all of net bank lending to Sub-Saharan African countries other than South Africa from 2003 to 2005. More recent data on syndicated loans suggest that bank lending has grown since, but mainly in resource-rich countries such as Angola, Liberia, Nigeria, and Zambia.
9. "Free riding" implies that new lenders might extend credit to risky borrowers, taking advantage of the improvement in the borrowers' credit risk following debt relief and concessional loans by official creditors (IBRD 2007).

10. Paris Club creditors provided $19.2 billion in exceptional debt relief to Iraq and Nigeria in 2005 and a further $14 billion in 2006 (IBRD 2007; World Bank 2007a). The HIPC Initiative, launched in 1996, has committed $62 billion ($42 billion in end-2005 net present value terms) in debt relief for 30 highly indebted low-income countries, 25 of which are in Sub-Saharan Africa. The MDRI, launched in 2006, deepens this debt relief by providing 100 percent debt cancellation by the International Monetary Fund, the International Development Association, and the African Development Fund. This debt relief amounts to $38 billion for a smaller group of 22 countries (18 of which are in Sub-Saharan Africa) that have reached, or will eventually reach, completion under the HIPC Initiative (IBRD 2006, 2007; World Bank 2007b). These two initiatives together have reduced debt service to exports from 17 percent in 1998–99 to 4 percent in 2006 (IBRD 2007).

11. The present value of debt stocks would eventually decline by 90 percent for the group of 30 HIPC countries. Lower debt-stock ratios, however, may increase free-rider risks (IBRD 2007).

12. Nigeria has benefited from both debt relief and the commodity price boom. Under an agreement with the Paris Club group of official creditors, Nigeria received $18 billion in debt relief and used its oil revenues to prepay its remaining obligations of $12.4 billion to the Paris Club creditors (and another $1.5 billion to London Club creditors) during 2005–06. This has resulted in a reduction of Nigeria's external debt stock by more than $30 billion (World Bank 2007a).

13. Speech by Chinese President Hu Jintao. Integrated Regional Information Networks, United Nations, November 6, 2006, http://www.worldpress.org/africa/2554.cfm.

14. One first step in this direction has been the memorandum of understanding between the World Bank and the Export-Import Bank of China to improve cooperation in Africa. Initial cooperation would focus on infrastructure lending in the transportation and energy sectors (interview with Jim Adams, Reuters, May 22, 2007).

15. Ghana, which benefited from over $4 billion in debt relief under the HIPC Initiative and MDRI, concluded a bond issue for $750 million with a 10-year maturity and 387 basis point spread. The resources will finance infrastructure and development projects. Some of the other Sub-Saharan African countries that are potential candidates for entering the international bond market include Kenya, Nigeria, and Zambia, all three of which have seen significant increases in the nonresident purchases of domestic public debt in recent years (World Bank 2007a).

16. Page and Plaza estimated that 73 percent of remittances to Sub-Saharan African countries were through unofficial channels. Using this estimate, remittances to Sub-Saharan Africa through formal and informal channels would be more than $30 billion annually.

17. Institutional remittances consist of current and capital transfers in cash or in kind payable by any resident sector (that is, households, government, corpo-

rations, and nonprofit institutions serving households [NPISHs]) to nonresident households and NPISHs and receivable by resident households and NPISHs from any nonresident sector, and excluding household-to-household transfers (United Nations Statistics Division 1998). NPISH is defined as a nonprofit institution that is not predominantly financed and controlled by government and that provides goods or services to households free or at prices that are not economically significant.

18. IDA countries (mostly in Sub-Saharan Africa) received an estimated $20 million from U.S. foundations in 2004, which was less than 3 percent of direct cross-border grants of $800 million provided by U.S. foundations in that year (Sulla 2007).

19. See Powell, Ratha, and Mohapatra (2002) and World Bank (2002) for the construction of capital outflows as the difference between sources and uses of funds in the International Monetary Fund's Balance of Payments Statistics.

20. Average annual capital outflows from Nigeria have been in the range of $2.5 billion since the late 1980s.

21. South Africa is reported to have launched a project to issue reconciliation and development bonds to both expatriate and domestic investors (Bradlow 2006). Ghana has begun marketing the Golden Jubilee savings bond to the Ghanaian diaspora in Europe and the United States.

22. Page and Plaza (2006) estimate that almost three-quarters of remittances to Sub-Saharan African countries were through unofficial channels.

23. Partial risk guarantees typically have been provided for private sector projects in all countries, including IDA-eligible poor countries, and partial credit guarantees usually go to public investment projects in countries eligible for IBRD loans. In addition, policy-based guarantees are extended to help well-performing IBRD-eligible governments access capital markets.

24. The Global Alliance for Vaccines and Immunization, a public-private partnership for combating disease, was created in 1999 and has received grant commitments of $1.5 billion from the Bill & Melinda Gates Foundation, with additional contributions coming from Australia, Brazil, Canada, Denmark, France, Germany, Ireland, Luxembourg, the Netherlands, Norway, South Africa, Spain, Sweden, the United Kingdom, the United States, the European Union, and the World Bank. See http://www.gavialliance.org.

25. Birdsall and Subramanian (2007) argue that international financial institutions have traditionally underfunded the provision of global public goods (GPGs) and have not been adequately involved in the development of new GPG products such as the AMC, preferring instead to provide loans and grants to individual countries.

26. See Skåre (2007), Trepelkov (2007), and the discussions of the Second and Third "Plenary Meetings of the Leading Group on Solidarity Levies to Fund Development," which was established in March 2006. (See http://www.innovativefinance-oslo.no/recommendedreading.cfm, and http://www.innovativefinance.go.kr.) Among the innovative financing projects, 28 countries of the

group are considering introduction of an Air Ticket Solidarity Levy to fund improved access to treatments against HIV/AIDS, TB, and malaria through the International Drug Purchase Facility of Unitaid.

27. The solidarity levy on airline tickets has been implemented by Chile, the Democratic Republic of Congo, Côte d'Ivoire, France, the Republic of Korea, Madagascar, Mauritius, and Niger (see http://www.unitaid.eu).

28. See http://www.gemloc.org for further details.

29. Under a more recent proposal advocated by the World Bank, sovereign wealth funds, which are estimated to hold more than $3 trillion in assets, would be encouraged to invest 1 percent of that in Sub-Saharan Africa. This proposed "one percent" initiative would use the Gemloc bond index and investability rankings (as well as promote the development of other market-based indexes) to encourage investments by sovereign wealth funds in African markets. If successful, this would translate into $30 billion of additional resource flows to African countries.

30. Such transactions also often resort to excess coverage to mitigate the risk of volatility and seasonality in future flows.

31. Obtaining a rating is important for raising not only bond financing or bank loans, but also foreign direct investment and even official aid (Ratha, De, and Mohapatra 2007). Any improvement in sovereign rating is likely to translate into an improvement in the rating of subsovereign borrowers whose foreign currency borrowing is typically subject to the sovereign rating ceiling.

32. The United Nations Office on Drugs and Crime (UNODC) and the World Bank (2007) reported that 25 percent of GDP of African states is estimated to be lost to corruption every year, with corrupt actions encompassing petty bribe-taking done by low-level government officials to inflated public procurement contracts, kickbacks, and raiding of the public treasury as part of public asset theft by political leaders.

33. For example, Nigeria has successfully recovered half a billion dollars in stolen assets from Swiss sources with cooperation of the World Bank, civil society, and the Swiss authorities.

34. Ratha, De, and Mohapatra (2007) argued that several factors may make it difficult for poor countries to get rated. The information required for the rating process can be complex and not readily available in many countries. The institutional and legal environment governing property rights and sale of securities may be absent or weak, prompting reluctance on the part of politicians to get publicly judged by the rating analysts. The fact that a country has to request a rating, and has to pay a fee for it, but has no say over the final rating outcome can also be discouraging.

35. Only five banks in all of Sub-Saharan Africa excluding South Africa (four in Nigeria and one in Mauritius) were in Standard & Poor's global debt issuers list. In contrast, South Africa had nearly 30 firms and banks in the list.

36. This literature models sovereign ratings as a function of macroeconomic and institutional variables (see Cantor and Packer 1996, Mora 2006). Interestingly,

the benchmark model of Ratha, De, and Mohapatra (2007) performs quite well for Sub-Saharan African countries. The predicted or shadow ratings for the 11 Sub-Saharan African countries rated under the recent United Nations Development Programme initiative were within one to two notches of the actual rating assigned by Standard & Poor's as of the end of 2006. The model successfully predicted the rating of the recent bond issue from Ghana.

37. Both rating agencies assigned Gabon a BB− rating, citing its relatively high income per capita and large external and fiscal surpluses derived from buoyant oil revenues. The proceeds of the bond will be used to buy back outstanding Paris Club debt (AFX News Limited 2007; Reuters 2007). Also, Kenya, rated B+, is reported to be planning a Eurobond issuance in the near future.

38. For the literature on aid effectiveness, see Collier (2006); Easterly, Levine, and Roodman (2003); Easterly (2006); Radelet (2006); Rajan and Subramanian (2005); and Sundberg and Gelb (2006).

39. Shifting remittances from informal to formal channels may require eliminating parallel market premiums, improving access to formal finance for poor households, and reducing regulatory barriers to entry of new operators.

40. Since this study has focused on mobilizing new sources of financing, it has omitted discussion of structural and investment climate factors that impede private investment in Africa. This literature is summarized in Bhattacharya, Montiel, and Sharma (1997); Bhinda et al. (1999); Gelb, Ramachandran, and Turner (2006); Kasekende and Bhundia (2000); and World Bank (2002).

References

Afreximbank. 2005. *Annual Report.* Cairo: African Export-Import Bank. http://www.afreximbank.com.

AFX News Limited. 2007. "Gabon Assigned 'BB−' Long-Term Issuer Default Rating with Stable Outlook–Fitch," October 30.

Ajayi, S. Ibi. 1997. "An Analysis of External Debt and Capital Flight in the Severely Indebted Low-Income Countries in Sub-Saharan Africa." Working Paper 97/68, International Monetary Fund, Washington, DC.

Aykut, Dilek, and Dilip Ratha. 2005. "South-South FDI Flows: How Big Are They?" *Transnational Corporations* 13 (1): 148–76.

Bhattacharya, Amar, Peter Montiel, and Sunil Sharma. 1997. "How Can Sub-Saharan Africa Attract More Private Capital Inflows?" *Finance and Development* 34 (2).

Bhinda, Nils, Stephany Griffith-Jones, Jonathan Leape, and Matthew Martin. 1999. "Scale and Monitoring of Capital Flows." In *Private Capital Flows to Africa,* ed. Jan Joost Teunissen, 19-46. The Hague: Forum on Debt and Development.

Birdsall, Nancy, and Arvind Subramanian. 2007. "From World Bank to World Development Cooperative." Essay, Center for Global Development, Washington, DC. http://www.cgdev.org.

Boyce, James, and Léonce Ndikumana, 2001. "Is Africa a Net Creditor? New Estimates of Capital Flight from Severely Indebted Sub-Saharan African Countries, 1970–96." *Journal of Development Studies* 38 (2): 27–56.

Bradlow, Daniel D. 2006. "An Experiment in Creative Financing to Promote South African Reconciliation and Development." American University Washington College of Law, Washington, DC.

Broadman, Harry G., Godze Isik, Sonia Plaza, Xiao Ye, and Yutaka Yoshino. 2007. *Africa's Silk Road: China and India's New Economic Frontier.* Washington, DC: World Bank.

Cantor, Richard, and Frank Packer. 1996. "Determinants and Impact of Sovereign Credit Ratings." *Economic Policy Review* (October): 37–53.

Chander, Anupam. 2001. "Diaspora Bonds." *New York University Law Review* 76 (4): 1005–99.

Collier, Paul. 2006. "Is Aid Oil? An Analysis of Whether Africa Can Absorb More Aid." *World Development* 34 (9): 1482–97.

Collier, Paul, Anke Hoeffler, and Catherine Pattillo. 2001. "Flight Capital as a Portfolio Choice." *World Bank Economic Review* 15 (1): 55–80.

———. 2004. "Africa's Exodus: Capital Flight and the Brain Drain as Portfolio Decisions." *Journal of African Economies* 13 (AERC Supplement 2): ii15–ii54.

Dadush, Uri, Dipak Dasgupta, and Dilip Ratha. 2000. "The Role of Short-Term Debt in Recent Crises." *Finance and Development* 37 (4).

Easterly, William. 2006. *The White Man's Burden.* New York: Penguin Press.

Easterly, William, Ross Levine, and David Roodman. 2003. "New Data, New Doubts: Revisiting Aid, Policies, and Growth." Working Paper 26, Center for Global Development, Washington, DC.

Economist. 2007. "Africa and China: The Host with the Most," May 17.

Financial Times. 2007a. "China Pledges US$20 Billion for Africa," May 18.

———. 2007b. "$5 Bn. S. African Bank Deal Signals China's Ambition," October 26.

GAVI (Global Alliance for Vaccines and Immunization) and World Bank. 2006. "Framework Document: Pilot AMC for Pneumococcal Vaccines." Document prepared by the World Bank and GAVI for the second Donor Working Group meeting, London, November 9. http://www.vaccineamc.org/files/Framework%20Pneumo%20AMC%20Pilot.pdf.

Gelb, Alan, Vijaya Ramachandran, and Ginger Turner. 2006. "Stimulating Growth and Investment in Africa: From Macro to Micro Reforms." Paper prepared for the "Inaugural AfDB Economic Conference: Accelerating Africa's Development Five Years into the Twenty-First Century," Tunis, November 22–24.

Gibson, John, David McKenzie, and Halahingano Rohorua. 2006. "How Cost Elastic Are Remittances? Estimates from Tongan Migrants in New Zealand." Working Paper 06/02, Department of Economics, University of Waikato.

Goldstein, Andrea, Nicolas Pinaud, Helmut Reisen, and Xiaobao Chen. 2006. *The Rise of China and India: What's In It for Africa?* Paris: OECD Development Center.

Hausmann, Ricardo, and Eduardo Fernández-Arias. 2001. "Foreign Direct Investment: Good Cholesterol?" In *Foreign Direct Investment Versus Other Flows to Latin America,* ed. Jorge Braga de Macedo and Enrique V. Iglesias. Paris: Organisation for Economic Co-operation and Development.

Hermes, N., R. Lensink, V. Murinde. 2002. "Capital Flight, Policy Uncertainty, and the Instability of the International Financial System." In *Handbook of International Banking,* ed. A. Mullineux, and V. Murinde. Cheltenham: Edward Elgar.

Hillman, David, Sony Kapoor, and Stephen Spratt. 2006. "Taking the Next Step: Implementing a Currency Transaction Development Levy." Paper presented at the Second Plenary Meeting of the Leading Group on Solidarity Levies to Fund Development, Oslo, December.

IBRD (International Bank for Reconstruction and Development). 2006. *Global Monitoring Report 2006: Strengthening Mutual Accountability—Aid, Trade & Governance.* Washington, DC: IBRD/World Bank.

———. 2007. *Global Monitoring Report 2007: Confronting the Challenges of Gender Equality and Fragile States.* Washington, DC: IBRD/World Bank.

IMF (International Monetary Fund). 2006. *Regional Economic Outlook: Sub-Saharan Africa.* Washington, DC: IMF.

———. 2007. *Regional Economic Outlook: Sub-Saharan Africa.* Washington, DC: IMF.

Kasekende, Louis, and Ashok Bhundia. 2000. "Attracting Capital Inflows to Africa: Essential Elements of a Policy Package." In *Finance for Sustainable Development: Testing New Policy Approaches,* ed. Juergen Holst, Donald Lee, and Eric Olson. New York: United Nations Department of Economic and Social Affairs, Division for Sustainable Development.

Kaul, Inge, and Katell Le Goulven. 2003. "Financing Global Public Goods: A New Frontier of Public Finance." In *Providing Global Public Goods: Managing Globalization,* ed. Inge Kaul, Pedro Conceicao, Katell Le Goulven, and Ronald U. Mendoza. New York: Oxford University Press.

Ketkar, Suhas, and Dilip Ratha. 2001. "Development Financing during a Crisis: Securitization of Future Receivables." Policy Research Working Paper 2582, World Bank, Washington, DC.

———. 2004–2005. "Recent Advances in Future-Flow Securitization." *The Financier* 11/12. http://www.the-financier.com.

———. 2007. "Development Finance Via Diaspora Bonds Track Record and Potential." Policy Research Working Paper 4311, World Bank, Washington, DC.

Matsukawa, Tomoko, and Odo Habeck. 2007. "Risk Mitigation Instruments for Infrastructure Financing and Recent Trends and Developments." Trends and Policy Options 4, World Bank and Public-Private Infrastructure Advisory Facility, Washington, DC.

McDonald, Calvin, Volker Treichel, and Hans Weisfeld. 2006. "Enticing Investors." *Finance and Development* 43 (4).

Mora, Nada. 2006. "Sovereign Credit Ratings: Guilty beyond Reasonable Doubt?" *Journal of Banking and Finance* 30 (7): 2041–62.

Ndikumana, Léonce, and James K. Boyce. 2002. "Public Debts and Private Assets: Explaining Capital Flight from Sub-Saharan African Countries." Working Paper Series 32, Department of Economics, University of Massachusetts, Amherst.

Oxford Analytica. 2007. "Nigeria/China: Deal Will Help Extend Banks' Reach," October 31.

Page, John, and Sonia Plaza. 2006. "Migration, Remittances and Development: A Review of the Global Evidence." *Journal of African Economies* 15 (2): 245–336.

Powell, Andrew, Dilip Ratha, and Sanket Mohapatra. 2002. "Capital Inflows and Capital Outflows: Measurement, Determinants, Consequences." Working Paper 7, Centro de Investigación en Finanzas, Universidad Torcuato Di Tella. Buenos Aires.

Radelet, Steve. 2006. "A Primer on Aid Allocation." Working Paper 92, Center for Global Development, Washington, DC.

Rajan, Raghuram G., and Arvind Subramanian. 2005. "Aid and Growth: What Does the Cross-Country Evidence Really Show?" Working Paper 05/127, International Monetary Fund, Washington, DC.

Ratha, Dilip. 2003. "Workers' Remittances: An Important and Stable Source of External Development Finance." In *Global Development Finance 2006: Striving for Stability in Development Finance.* Washington, DC: World Bank.

———. 2006. "Leveraging Remittances for Capital Market Access." Working Paper, Development Prospects Group, World Bank, Washington, DC.

———. 2007. "Leveraging Remittances for Development." Policy Brief, Migration Policy Institute, Washington, DC.

Ratha, Dilip, Prabal De, and Sanket Mohapatra. 2007. "Shadow Sovereign Ratings for Unrated Developing Countries." Policy Research Working Paper 4269, World Bank, Washington, DC.

Ratha, Dilip, and William Shaw. 2007. "South-South Migration and Remittances." Working Paper 102, World Bank, Washington, DC.

Reuters. 2007. "International, Domestic Bonds Likely in Gabon–S&P," November 9.

Rutten, Lamon, and Okey Oramah. 2006. "Using Commoditized Revenue Flows to Leverage Access to International Finance; with a Special Focus on Migrant Remittances and Payment Flows." Study prepared for the UNCTAD Secretariat, Geneva.

Salisu, Mohammed. 2005. "The Role of Capital Flight and Remittances in Current Account Sustainability in Sub-Saharan Africa." *African Development Review* 17 (3): 382–404.

Skåre, Mari. 2007. "General Remarks on Major Achievements." Third Plenary Meeting of the Leading Group on Solidarity Levies to Fund Development, Seoul, September 3.

Sulla, Olga. 2007. "Philanthropic Foundations and their Role in International Development Assistance." International Finance Briefing Note No. 3, Development Prospects Group, World Bank.

Sundberg, Mark, and Alan Gelb. 2006. "Making Aid Work." *Finance and Development* 43 (4).

Technical Group on Innovative Financing Mechanisms. 2004. *Action against Hunger and Poverty.* http://www.diplomatie.gouv.fr/en/IMG/pdf/rapportdugroupe quadripartite.pdf.

Trepelkov, Alexander. 2007. "Reflections on Innovative Financing for Development." Paper presented at the Third Plenary Meeting of the Leading Group on Solidarity Levies to Fund Development, Seoul, September 3.

United Nations. 2006. *Human Development Report 2006: Beyond Scarcity: Power, Poverty and the Global Water Crisis.* New York: United Nations Development Programme.

UNODC (United Nations Office on Drugs and Crime) and World Bank. 2007. *Stolen Asset Recovery (StAR) Initiative: Challenges, Opportunities, and Action Plan.* Washington, DC: IBRD/World Bank. http://siteresources.worldbank.org/NEWS/ Resources/Star-rep-full.pdf.

United Nations Statistics Division. 1998. "Recommendations on Statistics of International Migration." United Nations, New York.

Wang, Jian-Ye. 2007. "What Drives China's Growing Role in Africa?" Working Paper 07/211, International Monetary Fund, Washington, DC.

World Bank. 1999. "Sub-Saharan Africa Benefits from the first IDA Guarantee for Azito." *Project Finance and Guarantees Notes.* Washington, DC: World Bank Private Sector and Infrastructure Vice-Presidency.

———. 2002. *Global Development Finance 2002: Financing the Poorest Countries.* Washington, DC: World Bank.

———. 2004. *Global Development Finance 2004: Harnessing Cyclical Gains for Development.* Washington, DC: World Bank.

———. 2005. *Global Economic Prospects 2006: Economic Implications of Remittances and Migration.* Washington, DC: World Bank.

———. 2006. *Global Development Finance 2006: The Development Potential of Surging Capital Flows.* Washington, DC: World Bank.

———. 2007a. *Global Development Finance 2007: The Globalization of Corporate Finance in Developing Countries.* Washington, DC: World Bank.

———. 2007b. *"HIPC At-A-Glance Guide."* Economic Policy and Debt Department brief, World Bank, Washington, DC. http://go.worldbank.org/85B908KVE0.

———. 2007c. "World Bank Monthly Operational Summary Guarantee Operations." http://go.worldbank.org/R5XXEKDS70.

Index

Boxes, figures, notes, and tables are indicated by *b, f, n,* and *t,* respectively.

DATE DUE
